Dearest Carolyn

May you find These
stories inspiring!

IGNITE
Your
Inner Spirit

And Igniting!! ♡ I
Love you beyond The
moon + back!
XOXO
Paula

Additional International Best-Selling
Compilation Books by Ignite for you to enjoy

————————

Ignite Your Life for Women

Ignite Your Female Leadership

Ignite Your Parenting

Ignite Your Life for Men

Ignite Your Life for Conscious Leaders

Ignite Your Adventurous Spirit

Ignite Your Health and Wellness

Ignite Female Change Makers

Ignite the Modern Goddess

Ignite Love

Ignite Happiness

IGNITE Your Inner Spirit

LEARNING THE SKILLS TO AWAKEN TO, AND CONNECT WITH, THE MOST IMPORTANT PART OF YOU

INTRODUCTION BY **JB Owen**
Founder of Ignite and JBO Global Inc.

PROJECT LEADERS **Yendre Shen & Beejal Coulson**

PRESENTED BY

ALBERT URENA • ALEXIA GILESPIE • AMY HACKETT-JONES • BEEJAL COULSON
BRENT MARTIN • BRIAN SCHRIEBER • CAT FLOWERS • CHARLENE RAY
CHRIS PLOUGH • CLINT CARLETON • DEAN GRAFOS • DONATA S ELBER
ESTHER LÓPEZ • FRANCIS PICHÉ • GISELLE JENNAWAY • HINA MAHINDRU
JASON B. FLORES • JB OWEN • JEFFREY SORENSEN • JOANNE P. IMAI
JONATHAN V. REECE • KATRINA ROADS • LYDIA KNORR • MELIKE SULE HUSSEIN
MICHAEL TYLER • OLIVIA ÓDOR • PAUL BENSON • PAUL J PUNSHON
PAULA LAWRENCE • SAMUEL FISHMAN • SANTIAGO RAFAEL
SUSANA SEBESTYEN • TAMMY MCCANN • TRACI HARRELL • YENDRE SHEN

PUBLISHED BY IGNITE AND PRINTED BY JBO GLOBAL INC.

Published and printed by JBO Global Inc.
5569-47ᵗʰ Street, Red Deer, AB
Canada, T4N1S1 1-877-677-6115

Cover design by JB Owen
Book design by Dania Zafar
Designed in Canada, Printed in China
ISBN# 978-1-7923-4173-1
First edition: December 2020

Ordering Information: Quantity sales. Special discounts are available on quantity purchases by corporations, associations, and others. For details, contact the publisher at the above address. Programs, products, or services provided by the authors are found by contacting them directly. Resources named in the book are found in the resources pages at the back of the book.

THIS
BOOK
IS
DEDICATED
TO
EVERY
SPIRIT
IN
EVERYONE

TESTIMONIALS FROM AUTHORS

"It has been an absolute dream, writing for the Ignite team. From writing the first draft to the editorial sessions, masterminds, and the writer's nests, the journey and the insights have been wholeheartedly supported and crafted to bring out the very best of me in a nurturing and empowering way. I've thoroughly enjoyed the process. Thank you!"

~ Amy Hackett-Jones

"Being an Ignite author brings you the opportunity to impact the world, to leave your footprints, to inspire and ignite others through your experiences and learnings. But beyond that, writing your story becomes a remarkable journey of personal growth and acknowledgement; a tour in which you are brilliantly guided by a team of editors and gently supported by the whole community of Ignite authors."

~ Esther López

"I experience JB as a benevolent tsunami. Being carried by her impulse and the incredible team gathered around her has been a magical synchronicity for me. As a quiet observer of Life, I tend to hang back. Ignite has carried me forward into the world where my audience can find me. It has been a perfect marriage and a pleasure for which I have heartfelt appreciation."

~ Giselle Jennaway

"Writing the chapter for *Ignite Your Inner Spirit* challenged me to face parts of my past I wanted to leave behind, yet they had to come out for others to be healed. The editing process has helped me level-up my writing skills to higher levels and I'm truly grateful for that."

~ Albert Urena

"It has been an inspiring and supportive experience, working with Ignite. My inner spirit is ignited as I write this story. The people on the Ignite team are all genuinely kind and awesome people."

~ Cat Flowers

"Every time I write a story for Ignite, I become more aware of my own potential and the possibilities for my life. The editing team and JB make this a life-changing experience for the author. As a reader, be prepared to be inspired and transformed!"

~ Charlene Ray

"Thank you for igniting magical possibilities for all the authors to share their message and make an impact on the world. Loved the editing process. It was very enlightening. Much love to the family team!"

~ Francis Piché

"The process of writing this story was full of inquiry and self-reflection. Having to 'expose' myself to the world in writing my story for this book had me pause and doubt myself multiple times along the way. In the end, the incredible support throughout the process helped ground, for me, the validity of my story and experience, and that I am not alone and my story matters.

Writing is something I have done all my life, without any ambition of being a 'writer.' A few years ago, when I started to share my writings with people in workshops that I attended or facilitated myself, I was told that there was a book in me somewhere. I don't know about that just yet, but the Ignite process surely has added a significant feather in any writer's life — to be able to call myself an author. Thank you, Ignite!"

~ Hina Mahindru

"What an Amazing opportunity and experience. The process of digging deep and analyzing the past to develop my story in order to Ignite and share with the world has been life changing. Enjoying the process was the real lesson, as Life is all about the process of the journey and not the end. What a wonderful conduit to share my story with the world. Thank you JB, Peter, and the whole Ignite team."

~ Jonathan V. Reece

"As a rookie writer, I had a story in my head and heart but not yet on the page. My Ignite message would not have flowed out of me the way it did without the skill and magic of my fabulously kind, patient, and passionate editors. Writing was more emotional and cathartic and induced way more procrastination than I expected! My Ignite editors helped me to express my story while keeping my voice, though adding their essential polish. I've grown so much from the entire Ignite authoring process; it is richly supportive, very well structured, and provides so many opportunities for growing connections. I've loved it. The Ignite process has re-ignited me!"

~ Katrina Roads

"I had long wanted to get my words into print but had no idea where to begin. Then came along an incredible opportunity to work with some highly experienced editors and publishers at igniteyou.life and I now am able to add 'Author' to my list of accomplishments. The wisdom, support, encouragement and seamless process of the Ignite experience made my foray into writing such a joy. I am thrilled to further my passion for writing in my continued partnership with the Ignite family. My heartfelt gratitude to JB, Peter, and their incredible team."

~ Lydia Knorr

"Thank you so much for this empowering experience of being a part of the *Ignite Your Inner Spirit* book! Thank you for the amazing editors' encouragement and patience. This was truly a transformative experience in my life, putting my past in a different light and empowerment. I can not thank you enough for this opportunity!"

~ Olivia Ódor

"This has been a great experience with an amazing team of supporters and staff. Writing is definitely wonderful."

~ Paul J Punshon

"Being part of the *Ignite Your Inner Spirit* community has been a gift to my heart; the vehicle that has aligned me with the passions of my life and given me the thrill of co-creating with others!"

~ Paula Lawrence

"I felt like I took my life to another level through sharing my story on a global scale."

~ Samuel Fishman

"Working with the Ignite team to get my story out into the world has helped to make a dream come true! The support, love, and processes in place gave me the confidence to write and hopefully create a ripple in the world through the power of the written word. Thank you from my heart to yours!"

~ Tammy McCann

Message From the Publisher

Seldom does a book with so many individuals come together during such an unprecedented time in history. 2020 has been a year none of us could have predicted nor been prepared for. And yet, an amazing group of individuals, some of whom have never written before, stepped up in record fashion to produce a book that I know will become near and dear to your heart. These fabulous authors have blessed us with their stories and shown us the will, strength, and determination that lives in the human spirit. I know you will see the immense amount of work, sincerity, and love for humanity these pages reflect and feel the true desire they have to inspire and Ignite your amazing Inner Spirit.

May all our stories, going forward, be filled with the rise and restoration of the Earth and every single individual on it.

JB Owen, Canada, November 2020

Contents

DREAMER

VISIONARY

What is an Ignite Book?

The very word Ignite signifies the purpose of our books and describes the intention behind the stories we love to share. We see our books as gifts; as presents to the world. Every one we publish was born from the idea of inspiring, uplifting, and igniting the reader in the process. We believe we are the future, a bridge for human connection, and a beacon for what's possible for every person on earth.

As you read the upcoming pages, you will find every story starts with a *Power Quote*. It is a self-affirming, self-empowering statement designed to inspire. It is what you would want to hear to lift you up, push you forward, and help you step outside your comfort zone. Power quotes are phrases that you can use when you need a little encouragement or a tad of hope. They are statements meant to create thought, Ignite ideas, spark action, and evoke change. Every power quote is written to remind you what you have within you, what you can accomplish, and how your life is yours for the making.

Below the power quote, you will find each author's personal *Intention*. These are the personal insights and genuine wishes the author wants to share with you. They are their powerful messages filled with both purpose and meaning. Each author has the desire to IGNITE more of *everything* in you. They share their intentions to succinctly explain what they feel their story will do for you.

Then their Ignite *Story* follows. It is an honest account of how they found their inner truth and learned from it to become a greater expression of themself. Through their stories, they explain how their Ignite moment changed them and set them on a different path. They reveal their vulnerable feelings and share their authentic emotions of consciously awakening to the moment that resulted in a magnificent transformation.

We all have *Ignite* moments that change us, define us, and set us on a beautiful new journey of inner exploration. These stories derive from those moments told in the most honest and heartfelt way. They show that *life-altering* situations not only impact us but ultimately inspire us to love ourselves and those around us more completely.

Once you have read their stories, you will find a list of *Ignite Action Steps*. These are doable actions our authors took to overcome the obstacles and push past the hardships that can sometimes show up. Each author shares effective ideas, unique processes, and powerful practices that have worked in their lives. The idea is for you to implement them in your life to manifest great change. Each Ignite Action step is different and unique, just like you are, and each has proven to have amazing results when done diligently and consistently.

As you begin reading the book, know that many readers flip to a page at random and read from there, trusting that the page they land on holds the exact story they need to read. Others glance over the table of contents, searching for the title that best resonates with them. Traditional readers start at the beginning, while others will go directly to a story recommended by a friend. However you decide to devour this book, we believe it will be right for you. We know that you may read it from cover to cover in one single sitting or pick it up and put it down a dozen times over a long period of time. The way you enjoy an Ignite book is as personal as every story in it, and we give you complete permission to read it in a way that fits you.

What we do ask is, if a story touches you or in some way inspires you, that you reach out and tell the author. Your words would mean the world to them. Since our book is all about Igniting humanity, we want to foster more of that among us. Feel free to share your sentiments with the authors by using their contact information at the end of each chapter. There isn't an Ignite author who wouldn't love to hear from you and know how their story impacted your life.

If writing your own story is percolating to the surface, please reach out to Ignite. If you have a story to share (which we all do) and feel compelled to begin writing yours, we want to hear from you. We believe every person has a story and everyone deserves to be seen, heard, and acknowledged for their story. If your words are longing to come forth, we want to support you in making that happen. Our desire is to Ignite a billion lives through a billion words, and we can only do that together.

As you dive into the upcoming pages, a million different emotions will fill your heart. We love that about our stories and as you turn the pages, we feel a kindred spirit with you. We want this to be the book that awakens and blesses your life forever. May you be honored, loved, and supported from this page forward.

PREFACE

BY JB OWEN

It is no surprise that, today, with everything that is happening in the world, we *need* to believe in something more. With all the outside issues, pressures, and problems that are unfolding globally, we have both been forced and encouraged to look inside. It seems the Universe itself is asking us to go deeper than we did even a short year ago. It feels as though we were speeding along the freeway of life and got hit upside the head and forced to not just slow down but to get completely off the road.

Millions, I mean, *billions* of people are now at the place of asking, *"What is next?"* How do we pick up? Carry on? Or even just get started? Historically, we can see numerous times when the human race faced challenges of epic proportion. And, we can see in hindsight the steps they had to take to overcome and keep going. Often it was under the direction of a ruler or influenced by an institution shrouded in personal gain. For the first time in history, we are at a place where humanity is the captain, the planet is the guide, and *no one thing* rules over the other, other than the fact that we are all indeed *One*.

This book was created in the midst of an epic world revolution; a time when humanity is fighting for humanity itself. It holds within its pages the reflections of the individual and the wisdom of the many. It has birthed its way into being from the idea of just one person, and then grew and grew into what it is today: a beacon; a light; a marvelous message of hope. And from just one person, it has become a powerful spark with a mission to awaken the deep connections that define the very heart of the human soul.

This is how IGNITE works. An idea planted in the rich soil of the fertile imagination grows to become a wildfire of unlimited possibilities. You are about to become a part of that inferno. The one we have lovingly curated to impact others and uplift *all* of humanity. Our entire goal is that, amid a fury of uncertainty, confusion, and the unknown, the one thing you can feel for certain is our unwavering commitment to Ignite *your* Inner Spirit and the divine Spirit inside everyone so that we may all become the infinite potential we deserve to be.

INTRODUCTION BY JB OWEN

Founder and CEO of Ignite

You've picked up a book called *Ignite Your Inner Spirit*.

Excitedly that might mean... you are one of those people who is genuinely connected to your Inner Spirit. Someone who is deeply aware of the marvelous *will* that lives inside of them. You may be one of those individuals who *feels* your spirit deeply, *hears* from it often, and is *guided* by its wisdom on a daily basis. Your connection may be strong and you trust it implicitly. There are many people on this planet who *listen to* and are *connected with* the gifts their Inner Spirit provides.

Then there is the other reason you may have chosen this book... it is possible you are one of those people who are not so connected, not so entwined, not sure of their spirit's presence. You want to feel the connection, but only tend to hear a subtle whisper or just a gentle nudge. You might be one of those people who desire a better understanding and long for more consistent communication. They wish to *know* their spirit within and *be* deeply connected to its reverence.

Wherever you are on the spectrum, know you are not alone. Many people, at different intervals in their lives, have heard from, felt connected to, and been in tune with their inner spirit. Some describe those moments of joy as a great connection to their *true selves*. These people feel guided by Spirit and believe their connection exists with no proof or evidence. They are filled with bliss, responding to their calling, following their passions, and fulfilling their highest desires.

Then there are those that feel only the vacancy of spirit. They can't help but notice when their spirit is absent. When the messages are quiet and the instincts are reserved. They experience little conversation and mourn the moments that feel like dry spells and neglected silence. To them, a barren disconnection rules. They long to find the divine relationship that Spirit has with others.

To experience the powerful connection of one's Inner Spirit, many have gone on great pilgrimages and dangerous travels. They have searched new lands, encountered difficult circumstances, and faced challenges beyond belief. Spirit seems to reward them for their efforts and arrive exactly when it was needed.

Others have not been so lucky, they have sought spirit at both monumental and catastrophic times. They have pleaded for their spirit to arrive and suffered the loss alone, waiting for its presence. For some, when Spirit does appear, it is only as an infinitesimal tug of intuition or a sliver of new thought. It isn't the grand partnership they were hoping for and the emotions feel lost. They want those feelings where Spirit has shown up as a massive jolt to the system or an overwhelming burst of pure clarity. They'd welcome that! They have heard from others how Spirit chatters like an old incessant friend or looms lovingly like an enthusiast coach.

It is clear that Spirit shows up differently for every individual. There is no recipe or checklist that brings it forth, it rises simply when you are ready to hear what it has to say — or do what it wants you to do — or listen as it directs you — agree when it influences you — follow when it guides you. Spirit is not confined to one style of communication. Many have heard voices, felt gut-feelings, had the hair stand up on the back of their neck, or just simply *knew* on the deepest level.

Each one of us has our own unique connection to our spirit. It is cultivated over time, through practice, influenced by beliefs, and then fostered and refined through life experiences, trying new things, and listening from a place of know-ing, not processing information. The true voice of your spirit does not function on logic or practicality. It isn't influenced by cost, percentages, or rationale. It speaks in 'pangs of the stomach' or in 'ringing of the ears.' It comes in the form of 'gnawing questions' or 'emotional upheaval.' Nowhere is it said that Spirit speaks eloquently or clearly. In fact, Spirit has been known to offer riddles, execute conundrums, and reveal complex issues that require more than just our conscious or rational thinking. In fact, Spirit often asks you to go so much deeper, think without limits, and in many cases, bet it all.

If you have picked up this book, then I believe it is safe to say that you are ultimately looking to understand your Inner Spirit better. Possibly you want to have a richer connection with it or know its deeper purpose. Most likely you are intrigued by its presence and want to relate to it even more, expanding upon the uniqueness of that connection. If that is the case, you have chosen (by no coincidence) the right and perfect book.

Reading the many stories inside these pages will, without doubt, empower you and awaken that spirit-to-self connection. It will likely stimulate a new understanding of your Inner Spirit and inspire more ways of communicating with your truest self. We all have an *Inner Spirit*. It is in all of us. It is a richer, truer, greater, and more authentic reflection of who you were born to be. It is the rawest form of self and the truest essence of you. And, it isn't defined by anything else other than *you*. Yes, we could go into pages of religion, scriptures, dogmas, and beliefs on where and how 'the spirit' is defined, Yet, for our goal of Igniting your spirit, we have defined it down to this; your Inner Spirit is the inner *will* of you.

Your *will* for life, success, peace, love, acceptance, trust, recognition, pro-creation, survival, and a hundred more human experiences drive you toward and away from certain willful actions. Outside influences and conditional training often influence your inner *will*. Repeated setback, constant criticism, and a million other human flaws can shortchange and hinder the *will* you have. While at the same time, serendipitous encounters and magical connections can activate your *will*. Pride, perseverance, determination, and pure grit can awaken it. The simple *and* most enduring human conditions each have the potential to Ignite your Inner Spirit in a myriad of ways.

At some point in your life, a niggling, an itch, a calling may begin. Something new, like a sacred calling, can be heard speaking to your soul. That is when Spirit invites you to begin the journey — the long and unknown path to making the divine connection.

In this book, you will read the many amazing stories of individuals from around the world who have found their Inner Spirit and want to share it with you. These are their stories. Some are of precious moments and quiet connections, others of grand excursions and epic life-changing times. They each graciously explain their inner transformation and how it came to be. Some will be what you are looking for; others may make you cry. A few will hit home and be exactly what you are needing. All will reveal the beauty of the human *will*, the Inner Spirit we each have.

I invite you to treasure this book as a loving guide and trusted teacher. Every

Ignite story in it is designed to be just that; a leaning, a prompt, an awakening wrapped inside a story and destined to change your life. From the beginning of time, stories have had the power to impact us so greatly that they set complete societies on a new trajectory and turn the most ardent individuals toward a different path. This is that moment and it is right in front of you.

Get ready… because this book has been created to touch your soul and awaken your Inner Spirit. Every person in it gave a piece of themselves to make it complete. Their stories are your stories; they are *all of our* stories because they speak to the intrinsic need to connect to the *inner self*. They will touch that part of you that goes beyond the labels, past net wealth, and make you forget about the bling you may or may not wear. These stories supersede what the human mind values and honor what is so much more valuable: your *will*; your *essence;* the magical beauty of *Spirit itself.*

May each and every page be exactly what you need.

Much Love,

JB Owen

"Find the will to be completely you."

This is a story designed to awaken your Inner Spirit. It may not be an easy story to read. Others in the book may be more fun, introspective, and intelligent. My story shows how at times in our lives, when we are on the verge of emerging, we often have to crawl over broken glass to get to the other side. We have to swallow the heartache and endure the fury of the storm before there is calm. I wish for you to know that it is often through the most difficult moments that we traverse our reality and connect to the inner side: the side of self, of worth, peace, joy, understanding, and regard. The side where our spirit rules and our hearts follow suit, allowing us to rise up and be who we were created to be.

When She Stood Up, Everyone Rose

June 16, 2015

It has been a long and grueling day of dealing with all the drama and chaos that comes with being in a relationship with an addict and an alcoholic. My ex-husband is on another bender; on another runaway train down the long corridor of repeated relapses and alcoholic behavior. Despite my hellish day, I desperately try to smile and look as though I am listening to my children, who have just come home from school and desire my attention. I want to be attentive, but my mind is racing; adrenaline is still surging through my body from my visit to the police station less than 30 minutes ago.

I had hurried home to make sure I was waiting as they both got off the school bus. I act overly happy and exaggerated to camouflage the uneasiness I still feel inside. I plaster a fake smile on my face while making my voice singsong-like to mask the trembling in its tone. My hands are still shaking. I feel the tumultuous aftermath of having been forced to deal with a situation no one ever expects to face; but like I have so many times before, I function as best I can so that my children will have little to no idea that I have spent my day dealing with *another* relapse, *another* bender, *another* week filled with unbearable circumstances and agonizing events at the hands of my alcoholic ex.

Early this morning, after the children went to school, I had gone to the closet and started packing my ex's clothing for the umpteenth time. It is almost comical how many times I have done this. We have tried to reconcile so many damn times, and I have put these same damn clothes in these same damn suitcases a dozen times already. The first few departures, I folded his clothes neatly so as not to be vindictive or spiteful. I never wanted him to unpack his items and be angry at me. I would gingerly arrange them, sometimes crying at their departure, always regretting the events that had pushed him so far that he was leaving… again. However, today, I pack with a vengeance, shoving and stuffing his clothing into a black plastic trash bag with little regard. Not folding or sorting, just jamming everything in as fast as I can to get them out of my house and out of my sight.

Yet before I discard them, I hastily rifle through each pocket. It is a habit I have formed after finding crumpled receipts for liquor stores and pubs he swore he never visited hidden in his gym shorts or his hiking vest. Today, though, I am on the hunt for a different piece of paper: a pawnshop receipt. Last night, intoxicated and gloating, he confessed he had stolen my jewelry. He knows where I hide the diamond wedding ring my first husband gave me that I have been saving to give to my son. He has ogled over the many gold chains, gold coins, and 18-karat gold crosses my children have received from their grandparents at their baptismal day and on their birthdays. And now he has sold them all.

I am both frantic and furious, praying and pleading to God that I will find the ticket that will allow me to regain my children's heirlooms. I cannot find it in his clothing, so I flip open his AA book, his Bible, his Big Book study guide, all superficial signs of a goodly recovered alcoholic. I search every dresser drawer, pushing past a plethora of pills he uses to be able to sleep. I look in the bathroom behind the alcohol-laced mouthwash and find more pills, broken in half; his way of rationing the harder, more potent ones he has conned the doctor into prescribing. I have been here before — a dozen times; purging his things from my home, cursing him, and cursing myself for yet another round because I did not learn my lesson the last time.

This is not a new story in my life. The proverbial fly on the wall watching me for the last few years has seen it all before: the crying, the pleading, the shame and regret interwoven with hatred and spite. Yet that same fly also sits back in amusement to witness the romance, the love affair, the endless hours of canoodling amid star-filled promises during each reconciliation. Our back-and-forth relationship is like whiplash; the on-and-off-again is utterly dizzying. We are like ice and fire trying to live in the same space — and it is exhausting.

I sit on the edge of the tub to stabilize my body while my mind whirls frantically, thinking of where to look next. I am barely able to breathe from the sickening despair I feel at the thought of how much he has robbed from us. I can hardly live with myself for allowing him to return and inflict such horrific cruelty. I thought — like the last time and the time before that — that this time would be different. I desperately wanted this time to be different. To be better. To be filled with hope. But within weeks, his lying, grumpy, blame-filled attitude returned and I was busy appeasing him once again. It was a pattern I was used to, a constant downhill slide, and I'd give in, diminishing my spirit just to keep the peace and shield my kids from him.

The interesting thing is that if you met me face-to-face, you would probably never guess that this is my life. People say I am assertive and well put together. When they hear about my work, most are impressed with my business success. I have been acknowledged by organizations and awarded among my peers. I have traveled the world, done business overseas, built numerous homes, and took the clothing company I started with my kids' father to a million dollars in just four years. I am blonde-haired with a nice figure and I am told I have an infectious laugh. As a Gemini, I have great charm and retain cute little facts about lots of stuff. Most people enjoy being around me. Some have said they admire me; others have complimented me on my tenacious work ethic, creative energy, and beautiful life. From the outside, it all looks quite good — but behind closed doors, it is like an ominous freight train plowing its way through a parade route and leaving endless amounts of destruction and chaos in its wake.

There is my outside life and then my home life. The life I share with everyone and the life I can share with no one. I wear the mask of a divorcee at most social functions and I hide the truth that he is secretly back in the picture. I toggle between being with him and being without him. I look forward to his home-coming and I wish that he was gone. I want to be in love — but then question how living with a full-blown alcoholic can possibly be love? I want to *be* loved. I want it so desperately that no amount of lectures or parental advice, friends rolling their eyes, or therapists charging me hundreds of dollars has stopped me from being like a bee to honey for his charming yet destructive nature.

This recent reuniting was relatively nice. After five months of no contact, we resumed exactly where we left off — acting as if nothing had happened and he had simply been gone for the weekend. It amazes me, to be honest, the blank slate I offer every time he returns. I commit to a new beginning and somehow just brush away the past. I forget the lies, the assault, the hookers, the stealing, the threats. I see only the good or the calm and ignore the storm clouds I know are gathering on the horizon.

When anyone asks me why I take him back, I simply tell them that it is because I love him. I forgive him as God asks me to. I see his pain, where he came from, the horrors of his childhood. I am the only person he has; and since our on-again-off-again relationship first started when we were teenagers, I tell myself it's destiny and that we were pulled apart only to be reunited decades later. I believe I can cure him. That my love will heal him. That if I get it right, he will find the happiness that has eluded him his entire life. I feel it is my role, my *job* to support him; and I accept his disease as one would accept epilepsy or diabetes. No faithful person leaves someone who is afflicted and cannot help their condition. "Addiction is manageable," I recite; and if I were smarter, nicer, or more understanding, he would have no reason to be anything but happy and never want to drink again.

That *was* my thinking until today. It was the 'stinking,' 'stupid' thinking that brought me right here: packing, crying, fuming, and abused by him once again. It is the untrue, unrealistic, and undeniably incorrect dialogue that has continued repeatedly in my brain, justifying his return and forgiving his transgressions. I have sugarcoated, glossed over, and allowed the most deplorable behavior one person can do to another. And... I have endured it over and over again.

Seeing the stack of empty jewelry boxes pulled apart, broken, and strewn across my hiding place become the final straw. Others would assume the cheating, shoving, disappearing, or torrent of verbal insults would have got my goat; but like a single drop of water that finally tips the bucket, this was the denouement. Sweating with panic and fueled by rage, I drove to the station to file a police report. I give them all the details as I admit, furious with myself, to once again letting him back into my life. The police take down all the particulars and tell me they will issue a warrant for his arrest. I feel humiliated as they look over his record and see that this is not the first time I have been to the station about him. However, this is the first time I have decided that his actions are beyond excuses, and the first time I do not blame myself or believe that I had somehow caused it.

Instead, this time, with every fiber of my being aching from self-loathing and disgust, I feel something inside of me finally wake up. My Inner Spirit, the one that had been hammered down by his belligerence and torn to shreds by his assaults, finally starts to speak up and demand my acute attention. It begins as a whisper of doubt, rejecting his blame and rises to a wail of injustice, not tolerating his lies. There is no in-between. There is no soft, slow rise in volume. My Inner Spirit goes from total silence to wretchedly unfettered primal screaming. A deep *will* inside swells up to declare I do not deserve this, nor will I stand for it a millisecond longer!

While the kids do their homework, I bitterly gather all his belongings from this morning's packing and take them to the car. I try to be as quiet as possible, aware and ashamed that my children have seen me do this so many times before: stuffing their stepfather's things into my trunk and driving them to whatever house, hotel, or hellhole he is living in now. I can't keep track of all the reasons I have invented to explain to them why he's gone, where he is this time, or why I am removing his things. They have seen it before. Even at their young ages, they no longer believe that he is 'going to get help' or he 'needs time by himself.' Relapse, addiction, and alcoholic are words they commonly comprehend.

As I return to their adorable and loving sides, I curse myself once more. I keep playing over and over in my mind the disbelief I feel toward my situation. I cannot believe he has swindled me. He knows I was saving that ring for my son to one day give to his bride, and that the gold jewelry and coins were from their father's family ancestors. It seems unfathomable that he would steal these things from my children; but I do not have an addict's mind full of twisted rationale. I am cut from a different cloth. I am the enabler, the one who makes it easy for him to be wicked and destructive. I am the one who always blames myself so he is free to do even more.

Sadly, the kids are aware of my distress but say nothing, pretending to be happy. They know all the trappings of his antics. They are conscious that he has done *something* to hurt me, they just don't know what. I feel numb all over. My throat is so tight I can barely speak without wanting to SCREAM at his behavior that was more against the children than it was me. After putting them to bed, I crawl under my own covers, completely devastated. Although every cell in my body is hurting, my mind is racing, reaching, grasping at anything it can do to rise above these feelings. Between the tears, muffled by my blankets, I plead to a higher power to release me from this devastating pain. I ask Spirit to give me the inner strength to live a better way. I surrender every part of my knowing, asking God to teach me what I need to learn so that I can be the woman and mother the world needs me to be.

Like a beautiful wish granted from the most gracious and divine Source, something in me begins to awaken. I feel a deep stir; a driving desire. A fundamental need to shift. I feel compelled to stop hurting, to stop hiding, to stand up and be strong. I suddenly *choose* to no longer feel what I am feeling. I tell myself *it is time*. Time to connect to the *will* I have within and make the *changes* that will *change everything*. It is time to find a way out of this constant abuse. It is time to embrace my inner strength.

June 17, 2015

The next morning, I decide that today is the day when my healing must begin. It will be the first time I take a stand; the first time his departure marks my own arrival. While yesterday was filled with the fury, today is more about the reality that comes after the rage. There is a truth that sets in now that the anger is subsiding and a new inner conviction is percolating to the surface. I know that if I am to honor these new emotions, I need to do something productive. In fact, I feel a great sense of determination to take back my power and stand up for my own self-worth.

Yesterday, when I could not find the pawnshop slip, my rage was insurmountable, clouding all my hope. But today is different. While making breakfast for the kids, I devise a strategic and masterful plan. I know which pawnshop he frequents, as he has been pawning stuff for months. His camera. The racing bike I bought him. A 55-inch Smart TV. The $3,000 wristwatch I gave him as a wedding gift. He uses pawning as a source of income. It has been supporting him during the times he does not live with me. He pawns an item in order to pay his rent, then does just enough work to buy it back. Drink, pawn, sober up, buy it back. He is very proud of his ingenious way of keeping himself afloat; he takes all the valuable possessions I gift him and pawns them back and forth.

Privy to his pawning system, I decide to use it to my gain. A drunken alcoholic and a pawnshop owner can't be smarter than me, and I know if I am intelligent about it, I can get my items back. When my ex was boasting of his theft, he revealed that he received $5,000 from the pawnbroker for all my jewelry. He told it to me in a threat, demanding I give him the cash or I'd never see my items again. Knowing this, I go to the bank and take $5,000 out of my safety deposit box. I return home and, meticulously, in my craft room, cut the exact amount of blank paper to resemble the size and thickness of the cash. I put each stack in two identical white envelopes: one with cash, the other only paper. I empty my purse and refill it with only the two envelopes, my marriage certificate, my divorce papers, and my police report.

With the children safe at school, I go straight to the pawnshop. Walking in, I can feel the pounding of my heart coinciding with the clacking of my high heel shoes on the dirty cement floor. I feel grossly out of place. My sporty office dress sticks out among the fringed leather biker jackets and camouflage hunting coats hanging on the coat racks. Maneuvering past the drum set, row of power tools, and muddy mountain bikes, I approach the register. Immediately I take the envelope holding the $5,000 cash out of my purse and lay it, splayed open, for the man behind the counter to see. I tell him that I am here to pick up some items pawned by one of his regulars. Seeing the money and my fashionable attire, the man eagerly types the name I give him into his database. On the dusty old computer screen, I see the descriptions of my jewelry pop up in a neat little list. My heart starts thumping. My hands tremble slightly. I use my right foot to step firmly on the left in an attempt to get my body to toughen up and not be afraid. He glances down at the bills lying on the counter and shifts into being a delighted pawnshop owner — happy to meet me and delighted I am paying the entire amount for a customer he knows so well. He makes idle chitchat, having no idea that one of his favorite clients even had a wife, and only glances half-heartedly at the marriage certificate I provide. I share how excited I am to have my things returned and he scurries off into the back room to grab them from the safe. Holding my breath, I very casually take the opportunity to put the $5,000 in cash back into my purse and replace it with the other envelope filled with blank white sheets.

Seconds after completing my task, the man returns with all my items in tiny Ziploc™ bags and places them on the counter in front of me. I imagine my heart can be heard thumping from across the street. I am elated to have found my things, but seeing my valuable possessions in that disgusting place, in his sleazy hands, knowing that they were stolen, raises my emotions to a boil. I feel furious and violated! My disgust at his involvement takes over and gives me the courage to totally switch gears. I pick up all the baggies and step back from the counter to start dialing my phone. The man looks at me, perplexed.

I quickly ask for the police officer I was speaking to the day before, the one who was handling my report, then I look at the owner and boldly announce: "These items are stolen and I am calling the police."

What happens next is all a blur. As soon as I make my declaration, the man lunges across the counter, grabbing the hand that is holding my jewelry, and yanks me toward him, twisting and hyperextending my wrist clutching all the goods. The phone falls out of my other hand and lands face up on the counter. I almost topple over and have to bend at the waist as the shop owner pulls me toward him, across the counter, clawing at my closed fingers in an effort to release my grip. I start yelling into the phone, knowing that the police are listening.

"Help, I'm at the pawnshop! The owner is assaulting me! He's hurting me! He won't let go! Help! Help! Help me," I scream as he continues using all of his physical force to try and unclench my fist.

I yell the name of the pawnshop and the street it is on, all the while squealing in pain to emphasize that I am in one hell of a tug-of-war. I hang onto my jewelry with all my might, bracing my legs against the counter. Folded forward, I use my left hand to hang onto the arm that is extended outward and in his grip. I keep shouting as loud as I can into the phone, giving whoever is on the other side a play-by-play of the attack. The store owner realizes the police are listening and that he's creating bigger problems by accosting me, so like a wrestler giving up a fight, he finally lets go. I step a few feet back, out of breath from exertion, and immediately shove the little baggies of jewelry down into my bra. Huffing like a savanna rhino, I stare at him boldly, squaring off and waiting to see what he will do next.

With both of us panting heavily, the man starts yelling, "You're stealing from me! This is a domestic disagreement between you and your husband. How do I know *you* didn't give your husband that jewelry to get money out of me? You can't take it; it's communal property if you are married. He sold it to me and I legally own it!"

With a surge of righteous indignation and a tsunami of inner will, I reach inside my purse, yank out my divorce certificate, and slam it down on the counter like the catcher slams down his glove after the World Series winning catch.

"It's not communal property. It's stolen property! I divorced him two years ago," I shout.

To add to my claim, I pull out the police report and toss that to him, too. He looks over the papers, speechless and dumbfounded that some blonde-haired woman in open-toed heels is carrying this kind of paperwork in her white, patent leather purse.

As we stand there catching our breath, unsure what to do next, two police cars come tearing down the street and skid to a screeching halt on the sidewalk outside the front doors. Lights flashing, sirens blaring, four officers rush in with their hands gripping their guns, each one shouting at us to, "Freeze!" I comply. I don't even breathe.

I spot the officer I had spoken to the day before. He gives me a disapproving glare, a mixture of 'what the hell are you doing' and 'you should not even be here!' Yet I also recognize a flicker of concern across his brow. The situation is pretty precarious, I have to admit; a million things could have easily gone sideways.

The pawnshop owner immediately starts defending himself like a bully in a schoolyard playground. I say nothing, knowing better than to do so. My officer takes less than a minute to shut him up. He has no time for a third-rate dissertation by a pawnshop owner who thinks he knows the law. Already aware of my side of the story and that the jewelry was taken, the officer has us retrace our most recent events.

I meekly retrieve the stolen evidence that is hiding inside my bra and hand it to the officer. He lets us know that all of the items will be seized and be placed directly into police lockup. The officer explains to the pawnshop owner that he could lose his business license, be heavily fined, and face serious consequences for buying stolen merchandise and not doing his due diligence on whom he purchased it from.

I keep quiet. All that matters to me is that I eventually get my jewelry back. The pawnshop owner apologizes, knowing his attack on me could be added as an assault. He wipes his sweaty forehead, mumbling about losing five grand to my lying ex. Acting on instinct, I use my phone to take pictures of them rebagging and cataloguing my items. I want proof to send in the next scathing email that comes from my ex. I want him to know that the cops are involved and that I have my jewelry back.

Once everything is in order, I am escorted out of the store. At the curb, I am given a warning not to come back to the pawnshop and leave things to the police from now on. I am also told not to mention this to anyone, especially my ex, because now that the items have been recovered, there will be additional charges added to the warrant issued for his arrest.

I want to hug all the officers but stop myself from doing so. I say my good-byes and walk to my vehicle — the white mommy-van parked down the street. I feel a little like Tom Cruise's character in the movie *Jerry McGuire* as I drive home, flipping through the radio to find the song that will match my mood. I want some rap number that has a bunch of "Don't f**k with me" and "Look out mother-f***er, don't steal my s**t." My body is surging with adrenaline and I feel empowered and slightly giddy. Banging to the beat on my steering wheel, I turn the music up as loud as the volume will go. I bask in the prideful feelings of taking my power back, reclaiming my things, and outsmarting both the thief and a slimy pawnshop owner.

That evening, I want to tell everyone about my crazy encounter at the pawnshop; how I cleverly outsmarted my deceivers. In reality, though, I feel silly taking pride in those actions. Instead, I curl up under a blanket and watch a Disney™ movie with my kids. They have no idea what has happened and a long-sleeved sweatshirt covers my tattered wrists. Yet I can feel a new sense of calmness in them; they can feel a new sense of strength in me. My Inner Spirit has risen and it has brought a surge of comfort to each one of us. I feel stronger, clearer, and deeply resolved in who I've become. What was dormant is now awakened. I am content watching over them, giving them the love they deserve. Freeing myself of the shackles of the past and knowing that while it may not be easy going forward, it is going to be on my terms.

We never know what will stir our Inner Spirit to rise triumphantly to the surface. In my case, it was what one might consider the lowest and most horrible of experiences a person could go through. Except, I have found the gratitude and gifts that came from enduring that and they have enabled me to connect to and honor the spirit I have within. We all have a magnificent, powerful, benevolent part of our being that wants to be known, and in knowing it, we become it. We step into the strength, conviction, and reverence for who we are meant to be.

You have a *will* in you that you can call on at any time. A strength. A power. A pride that stems from your Inner Spirit. Allow it to come forth. Let it surge like an excited volcano and shower down on you like a beautiful array of fall leaves. Awaken your greatest strengths. Bring forth your inner determination, your genuine spirit, and your complete power. It isn't easy, but it is worth it. *You are worth it.* Tap into the rebel, the dreamer, the adventurer, the warrior, and the visionary who guides your Inner Spirit. My darling friend, be all that you can be.

Ignite Action Steps

Purge your home of all the things that you no longer enjoy or that hold unhappy ghosts and painful memories of the past. Things have energy, and when we hold onto old items, momentos, and possessions that are intertwined with negative energy, we keep that energy in our lives. Get rid of anything that no longer makes you feel good. Thank it for being in your life, say goodbye, and recognize the lessons it taught you. Have a ceremony if you need to, and then send it on its way, cleansed and purged of all the old vibrations that no longer serve you.

Many of us hang onto items, possessions, memories, and even people that no longer serve us. Habit, comfort, and convenience keep us holding onto an old story or a limited, outdated belief. Be mindful yet discerning. If something doesn't feel good when you wear it, get rid of it. If you feel uneasy about having a dutiful gift or guilty about owning an item, allow yourself to remove it from your life. Your space is sacred and deserves to be filled with positive energy so you can create enjoyable thoughts and have a supportive purpose in your life. When everything around you is in harmony with your beloved Inner Spirit, it will create pure and utter happiness.

JB Owen – Canada
Speaker, Author, Publisher, CEO of Ignite, JBO Global Inc. & Lotus Liners
www.jbowen.website
www.igniteyou.life
www.lotusliners.com
jbowen
jbthepossibilitymaker

Yendre Shen

"From your pain, you will find your destiny."

Dear reader, trust that your life has been preparing you for something you're meant to do. From the start you would have no idea what this is, perhaps there were little inklings along the way, but you're often left wondering and searching, feeling like you've been forsaken in a vast empty land with no one to give you directions. You may want a hint as to why you're here and what your purpose is. Believe me when I tell you, you're born equipped with the inner knowing of your destiny; the only thing required of you is that you listen and then take the steps toward it.

Don't Be Afraid to Feel

The lady at the desk looked up and smiled, "Hello Dr Shen," she said. "Welcome, we're so glad you're joining us." We exchanged greetings. I signed in and she handed me a binder of course materials. I walked through the doors into the next room with several round tables staggered in a zigzag order. I settled into a chair near the back and surveyed the people milling around — some got up and approached the table with a wide spread of breakfast options. The delicious smell of coffee wafted from the corner of the room with people clustered together to pour themselves a cup. I decided to join them. Having a preference for teas, I took a spot by the hot water thermos, awaiting my turn to choose from the selection box.

As I made my choice, I wondered what brought each of these health practitioners to this intimate gathering. What did we have in common that drew us together? I could understand the presence of the homeopaths and naturopaths, as I'm one of the latter. But the room also had medical doctors, optometrists, nurses, nurse practitioners, and pharmacists. They had the right to prescribe and dispense pharmaceutical drugs, but they were here at this course to learn about the clinical applications of homeopathy — a form of medicine that uses minute doses of substances to treat diseases. It was one of my favorite subjects when I was a student at the naturopathic college. Homeopathic medicines have been used for over 200 years. But it has fallen out of favor in North America due to debate over its scientific basis. It ventures into the unseeable unknown to acknowledge that we are energetic beings as much as we are physical beings. Its prescription takes into great consideration the mental and emotional status of the patient. It honors that our feelings reveal much more about us and our state of health than western medicine realizes.

I curiously pondered how each of these practitioners found their way into their chosen professions. I have grown accustomed to things not happening by chance. I wondered what I would discover if I retraced my steps back to what sparked me down my own path. For a while, I have been feeling restless and unsure whether my profession really suits me. It felt odd to think this, as it seems such a perfect marriage. I had fallen in love with nature and plants from growing up in the untamed wildish landscapes of South America in British Guyana. The events that took place there shaped my childhood; it shaped me.

I was 4½, and together with my two sisters, who are seven and 13 years older, crossed the Atlantic Ocean from China to Guyana to be united with our father. Growing up without my mother, I was often left on my own to tend to myself. I spent a lot of my time in the vast openness of nature that *lived* behind the noodle factory owned by my father. It was a place I felt the presence of God, but didn't know it by name then. I could sense there was no judgment in nature. Nature nurtured me. Our mother had died three years earlier; I couldn't remember what it felt like to be nurtured by her. The plants were my playmates as I explored, inspecting and examining their unique features and beauty. On occasions, I came back with wildflowers I collected from my adventures. Upon reflection, I saw how formative that period was in shaping my connection with nature. Spending so much time alone in my inner world fortified my awareness with my intuitive senses.

My father's noodle factory produced the noodles for the local Chinese restaurants. On weekends, our father would take us into town. He would buy us tickets to the cinema, which often showed Bollywood movies. I loved the singing and dancing of the Bollywood stars, and I emulated them by dressing up in saris and copying their dance moves. On one such trip to town, when I was 7 or 8, we saw a film about a plane that crashed in the jungle. It was not a Bollywood movie; it stood out for me. In it, there was a lone survivor of the crash, and he was nursed back to health by a medicine woman using plants from the jungle. I felt the strong impression this had on me, the revelation that plants have healing powers. It left me in awe realizing the plants I've admired and played with in the wild had possible restorative properties. I remembered afterward I reenacted the scenes with my cousin, who was my age, and played make-believe games creating medicines from plants to heal each other with.

Clearly I can see the reason for my choice of becoming a naturopath. But why was I feeling restless about my work? At the course they were discussing the uses of the homeopathic medicine made from the German chamomile plant, Chamomilla, which is great for cranky and difficult-to-please teething babies. The presenter described a child who found the pain so intolerable, they would indicate something they wanted and, when given it, would still be mad and push it away or throw it at you. They would want to be held, but at the same time would push you away. They were inconsolable in their pain. I thought there were times I could have used that medicine as a child.

My oldest sister used to tell me stories of how I had tantrums that wore out the heels of my socks from kicking my feet on the floor, and how I cried so long I would lose my voice. She said I was unreasonable and willful. It was difficult for our mother. She told me of an incident when, coming home from visiting relatives, our mother was carrying me in a basket. As we passed over a bridge, our mother paused, and in her emotional distress, she wanted to drop the basket with me in it into the river. My sister grabbed our mother's arm, begging her to not do it. I used this story to comfort myself for our mother's unexpected death. It helped me to not feel sad for her absence, as I convinced myself it was better not to have a mother who didn't want me. Perhaps some of my inconsolable crying was from feeling my mother's hardship and not being able to have her when she died. I didn't have the words to understand my emotions as a child.

Being a mother myself now, I understand the joys and pains of parenthood. There are moments I would happily give away my own child. I have endured my daughter's tantrums that lasted hours as she insisted on having her way, from her views of fairness. How perfect that I have such a child to practice confronting my own feelings on the giving and receiving ends of this experience to come full circle in understanding its purpose for me. There is no reasoning with a child, sometimes you have to find your way to be loving no matter how difficult. I believe we act out in our relationships to test the limits of our safety, daring how much the other person can handle and still love us in our worst moments; to trust we can be ourselves freely.

My father didn't tolerate my stubborn defiance kindly. He was a tall, thin man, stoic and private. We had a battle of wills. He dealt with my willfulness with brute force. He demanded my obedience with the use of his hands and when I wore them out, he used the bamboo handle of the feather duster to whip me into submission. Obviously, this method didn't get me to comply — I just grew more defiant in silence, more determined in my mind to not surrender my will to him. I was aware he was beaten as a child. My grandfather was a bully and called him a weakling for often being sick. My father was not shown kindness or understanding in his times of need. He didn't know how to contain his anger and rage when I provoked him.

My father was born in China during WWII, when Japan invaded and occupied it. He remembered the cruelty of the Japanese soldiers. He told me horrific stories of how the Japanese people treated the Chinese. His own father left him, when the war broke out, to evade being drafted. He had an older brother who was his protector. One day, his brother drowned while they were swimming together. He relayed this story to me often, of how he lost his brother. He witnessed the drowning but was too little to do anything to help. The care, love, and protection he had felt was lost forever when his brother died. He was left feeling even more scared and alone. I know he didn't feel safe or secure in the world. I felt those emotions from him as a child and still I feel them in my life now.

There were tender moments I had with my father, when he used to take my hands and study them, peering into them like he wanted to see into my future. He examined my palms one after the other, looking carefully at the lines. I waited patiently, rarely getting this kind of attention from him, to hear what he saw. Sometimes he would say nothing, on a few occasions he'd tell me I had too many emotions, I felt too much, and that it would be hard for me to make decisions. I took this 'feeling too much' as something bad, a curse, like a kind of liability I had to bear in life.

I do feel my emotions easily and deeply. At the homeopathic conference, we were talking about Pulsatilla, the homeopathic medicine made from the delicate wind flower. It's especially beneficial for abandonment issues and traumas where the fears of separation would have the child clinging and hiding behind their mother. I've used this medicine for my son. He's a kind and affectionate child, easy to show his emotions. Because he cried easily, his father has on occasions called him weak. I wondered if this was a medicine my father could have used. Perhaps he was a tender, delicate child who was told that boys don't cry, that he shouldn't show emotions, as being emotional was a weakness and it was dangerous to show weakness. It was dangerous to feel too much.

Without fear, my cuddle-loving son innocently asked me one day, "Mommy, if I killed you, would you still love me?" I paused and thought about what he was asking me. I know his question was not about killing me. He needed to know if he did the most horrible thing he could think of, would I still love him? I told him, "Yes." He needed the security of my love; to know that no matter how terrible an act he committed, I would still love him. Our emotions can grasp the holistic nature to the nonlinear logic of things that our minds can't comprehend with reason alone. Fear of separation and abandonment starts in childhood, because of the withdrawal of love and security. A child needs to know they can make mistakes, be different, and not be forsaken.

On our break, I chatted with a medical doctor who has changed her practice to solely using alternative medicine. She didn't want to prescribe drugs anymore. It was ironic and I realized what had been bothering me about my profession. In wanting to be mainstream, for the sake of belonging and the privilege of having the doctor title, my profession sold out — we sold out on the soul and spirit of the forefathers of naturopathy. To me, we were sacrificing our spirit for acceptance. It was evident by the public disowning of homeopathy on national TV with members of my profession claiming it was not scientific evidence-based medicine. 'Evidence-based medicine' is a code word for the collective agreement of what's true. Much of what's true is unknown to us. There are far more things we don't have evidence for than things we do.

Children come into the world with their spirit intact, a spirit that's untamed and wildish in nature. Feeling not accepted for who they are is like a form of death to their spirit, yet sacrificing themselves for the sake of belonging is another kind of death. My rebellion with my father was a test of his love. Not being accepted for who I am was the source of my defiance. Defiance was a form of self-preservation. I was aware of my inner spirit since I was child. My intuition is the voice of my spirit which speaks to me. It's been my source of inner guidance without having guidance from my mother or father. I sense much more information from my intuition than I'm capable of explaining or proving. My life has been a search for truth. I trusted more what I could *feel* than what I was *told*. Things came to me from feelings first before I could articulate them into words. My spirit accepts me unconditionally and honors my every choice lovingly.

My work with my patients has always involved helping them develop their intuitive abilities. My goal was for them to be able to make good choices independent of me. Something beautiful comes from this. As my patients develop confidence in their intuition, they trust themselves more and make decisions that align with who they are. They were able to recognize their gifts and abilities and use them naturally, therefore making them more happy in their lives. Our spirit always wants what's in the highest good.

I was beginning to see what was common in the practitioners who attended the homeopathy course. It was their inner spirit of not wanting to do harm that drew them to homeopathy. Homeopathic medicines are gentle and don't impose on the vital energy of the person. There's no battle of wills. It aligns with nature, by respecting the individual's uniqueness, and the spirit of the organism. It trusts in the innate wisdom of the body and supports how our spirit heals without harm or force.

I was seeing why I felt disconnected from my work. I no longer found fixing people's chief complaints satisfying. I wanted more than helping people get rid of their allergies, digestive issues, hormonal issues, or bodily pains. Illnesses were messages from our bodies and manifestations of the mind. Our whole life is captured by our emotional record stamped onto time. Ultimately the patients who are willing to do the deep inner work with me find themselves back in their childhood. I have one such patient who has worked with me for over a decade. She courageously dove into her emotions and found the obstacles holding her back from her self-expression. Last year, she invited her partner to work with me as well. He confronted his anger issues and worked on his communication skills. He saw he didn't know how to honor his emotions. They have grown so much together in accepting each other's vulnerabilities. In October, they welcomed their first child into the world. Watching them together, seeing how much unconditional love they're able to pour into that new soul, how much respect they have for that unique and wonderful new Inner Spirit, I felt fulfilled and understood the purpose of my work. It was gratifying to be a part of their baby's birth and see the fruits of my labor as two conscious spirits created a third. I feel my two patients, through their journey and child, have been reborn themselves, awakening to their union and oneness.

Healing their childhood wounds meant they could be more present in honoring their child's spirit. They could learn from their child, as well as be a role model. This experience made me realize deep down what I wanted was to give people the childhood I never had. I wanted children to be nurtured by a mother and a father who unconditionally accepts them. In this loving environment, a child can tame their inner spirit from within and not have to shut down or act out in defiance. Defiance is not necessary when our emotions are acknowledged. A parent's task is to love the child without killing the child's spirit. Parents who do their inner healing work can teach their child the unspoken, innate, and universal language of their spirit, in which deciphering our emotions is the key to understanding this language with our bodies and intuition.

The love gaze of parents on their child bestows on the child the sense of themselves; that they are loved and accepted for who they are. It gives them the security within themselves to trust that the world is a safe place. I want children entering the world to know they are wanted and valued. To know they can be loved unconditionally by their parents; loved for who they are. This is the spiritual work of parents and children. Feeling too much is my gift to helping people. I give people permission to feel their emotions; as we can't heal what we don't feel. Helping people heal their childhood wounds healed my own childhood. Our pain helps us find our meaning. Our life story contains the pieces we need to know what our destiny, purpose, and gifts are. The purpose of your inner spirit work is to have the best relationship with yourself.

Ignite Action Steps

- Be kind and present with your feelings. Don't be afraid to feel.

- Nurture your inner child and cultivate the parent within you. You can be the parent you never had. Love is attention, focus, and presence. Have time, space, and patience for yourself, your children, and for your own inner need for tantrums or childish behavior.

- Surrender to your Inner Spirit's wisdom. Trust that every part in your life's journey is necessary in discovering your destiny, your purpose, and your gifts.

Yendre Shen – Canada
Spiritual Mentor and Naturopath
Innerguidance.ca

OLIVIA ÓDOR

*"Our soul power is an untouchable beautiful force; let it
flow as an unbounded river of love and freedom."*

**My intention is to help you see that we are not *powerless* in any situation.
We are *powerful* when we allow ourselves to trust the unseen, that inner
voice; our senses. The outside loudness and reality can run its course,
but nothing matters more than connecting to our own internal truth and
standing our ground. We can heal ourselves and shift reality by connecting
to our soul's power. It is untouchable.**

MY SPIRIT AND MY HUMANNESS

Flying into the heart of the Grand Canyon in a small helicopter with my
friends, I felt a strong sensation of being fully alive. The view, open space, and
freedom of speeding through the air was like being on the top of the world.
It was the first time I felt the lightness of life. This is how life is supposed to
feel, I thought.

Walking in the canyon, my friends were taking pictures, posing, and in a
hurry, seeing everything very quickly. They got so far ahead of me that I could
not hear them anymore. I sat down on a big rock and fell into the awareness
of my soul. Being in such beautiful surroundings, and away from my friends,
opened me up to allow me to be truly me. For the first time in my life, I was
able to look inside, beyond the curtains, and see the inner side of myself. I
was struck with the realization that my heart was holding so much pain. A

storm opened up in my internal unseen world. I just sat there with the silent magnificent surroundings, the stillness, the depths and the heights of the rocks, and allowed myself to feel it all.

I know there was *love* in that perfect imperfection. The presence of nature allowed me to be completely present within myself, and I was given the space and freedom to feel it all, and I sensed it was okay to be me. I promised myself that day I wouldn't let the point of my life be about only looking good on the outside! I only cared about how I feel on the inside, my raw truth. I made it a priority for myself. I never told anybody about my experience, but I knew it was a '*soul call.*' That experience taught me to always turn internally — even though it would take many more years and challenging experiences before I would learn to honor the power of my soul and stand up for my real truths.

I had to learn to hide my feelings in order to survive my childhood. I was a quiet child, not making any noise, behaving perfectly all the time, so they treated me as if I was a shy girl — but nobody saw who I was on the inside. I was not shy. My parents were highly educated and well-known in the community. My mother worked as a school principal and my father trained as a professor, but sadly wasn't able to work as one because of his unpredictable crazy behavior. It was much later in my life that I discovered he had schizophrenia but always refused to take medication. My grandma worked in a courthouse, and my grandpa had a business selling wine. In the community they were seen as a loving couple and loving grandparents but behind closed doors it was a totally different world. They hid their true selves from everyone. I was part of a family of pretenders.

One day when I was 12, a short time after my parents divorced, I had to spend time with my father and his family. My cousins and I were playing outside, and then all of the sudden my father started screaming. My family members and I ran to the house and away from my father, locking all the doors. Far across the street, the construction workers building a school all stopped their work and put down their buckets, their tools, not knowing what was happening. My father was standing alone in the middle of the yard holding the axe, very angry. Out of control. His large body was in rage as he screamed, "Give me my daughter!"

I felt a hand on my back. My grandmother was pushing me out of the door without any motion to protect me. I thought, "If my mother was here, she would never expose me to any danger." I was scared and ashamed that my own family treated me like this. I felt unworthy. The door closed behind me fast. I started to walk to my father, not knowing what would happen. I totally dissociated from my feelings and disconnected from reality. There was nothing left to do but surrender. I slowly walked toward him.

"You belong to me not to them!!" he said. Since they had pushed me out and hadn't protected me, I completely believed him. We walked across the yard together and into a small house. I had grown up with my father. I was familiar with his craziness, so I knew how to relate to him so he could calm down. I had learned to go along with whatever state he was in. I didn't resist, I didn't argue, I was just a rag doll, I was nobody, in complete survival mode. I didn't reveal any part of myself — I had learned that he was dangerous; I never knew what he would do. My father was speaking crazily, expressing his anger. I just let him be and he slowly calmed down, turning into a little child who never wanted to hurt anybody. In that state, he became a completely different person: innocent, scared, naive.

I don't know how many hours passed, but it felt like many, then there was a knock at the door. My father happily ran to open it. The man outside asked where his brother was, but it was a trap. Other men came in and my father was handcuffed. Everything felt unfair. Felt so wrong — he had come back to himself but he was still being punished. Standing there in handcuffs, he promised me that he would take me home the next day and part of me believed him. I felt completely alone. The father that I loved was about to be taken away.

Nobody asked how I was. No one saw me or knew how I felt. My grandma came and did not say a thing, ignoring me and pretending as if nothing had happened. I was being punished for no reason and felt so unloved and singled out. I had to spend that night in the house with her alone. I was a good kid, not saying anything, but I felt twisted inside.

That night, during my sleep, I suddenly jumped up, choking and trying to breathe. All I knew was that it was pitch-dark and I was in a panic. There was no air getting into my body, and I felt like I was on the edge between life and death. I was completely alone. Pretending I was okay was too much for me. I had to keep it all in, but my body wanted to give up. At that moment, I paused. I thought, "I am only 12 and this is my life?" I had the inner knowing that I didn't want to start all over again from the beginning if I have to be born again. I had nowhere to turn but completely inward, toward my own Being. I had an inner knowing that the choice to live or die was in my hands, and that made me see that I was not powerless in my situation; my own soul force was present, bigger than life, bigger than all the human experience. I became one with it. My soul wanted to be alive even though not showing my emotions was nearly killing me. I could see that I had a choice to make — either follow the family pattern and be a pretender, which would destroy me, or connect fully to my own soul and truth. I chose my truth.

It wasn't until my visit to the Grand Canyon that I realized how much I was still carrying the pain of my childhood around and how much this pain was impacting my relationships. I hadn't realized how much trauma I had experienced at a young age; instead I had believed my childhood had been normal. My visit to the Grand Canyon and the feeling of knowing my soul prompted me to want to learn more. This questioning led me to go soul-searching. I became interested in healing modalities and connections with other realms and dimensions. I searched for answers and met a spiritual teacher working in a yoga center, a fancy place full of curious people, also searching for healing and direction. The teacher was a speaker, healer, and successful person — a published author and authority figure that nobody could question. I loved to go with her to different gatherings. I didn't recognize why I was attracted to her but she felt very familiar and I felt at home with her. I wanted her to see me being a good student because I felt that this would keep our connection strong.

I followed her on the spiritual road that she took me down, but I was not myself. I ignored my internal voice, the same way I had in childhood, in order to survive. The pattern of being 'good' for others was familiar to me. I trusted her deeply, I trained with her as a very disciplined, receptive student. I became a mentor of her process, and I was allowed to attend her private meetings. I even helped her give out free healings at public expos. I felt special being in a close relationship with such a person. But, I was getting more isolated from anyone who wasn't a part of this closed group. I moved to her house, away from my place. I became more isolated, further away from my original life. I didn't feel any joy. I could see other people out in the world, having fun. I had no freedom at her house, nothing felt good — I could see that the stories she was telling weren't reality. Then, when she escalated her demands one last time, I hit my limit. I was not an obedient sheep anymore! I refused to follow her demands ever again!

Because of my refusal, she humiliated me in front of the others saying, "Her soul is gone. She has no soul." That was it for me! I become that fighter's soul energy, nobody decides for me! No one rules over me, nobody could ever tell me that I don't have a soul. Who was she to make pronouncements about my soul? But it was dangerous. I was in her house, giving up on my life, and having nightmares already. At that point I knew I was done and I needed to escape from her. It was for my own sake that I turned against her and left the group. This was a very long, intense, and traumatizing experience. I traveled far from myself; physically and spiritually. I did not feel a rebel or a warrior at all.

My life turned upside down. I had to move to a very cheap rental room — it was a wreck. Sitting on that filthy bed in that scary house, I felt ashamed about the situation I was in. In that horrible room, as my back pushed against the dirty walls, I looked around at my terrible surroundings and meager belongings and reflected that everything I had built was completely gone. My old life was over, my personal special belongings were lost. I had to ask myself, what had happened to me?

In that moment, I recognized that everything I had lost was just my own creation as a reflection of myself. I became completely present within and I saw the most *wonderful* thing — that there was a part of me that no one could touch or break!! My Inner Spirit. I witnessed my own creative power. It had never been lost, just buried. I recognized that inner untouchable power I had and that I would not need anything else in this world as long as I was connected to my own internal self!

The hardest part was releasing my resistance toward the present undesirable situation. The moment I had no resistance toward it, I had a clearer focus on what I wanted. I found a new beautiful house to live in. New friends came along and new jobs. I could manifest the material world so quickly when I let go of my identification and focused on creating the things that I wanted — even better things than I had experienced before.

But, I wasn't able to do this with my *body*! My body was holding the old truths. I was wounded emotionally. The fact that I had no support and I had to move on with life, happiness skipping over the past as if nothing ever happened, made me feel like I was running in deep water. Invisible to the outside, I collapsed inside. The pain of being unseen and alone was intense and overwhelming causing third stage rosacea to appear on my face and skin. That led to inflamed bumps with liquid and blood running out of control, down my face. It was a sign from my body, an alarm. There was so much tension in me. People advised me to move on with a happy life and never look back. Sadly though, this is not how it works. I could not move on because I could not *feel*.

I had to go back emotionally and release the sorrow, fear, and anguish. The healing began with focusing on my truth, just like I had experienced in the Grand Canyon. I had to connect to my body sensations and emotions. I used alternative healing modalities, years of practicing trauma integration while being present with my body and doing inner child healing.

Throughout my healing journey, I recognized I had never allowed myself to feel anger as a young adult. Being a good child, anger was not acceptable, and I was frequently shown that anger can make you a bad person. The moment when I allowed the burning sensation of anger and permitted myself to go even deeper into the painful suppressed emotions, I suddenly experienced a miraculous sensation of being cooled down internally. That changed my skin immediately. It was an amazing transformation. I continuously healed myself by turning inward and only listened to my complete truth, honoring my body's emotions, regardless of how painful it was to bring them up. I had given *space* to express myself in a healthy way through imagination, writing, and music.

By being fully open, I found my way out of the old patterns that made me sick, closed off, and stuck as the quiet numb girl. That was not my soul's energy. My 'soul energy' was the untouchable, strong, beautiful force that I allowed back into my body, recognizing it as the same feeling I had when I survived in my childhood. My body alarm opened the floodgate, guiding me to break free and embrace the expressions of my soul and my intense emotions, leading me to breathe life in deeply.

Despite many years of healing, subconsciously I still identified negatively with myself, feeling badly about my past. I wanted to stop struggling with this. Miraculously, I met Beejal Coulson, the creator of Quantum Life Technique™. Her method turned me back to my 'soul energy', as though I was an out of tune *instrument*. Her method was so intensely powerful that I could not believe what I experienced. I was not prepared for the awe that I encountered. I connected with my 'soul power' with exactly the same feeling that I had as a child on that night reaching for air. Beejal brought me back to sensing my power as if it was a *forgotten sound*. It was unbelievably transformative. It was such a deep experience! It put me back in alignment and provided instant healing on all levels.

I have learned that we cannot skip our humanness, we have to bring our true human stories into the realm of who we are. Listening to my soul's guidance, I made a choice to break free from my family pattern. I came here to express the truth, to create a life that matches the inner beauty of my soul, and to find authentic happiness.

Reality can be a huge tornado all around you, but your heart and soul can stand untouched and strong. Allow the human part of life to run its course and trust the unseen, to uncover the depth of your soul. Your soul knows the plan, when nothing makes any sense in the moment. Let it be. Stand your own truth and nobody can bring you down or break you. Reality will shift on your behalf according to your soul's plan. We can turn anything around by connecting to our Soul power. May you be blessed to connect to yours.

Ignite Action Steps

Practice releasing resistance and creating the state of allowing. This helps manifest the desirable outcome, instead of being stuck. Without resistance our focus is powerful and clear.

Meditate to connect more deeply with your thoughts, emotions, and body sensations. The point is not to 'feel better' but to gain a deeper awareness. Be where you are completely validated; where your truth is *not fixed*.

Listen to the sensations of the body, notice them, *never* allow your thoughts to dismiss or diminish your body sensations and emotions. Only you know your truth and how you feel. Deeper awareness will bring you to solutions and clearly show the old patterns.

Trust the unseen realm. Trust life, surrender, have the desire in your heart, but never control reality. Life will always support you; it will flow when you are on your path, even when it's absolutely illogical from understanding. Life puts lots of obstacles and hardships in the way when you are not trusting your intuition and are going against yourself. Obstacles try to force us to turn inward and make limiting choices.

Surrender to the Higher Power, let it unfold. This releases the resistance in reality. When you trust completely that you can be okay with any outcome, then the situation is completely in your hands. Reality will shift and life will blossom on your behalf.

Olivia Ódor – Hungary & United States of America
Metaphysical Integration Coach
www.oliviaodor.com

Paul J Punshon

"By being aware and still, you can achieve what you believe."

My intention is that my story brings you light and hope. When you are in complete despair, when you feel consumed by fear, know that you can overcome anything. Know that letting go and ultimate surrender is the start of a new path to a vibrant, meaningful life.

The Power of Powerless

When asked if I'd be interested in writing for this book, I jumped at the opportunity as I never thought this would be a reality, rather just another unfulfilled dream. This is my first attempt at writing; I intend it not to be my last.

By the time I was 17 years old, I was a hustler. I was sleeping in bus shelters and doing whatever it took to survive. While I attended school through the end of grade nine, I don't feel like I had a formal education, but rather a 'street survivor' education. This led to many life experiences and I had to reinvent myself often, whenever the situation dictated, as I never really knew who I was. I seem to have always done things the hard way, which always led to stress, drama, and uncertainty. And the harder I tried, the further behind I got. I was caught up in blame, shame, and being paranoid of the world around me. It was a bleak situation for a teen to be in.

I used the excuse of never having met my biological father to justify feeling out of place, broken, and victimized. His absence became my reason for my out-of-control lifestyle. Little did I know that every decision I made was solely my choice. I thought everyone else was the same and I was the only person who was different. My mother married when I was 3 years old, and they had a son soon after that, my brother Rob. I was now in a family that didn't seem totally mine. I suddenly had new cousins, aunts, and uncles. Later, as the insecure adolescent I was, this felt like a lot of pressure. Being a skinny kid, surrounded by my 'new' family of masculine, tattooed, tough guys, and wanting to be like them but not being able to just added to my despair. I was in a total identity crisis.

I was so full of fear at a young age. Even recess could be terrifying. I can clearly remember, in grade one, being swarmed by older girls time and time again. They were kissing me and grabbing me, forcing me to the ground. I felt small. Helpless. Violated. This went on for what seemed like an eternity but was probably only a couple of weeks. It had me so freaked out that I would ask to go to the washroom right before recess, then hightail it out of there and run all the way home, begging my mom not to take me back, which of course she did.

My mom would march me back to school, and with that came embarrassment as the teachers and students all knew what happened. I became the center of attention for everyone to talk about and that felt humiliating.

In trying to avoid attention, I wouldn't raise my hand in school. This of course contributed to my poor grades, but I was pushed through elementary school on the pretence that maybe I'd do better in my new middle school. Well, that didn't work! I was held back in grade seven and that started raising flags that maybe there was something wrong with me academically. The school sent me for psychological tests and set up regular counseling meetings which made me believe that something was seriously wrong with me. It was a terrible thing to do to a child's self-esteem.

I believed I must be defective, so I started to act that way. I began by lighting small fires. I wouldn't do any homework. And I moved up to petty stealing. This was the beginning of a long dark road ahead of me, but at least I had an identity: one of being troubled, crazy, or nuts (names people would call me), but I was okay with that as people soon began to fear me. Rather than *me* being in fear, I was in the position of power. It felt like I was being respected. I then started hanging out with other bad kids, and doing bigger crimes, moving up the respect ladder, being crazy and more of a bad ass. Funny thing was, *I wasn't respecting myself.* The only classes I tried in were gym and shop, two interests which are still prevalent in my life today and are part of what saved me.

I ended up quitting school at 16 and found drugs and alcohol, which I fell in love with. They took away all the shame, doubt, and insecurities. But they also led me to make many bad decisions. I embraced recklessness, did things I regret, and faced bigger troubles such as jail and homelessness. On the one hand, my life seemed better; but on the other hand, it was actually getting worse. Nothing some drinking and drugging couldn't fix. But my troubles never went away; instead, they accumulated. I had become an addict and an alcoholic.

Uncertain of where I'd sleep each night, I was getting used to sleeping outdoors. Meals were equally uncertain and sometimes only consisted of red licorice. That's all I could afford as drugs and alcohol were more of a necessity just to survive. Even when temporarily sober, all I could think about was finding my next drink to oblivion. There's a familiar saying, "One drink is too many and a thousand not enough." This was certainly what I felt to be true.

I became a good talker. Lying and making false promises meant nothing to me as long as it got me what I needed to make it through another day. I picked up the odd handyman job where the work was short and got me drinking money. I liked this kind of work and I acquired skills along the way, taking on bigger projects as time went by. I was feeling useful and it seemed like everyone needed something done around their house, especially single women of all ages. I would use this to my advantage, talking my way into a place to stay while I worked on the house. Not a lot of work got done, but I had a warm bed, a shower, and food in the fridge. This became a pattern in my life, especially when winter was approaching. Not surprisingly, I got one of them pregnant, and the funny thing is that I was a vegetarian at the time and she was the butcher's daughter. I was 23, drinking more than ever and working as little as possible.

I first met my daughter Tianna when she was 3 or 4, and I was as out of control as ever. I tried to take on a father role — rather, a drunken father role — trying to do what I thought I was supposed to do. I eventually separated myself from her and her mother, and it would be over 15 years before I saw them again.

Winter in small-town Canada was harder than living in the big city. It was colder, with more snow and eight hours from the familiar concrete streets and hectic pace of Toronto, my previous stomping ground. I needed money to escape and get back home, so I broke into a store. I was unsuccessful, but still determined, and stole a vehicle. It had no gas so I filled up at the gas station and drove off without paying, then decided I'd better ditch that car to avoid capture and found another. That one turned out to be a school bus; I stole it while the driver went into the school. I drove that for a bit before I put it in the ditch. Very drunk at that point, I hitchhiked for four hours and only made it 79 km, where I slept in a men's hostel.

The hostel was an eye-opening experience. Massive body odor, terrible personal hygiene, and things you never want to see. Upon waking, half asleep, with one eye open, sober and realizing I was not going to make it to Toronto, a five hours drive away, I hitched a ride back to Manitoulin Island where the police were waiting for me. They gave me a cell for the night. I was charged the next day and thankfully released into the custody of one of my many female friends.

Since I marked myself a pro at beating the system, I knew I could avoid jail if I attended a 12-step program, got a haircut, and faked being a good contributor to society by getting a job. It felt like I was putting on another one of my personas. But this time had me scared — The Queen's Crown Bench was asking for two years, meaning I'd moved my way up to the beginnings of prison time. I was no longer small potatoes. I remember thinking to myself, "What's next? Five to 10 years?" It was a place I didn't want to be.

I started attending meetings where I met people similar to myself, heard crazy stories, and saw men cry. I wasn't alone anymore. Those folks were just like me. I learned that I wasn't a bad person. For the first time, hope was shining through in my life. I knew I still had time to turn my life around. We didn't talk about how to quit drinking; we talked about spirituality and how to dig deep into our conscious selves. I learned how my ego was running my life, how my reactions were *overreactions* based on my emotions. The desire to drink just left. I started praying. The only time I had ever prayed before was when I was in trouble and begged God to get me out of it and promised never to do wrong again. I enjoyed the meetings so much. I was attending every day, making actual friendships, and working the steps.

I earned my first chip, and then my second. Before I knew it, I was two months sober. That was the longest I had been sober since I had my first drink seven years prior. I had a ton of work to do, but I wasn't afraid to do it. As long as I stuck to the spiritual plan, I knew it was possible. It meant making amends to those I had wronged and the great thing is, it gave me the courage to do so. I was on a new journey, discovering and uncovering my true self, and it was great. Suddenly, I was three months sober and started going to the gym. Now that my physical health was improving, I was thinking clearer. Amazing things started happening in my life automatically. All I had to do was surrender, admit I was powerless, and that gave me power! Resentment became passion, regret became acceptance, anger became patience, and hate became love.

A few years later while at a friend's house, I ran into an old girlfriend. She was a tiny woman and down to earth. She was different, in a good way, and so independent. We got along and started dating; not too long after that, we were married. We had two awesome daughters within fifteen months; Indi and Carlye whom I'm extremely proud of. We would go to the park and the first thing we would do is pick up at least one piece of litter. With our kids putting their hands in their mouths or wiping their noses, we changed that to the last thing we did. We always had fun together. They were my champs, they gave me purpose, a reason to get up every morning and keep going.

I loved teaching them about nutrition when we were grocery shopping. Pretty soon they were making the food choices. This was important to me as I wanted to prepare them to make their own decisions in all aspects of their life. I taught them to be sure of themselves, to trust their actions, to build self-esteem and confidence. One of my favorite memories was of the best fishing story ever. I was with them, off the docks on Lake Muskoka, when one caught a turtle and the other a seagull, shocking the seasoned fisherman sitting on the dock.

Our marriage ended suddenly, lasting seven years to the day. Superstitious or what? Its' end sent me into a depression for a year. I cried everyday and my drinking and drugging started up right where I had left off years earlier. As much as I missed my kids, I had to accept being separated from them and look at it as it was meant to happen. I had to trust in my Higher Power and get back to making me number one, believing that everything would fall into place, which it of course it did. Not exactly as I would have liked it to, but at least I returned to sobriety and I will be ready when the time comes to be with them again. Letting go can seem like the most difficult thing to do, yet it's actually quite simple. I trust in my heart and look forward to reuniting with my girls. Universal timing will be divine.

Everything I always wished to do was happening in my life. Playing guitar again, taking part in a few triathlons, writing in this book. These things never would have happened if I had stayed on my path of disconnect to my inner spirit. I'm now 54 and to this day, I practice meditation to slow down and control my thoughts. I go to the gym five days a week. I live a healthy lifestyle. And, I honor my true self.

Now, I focus on balance, harmony, and self-worth. I eat right, listen to my body, constantly rearranging my eating habits. I read, even if just a little bit, and eventually a book grabs me so strongly that it's hard to put down. I meditate periodically, slowing my mind, controlling those negative thoughts that sometimes enter my head. Meditation has proven very useful in catching myself in a self-serving pattern or ego-driven thoughts and redirecting them to a positive outlook. I listen more. I talk less. There's a good saying I've heard, "We have two ears and one mouth so that we listen twice as much as we speak."

Of course, staying sober is the first and only step I need to take; all the rest comes to me automatically and I find I get more accomplished and keep my word more often than not. I surrender myself to my Higher Power and trust that all is unfolding as it is meant to.

My eldest daughter is now 30 with two kids of her own. Being a grandpa is like a second chance and I feel so much love and joy. My daughter is an amazing woman, considering my absence. I wasn't a very good influence and made many bad decisions, which I carried as regret and shame for decades. The drinking and drugging obviously clouded my thoughts and judgment, but I also went through a deep and profound physiological change. Things from my own childhood that were buried so deep I didn't realize, came to the surface. Only through re-enactment after the fact did I realize what I was doing. I am grateful that I decided to sober up, find my way, and get in touch with my inner spirit. Today, my daughter and I are getting closer, and I am astonished at her capability of forgiveness and for love.

As I go through life, I'm always learning. The world and the people in it are my best teachers. I love myself more than ever and realize I'm a leader, not the follower I was always told I was. I know now that life is a journey, whether bumpy or smooth, planned or not, and I must trust in the process of the Universe and know *my spirit* is a part of it.

I live passionately. I have freedom; I have gratitude. Again, I might not be perfect, but it's progressive. It's all practice for me. If I keep at it, it's guaranteed to work out.

I am now semiretired after being self-employed most of my life. I'm grateful for my past and my experiences because they have taught me survival and simplicity. I don't have much, but I have what I need. You do, too. Get in touch with your soul and fill it with love. Take care of yourself, respect yourself, honor your inner spirit and your higher power. When you do, the rest falls into place.

IGNITE ACTION STEPS

Once we've had enough of being sick and tired, lonely, or fearful:

When we've hit a complete bottom is the perfect time to completely surrender, to give up, to stop trying to do it on our own. It's okay to admit defeat. It's okay to stop doing what you've always done as a new you is about to emerge. And the new you is so much better than you could imagine. Next, you must believe in something mightier than yourself. Call it God, your higher power, the Universe, etc. It doesn't matter what you name it. We must have faith. This will release us from our sensitive egos and allow us to listen more and react less. With our head now thinking more clearly on this new journey, this is a good time to take a personal inventory of our lives and feelings, both past and present. Take a true honest look at yourself, who you were, who you are today, and who you want to be.This can be a painful process and take some time. it teaches us humility. This is the start of the growth process, from the ground up… Your foundation. When you do the work, stability, strength, and courage start to blossom. Now you're ready to clear up the past, make amends. It doesn't have to be all at once; divine timing seems to present itself when the time is right and your inner spirit will let you know when that is.

As we continue to grow, keep the faith, practice living on a spiritual level, we will see our lives change before our eyes. We will overflow with love, we will know gratitude, we will thrive in simplicity and expand and live our dreams.

Paul J. Punshon - Canada
Motivational Speaker / Life Coach / Mentor

ADVENTURER

BEEJAL COULSON

"You are in the Universe and the Universe is in you."

My deepest desire is for you to increasingly discover and connect with your Inner Spirit to awaken, heal, transform, and evolve. With an awareness of the inner world reflecting the outer world, you can intuitively invite synchronicities and embody a life aligned to your soul's purpose.

GO WITHIN

I was not aware of my inner world until my late 20s. My initial connection with my Inner Spirit was during my first kundalini yoga class. I felt displaced – it had been an unpleasant day as I had learned that I had been the victim of credit card fraud. Even though I was usually more into faster movement exercises regularly doing kickboxing and aerobics classes, dismissing the yoga class as some kind of cult, the stress of the day led me to give yoga a go. As I entered the room, the beautiful soothing tones of Snatam Kaur flowed out through the speakers and the sweet scent of jasmine incense was wafting through the air. The teacher was calmly seated in a lotus pose on a soft cream sheepskin rug at the front of the yoga studio. She was wearing a delicately-embroidered traditional white linen Indian *kurta* with her hair wrapped in a white turban. I could feel her strong vibrant presence. Her eyes smiled at mine as she nodded her head toward the one space available for me in front of her. The class commenced with an opening chant, *Adi Mantra*. We did a number of *kriyas* and a variety of breath techniques. It was during the meditation that

I had my first wondrous inner experience. Even though my eyes had been closed, I sensed hues of green waves engulfing my heart, and whispers of violet danced around in my forehead. I felt at peace. As I slowly opened my eyes, tears trickled gently down my cheeks. I had witnessed energy within me and what felt like me weeping from the inside. Everyone rearranged themselves so we were seated in a circle with our hands in prayer *mudra,* singing the song *Long Time Sun.* My body felt light; as if it was floating. That experience of my inner world left me curious.

I continued with the yoga class religiously, attending twice a week. Each time, it was different and always interesting. I loved that there was not just a focus on body movements, but also on breathwork and meditation. It was an exciting opportunity for me to advance my awareness of my inner self by going within to connect with my mind and body. It was in one of the classes soon after that I began to explore the question of "Who am I?" This curiosity led me to an exciting spiritual journey of discovery.

The biggest leaps in my spiritual awakening arose when working or traveling abroad, alone. These magical trips resulted in a deepening connection within myself. I felt a wonderful sense of freedom when I was away from the normal stresses of life and invited in synchronicities without even the realization that I was doing it. People, places, adventures, and opportunities all seemed to line up effortlessly. Something greater than me was collaborating for my highest good. When I turned 30, these experiences resulted in a yearning to travel the world for an extended period of time. My role and responsibilities as a Senior Lecturer at London College of Fashion were getting more expansive and life was becoming more challenging to balance as a consequence. My social life outside my work had shrunk. I was also diagnosed with irritable bowel syndrome, which seemed to trigger directly in proportion to my stress levels. In moments of self inquiry, my inner self started to whisper, "Do something out of the ordinary." I trusted it and listened to it. This took some courage and defied convention, as I was heading into the unknown.

I handed in my notice at work, left my apartment empty, and headed to the other side of the world with an open ticket. It was to be one of the most incredible years of my life with so many magical experiences that went beyond my fears and imagination. Nature became the gateway to activating my Inner Spirit. The year was suffused with adventure, fun, joy, wonder, and synchronicity. The symptoms of irritable bowel syndrome miraculously vanished. I had many life-changing adventures, especially in New Zealand, such as paragliding over a lake, horse riding in Queenstown, skydiving at 12,000 feet in

Taupo, ice hiking on Fox Glacier, kayaking and hiking in the beautiful Abel Tasman national park. My most challenging and most memorable adventure that took me far beyond my fears was when I did a PADI scuba diving course on the Great Barrier Reef.

Reflecting back, the magnitude of freedom I had felt while away was from the *present-moment awareness* I was experiencing; not just from the incredible adventures but also from smaller moments, such as skimming stones on a lake and delighting in the cascading ripples they created. I examined each pebble deeply, its shape, its color, its pattern. I touched it, feeling its solidity, its smoothness. Listened to its sound as it danced on the surface of the water. There were many incredible synchronicities from the people I met to the places I visited. I would place my attention in a particular direction and an invitation in that area would appear, often rapidly and seemingly effortlessly. I learned during that time that my Inner Spirit graced its presence whenever I tapped into the source and vibration of joy.

There were also an increasing number of synchronicities along my spiritual path as I was inspired to attend spiritual workshops, *satsangs*, concerts, festivals, and retreats in the UK and abroad. I encountered awakened souls who were embodying unitive consciousness. I had mystical experiences. The more I connected to my Inner Spirit, the more choices I made to seek experiences that catalyzed that connection.

Then, life took over for the next few years — I met my husband, moved out of London, got married, and became pregnant. I experienced a profound birth moment when my daughter Sienna was born. The midwife scooped her up and laid her in my arms. I felt the warmth of her skin on mine; the umbilical cord still connecting us. She was silent and peaceful. Her big beautiful light brown eyes shone up into mine and she held my gaze intensely as they reflected the diamond-like light from the divine. Filled with love and grace, I felt mesmerized and in complete awe in the miracle of life. My Inner Spirit rejoiced. It was her first recognition of me as her mother and the beginning of a beautiful bond connecting us. This special moment is etched in every fibre of my soul; one that I will always cherish.

I had another profound spiritual experience the following year, this time connected to death. I was with my grandmother, holding her hand during her final moments. When she took her last breath, a tear rolled out of her right eye as her soul passed to the next realm. The heart of the family was gone. In meditation, I met with the essence of my grandmother's energy as she appeared as a radiant being of light. A deep sense of peace washed over me. Experiencing birth and death in these ways enriched my inner world, connecting me to my Inner Spirit profoundly.

Then, from my late 30s, I experienced many adverse challenges in my outer world. My mind and body were finding it difficult to cope with life.

In an attempt to seek healing, I booked a space at a 5-day retreat, hoping to get healed during that time. I figured that daily yoga, a good cleanse, and lots of meditation would do the trick. Little did I know that healing is a process. I booked a session with an intriguing spiritual coach. She instructed me to lay down and close my eyes. My third eye was enshrined in indigo. I visualized a red heart, the shape of a brain, and then fluttering iridescent butterflies. As I sensed a swirling energy of light above me, I was asked where the pain resided the most. I pointed to my head and my belly. A shimmering blue mosaic emerged in my mind's eye and dispersed downward into many pieces, then my hearing changed pitch, as if it was tuned to the calming sound of the ocean. Blue energy appeared to be flowing out of my head. As the session ended, it was made clear that I needed to welcome and accept pain as if it were my friend; that I had spiritual healing powers and a higher mission to fulfill. That's when I learned that my purpose was to show people to the light.

After the retreat, I continued in my professional life as a university lecturer even though I had lost the passion I once had for teaching. It had become more challenging and I was just getting through it. My body was screaming for attention as I encountered further mental and physical symptoms. I experienced a breakdown a year later and was signed off sick. As I took time out to recuperate, I returned to practicing yoga and meditation, and I went swimming daily. My intuition slowly returned and a series of serendipitous discoveries, experiences, and opportunities took place that forged the path to activate my healing, transformation, and evolvement. Simultaneously, my soul purpose began to reveal itself in the holistic arena. I retrained in rapid transformational hypnotherapy and reignited my coaching services.

By allowing the opportunities for my body to communicate what it needed to, I experienced a revelation of subconscious memories that had been buried deep: from the near-death experience when I was hit by a car as a pedestrian when I was 17; to why I was born in breech position; and why I had inflammation in my body with autoimmune conditions. I uncovered deep-rooted limiting beliefs and, as they emerged, tremendous healing took place, allowing transformation and integration of the self. Learning to master myself at the level of pure consciousness and explore life from the inside out at this invisible energy level was a game changer. My inner healing drove my physical healing, leading to massive gains in my health.

As part of my recovery program back to health, I experienced transformational breath sessions. In one of them, I felt a sense of surrender in my body and my breath took on a life of its own. I was breathing deeply and effortlessly through my diaphragm. A bright light shone over me and the warmth embraced my soul like a big blanket of unconditional love all around me. I was in the presence of divine love. This connection felt like a soul remembrance. The divine was eternal and always present.

I discovered in my own healing journey that when I hear the message of my pain, then my pain can be released. This is what the spiritual coach was referring to when she said, "Make pain your friend and listen to it." This inner wisdom was the catalyst to regaining my health. My Inner Spirit guided me in my healing when I allowed it the opportunity by going within; all the while enabling my deep devotion to helping others to come into fruition more and more by aligning to my soul purpose.

My life transformed to another level of awakening, healing, growth, and evolution — inside and out — after experiencing Dr Joe Dispenza's teachings, which emphasized the connection between science and spirituality with the goal of coherence. My first live meditation experience with him focused on aligning the energy centers. It had such a dramatic effect on my body's responses that I experienced a strong healing sensation. It was incredible, and I was curious to experience more.

I attended Dr Joe's meditation retreats, immersing myself in the profound meditation experiences and diligently attentive to his teachings about quantum science and neuroscience. During my first pineal gland meditation, I discovered the truth of my essence as an energy being. It was as if there was a screen projector in my mind and I was visiting varied historical landscapes. There were wild scenes by the sea with cliffs and rocks inland with ancient ruins. It was a journey across past timelines. I was flying. I was not in human form and far beyond my senses. I was an eagle, a peacock, then formless. I felt free, with an inner sense of knowing what I was experiencing. The concept of energy took on a deeper meaning. I realized that I was undefinable and beyond form; my soul was eternal and I was pure infinite intelligent energy beyond time and space. The quote by Thich Nhat Hanh resonated: "I am not limited by this body. I am life without boundaries. I have never been born, and I have never died."

I increased my time commitment to a daily practice of meditation, enabling the opportunity to heal, transform, and grow. I also incorporated regular breath work, kundalini yoga, and sound baths into my schedule. My healing powers grew exponentially as a result. My soul purpose to guide people to the light as a hypnotherapist and coach evolved.

Life was unfolding in a magical way, aligned with my life and soul purpose. Energy was flowing through me and my compass, over time, no longer needed input from external sources to validate my choices, as my intuition flourished. I was more energetically attuned and my senses became more heightened. This became increasingly apparent in my therapy sessions with clients. I discovered that when I tapped into the source of joy, creativity, and inspiration, my Inner Spirit accompanied and guided me. A higher wisdom had come into play that exceeded the limited vision of my conditioned mind. This resulted in inspired action and achievements beyond my imagination in my outer world.

The inner dance from going within was reflecting in my outer world in the most wondrous of ways, inviting synchronicities aligned to my soul purpose. I was able to realize and reclaim my magnificence and embrace myself as the powerful energy being I am. I created a modality called Quantum Life Technique™ to enable people to discover their highest potentials with their higher mind and embody a life they loved aligned to their soul purpose. It synchronised the energy of the future with the present. I trained therapists and coaches in QLT. I also discovered my gifts as an energy healer after participating in a weekly coherence energy healing group.

Fulfilled by the wisdom and love I am learning to embody, the skills I have cultivated throughout my course of mastery are made tangible to help others to further a mission of planetary evolution, raising consciousness.

When I meditate in nature, in front of a beautiful sunrise or waves lapping on the shore, I often merge with my surroundings and experience oneness. When I embody within me fully my intentions, I have the power to create them in my outer world.

Our original and natural awareness of ourselves as spiritual beings has been replaced by the illusion that we are the bodies that we occupy. We identify with our form and the outer world becomes our main focus. The loss of soul consciousness creates suffering. It is more often than not that our suffering is our messenger to our truth; our wake up call. If we go within and gain a greater awareness of our outer world, we have the opportunity to continue to heal, transform, and grow. It is an infinite process.

Connect the dots to those deep moments in your life that revealed your powerful inner world and, in the process, indicated something far greater in existence in your outer world. Seek connection in discovering and creating a life aligned to your soul purpose. Enjoy the synchronicity at play when the Universe works with you and supports you on your journey to living a life that you love.

"In oneself lies the whole world and if you know how to look and learn, the door is there and the key in your hand. Nobody on Earth can give you either the key or the door to open, except yourself." — Jiddu Krishnamurti

The answer to the question I had asked myself years ago, "Who Am I," became crystal clear. Just like the poet Rumi beautifully reminding us that we are not a drop in the ocean, we are the ocean in a drop, I discovered that when I ask myself, "Who Am I," my Inner Spirit whispers, "You are the Universe."

This applies to you… you are the Universe in your own expression. You have the Inner Spirit guiding you. Invite all synchronicities to blossom in your life. You are far greater than you think you are. Everything you need is within you.

Ignite Action Steps

1. Go within; connect to your inner world. Invest quality time daily on an activity such as meditation, chanting, dancing, or painting that will enable you to be in a lower brainwave state and access your Inner Spirit.
2. Heart breathing — feel into your heart and breathe in and out from there. Sense your heart to draw in the frequency of love from the Universe and radiate an energy of compassion outward beyond your body, beyond your energy field, and out into the Universe.
3. Pick a sign, e.g., color, shape, animal, flower, number sequences. Be playful. Be open to receive. Observe the synchronicities you encounter with this sign.
4. Listen to a music track that evokes feelings of bliss and raises your vibrations.

Embody the life you love.

Beejal Coulson – United Kingdom & Mallorca
Creator & Founder Quantum Life Technique /
Clinical Hypnotherapist / Author
www.beejalcoulson.com

TRACI HARRELL

*"Loving your life's journey and connecting to the
power of your Inner Spirit is an inside job."*

It is my greatest desire that you will enjoy my story and find some magic and majesty in the lessons I have learned about how to love the journey of life while living out your dreams. My goal is to leave you feeling energized, inspired, and empowered to face any situation with courage and confidence. I offer steadfast assuredness that the Universe will provide for your greatest good, no matter what obstacles you encounter in life. Tapping into your Inner Spirit is how you experience joy along the journey of life and how you can fulfill the true desires of your heart, finding perfect peace that can only be sourced from within.

LOVING YOUR JOURNEY OF LIFE IS AN INSIDE JOB

Throughout my life, there has always been a flow, a knowing, some type of force that guided me. This force felt external to my being, yet it was clearly a force from *within*. I came to know it as my Inner Spirit. It seemed to be all-powerful yet unapologetically weak. It was all-knowing yet also open to infinite possibilities. Somehow these seemingly opposite forces lived perfectly within me and brought me indescribable *peace* and *joy*. It was weird and awesome, and I've never tried to explain it, or to fully understand it, until now.

We can all love our journey of life *and* live out our dreams despite any obstacles that might *appear* to get in our way. Peace, power, and pure joy are the product of connecting to your voice from within… connecting to your Inner Spirit. It's an inside job. This is a fact that I discovered as a young girl and my journey to explore this inner wisdom has continued to uncover new depths of higher learning.

When I turned 50, I began to struggle with the idea of my own mortality… my legacy… my journey of life. I asked myself, "What would be my legacy?" We can all offer the world a gift in telling our stories. I wanted to share with others the power of Inner Spirit. I had done the work… I continue to do the work… and I knew I could share how we can all love the journey of life while living out our dreams.

As I sat in my garden, surrounded by beautiful plants, the sweet smell of lilies reminded me how much I love spending time in nature. This is where I first discovered my personal definition of Peace, Happiness, and Adventure, all in one. It was in nature where I discovered the *power* of connecting to my Inner Spirit. It's where I learned to enjoy the journey of life, no matter what was happening around me.

When I was young, I used to bury my head in books, often while outside in nature, instead of playing with dolls or other games kids my age seemed to enjoy. I remember believing that I could go anywhere or do anything between the covers of a book. I soon defined that success, for me, would be when I had enough money to travel the world to see the places from my favorite books.

As a young girl, I didn't have money that I could spend on my own, and I always thought that having money would solve my problems. I remember feeling tortured when I had to eat foods I didn't like, over and over — wishing that someday I would have more choices in life. I now understand that having food, any food, is a blessing (even if I don't like the taste). I also recognize now, that what I thought were my childhood problems, were really just 'first world' issues (much greater concerns exist in the world)… but at the time, I wanted *control*. I thought that *choices* could only come with having *money*. I also assumed that wealth would come with some degree of happiness and peace.

My journey to leave a legacy required that I reflect on how I first learned that I possessed the power of the Inner Spirit inside of me. Ms. Ward was the first one to open my eyes to the existence of the 'Inner Spirit.' She was a quiet, regal woman who was like a surrogate grandma for all of the kids in the neighborhood. I was 6 or 7 years old and I used to attend a weekly Bible Study in Ms. Ward's screened-in garden patio. She lived in a simple white house across the street, with the most beautiful flowers that seemed to always be in bloom. She would allow us to visit her garden anytime, and for me it was one of the most wonderful places in the world. We also had beautiful plants and a vegetable garden at my house; but as a child, what first drew me to Ms. Ward's garden were the treats that she used to give us during our Bible Study. My favorite were these delicious butter cookies shaped like a daisy with a hole in the middle, which perfectly fit onto my finger. I used to nibble one petal off at a time and allow the soft butter cookie to just melt in my mouth. I don't recall us having many treats at home unless it was a special occasion, so for me, every Sunday at Ms. Ward's house was a special occasion.

As I nibbled off each cookie petal as slowly as possible, I would sit contently, listening to Ms. Ward share amazing stories with us from the Bible. We all sat in a circle on the patio, surrounded by beautiful trees, plants of all kinds, and a sweet fragrance from the bouquet of flowers planted around us. Everything was always just perfect in Ms. Ward's garden. There were gardenias, magnolias, roses, and lilies... I loved them all, but one particular lily was my favorite. She called it the Asian Stargazer lily. It stood taller than I was. It had a firm stalk that I could lean down to my level. I used to bury my face inside of the huge white flowers, which had a bright pink star-shaped center, until my nose touched the middle and the fragrance filled my heart with joy.

In Ms. Ward's backyard Bible Study, she planted the first seeds inside of me that made me aware of the oh so powerful Inner Spirit that lives within all of us. At Ms. Ward's house, we used to sing songs like *Jesus Loves Me* and *His Eye is on the Sparrow.* How cool was that! I learned that we were all special in *His* eyes. I loved the songs, but even more, I remembered the Bible stories. We heard about individuals in the Bible who tapped into their Inner Spirit and experienced miracles — from Moses parting the Red Sea (to save his people), to Jesus raising people from the Dead (and healing the sick), and the Holy Spirit protecting Daniel in the Lion's Den. My favorite was the story of Noah and the Ark, a man hearing from the Holy Spirit, from God, that He wanted him to build a huge ship on dry land. Noah knew it would make him a mockery of those in his community, but he did it anyway. I loved that he had FAITH and he *believed.* And when it rained, it poured... and then he had proof that what he heard from his Inner Spirit was true. His truth was *THE* truth, and there was such comfort in that. Ms. Ward reminded us that these were not fairytales or fantasies. She shared that these stories were about real people. We learned about a real LIVING force and about the option to have a real relationship with what she called the "Holy Spirit." This made the Inner Spirit real for me.

How perfect that my Inner Spirit had blossomed during that time. As it clarified for me *exactly* how I should live the rest of my life: 100 percent on

purpose! Living intentional, fearless, activated, with the sole purpose of helping others to live their best life. I really wanted to gain new personal insights
and to bring joy and love to my family, to my community, and to the world.

I never could have imagined that I would be sitting in my garden decades
later, and that the ideas of *control*, *choice* and *money* (which had meant so
much to me growing up) would now all have such different meaning to me...
a deeper meaning that had bloomed from my ability to trust in the power of
my Inner Spirit. I have lived a life of joy, with dreams fulfilled, but it wasn't
for the reasons that I had thought.

Throughout my corporate career, I had accumulated some money and financial security — yet today I am willing to risk it all, just for the honor of doing
what I know to be the 'right thing.' I had seen more *choices* than I could have
ever imagined — yet today I realize that the only choice that matters is the one
that aligns with my core values and the calling of my Inner Spirit. I've done
well in school, have worked in top companies, and have traveled and lived all
around the world. I have felt more in *control* in the past than I thought possible
— yet today, my ability to surrender to the calling, to the knowing of my Inner
Spirit, is what brings me the greatest sense of *peace* and *joy*.

Most of the things that I dreamed of as a child have already come true. I've
had dream jobs, including one that allowed me to live on the beach in Rio
de Janeiro. Despite all of my apparent successes, the job I'm most proud of
is the 'inside job' that I have cultivated over time by investing in, trusting in,
connecting to, and surrendering to the power of my Inner Spirit.

What I've learned along my journey of life is that the 'true treasures' that
bring the greatest joy are from those unique lived experiences. When the
power of Inner Spirit is embraced, then every decision, every 'next right action'
becomes crystal clear. You feel it in your bones, in your heart, and in your
mind... you just know. When you focus on and tune into that *knowing* and into
that *feeling* — that is the 'inside job' which serves as the gateway to miracles
in one's life that are sourced from within.

There's no real mystery to the power of the Inner Spirit. You can practice
it to make it more powerful and more natural for you. Like any muscle, the
more I practiced and used it, the stronger it became, and the easier it became
to do things that I couldn't accomplish before. With the practice of connecting
to your Inner Spirit comes *clarity*... and with clarity comes *peace* and *joy*.

The concept of using the power of the Inner Spirit sounds super simple;
that's because it is. Simple but not easy. It's like losing weight. We all know
what to do. Success may look different for each person, but your body will

help you to find the 'path made clear'... if you are willing to do the work. That's how the Inner Spirit works... It's an inside job. It doesn't matter what's happening around you. All that matters is your ability to *focus* on what comes from Inside of you.

As I sat in the garden contemplating how I had just endured my most recent battle for my life, for my safety, and for my sanity, I knew that I had been guided by the Inner Spirit every step of the way. I felt overwhelmed with gratitude at that moment. I knew that the outcome would have been extremely different had I not already invested in learning to hear from my Inner Spirit. I flashed back to the memory of my traumatizing experience with exclusion and bias at my last job, and I remember how I had felt suffocated, belittled, sad, angry, and powerless. Then I recalled how it was the power of the Inner Spirit that gave me the strength to speak 'truth to power.' I had perfect clarity in knowing that it was 'my calling' to stand up and fight for *inclusion for all*, for something that was 'Bigger Than Me.' It was both scary and exciting.

I was a *visionary*, faced with ongoing opportunities to create a vision that I knew was right. I was also a *warrior*, sacrificing my livelihood, jeopardizing my job, going into battle to follow my Inner Spirit. I was an *adventurer*. I didn't know what to expect. And all the while, I was a *rebel*. Each day some new miracle allowed me to 'soldier on' and to 'take a stand,' and it felt amazing to follow a *divine calling*.

When I felt the initial realization that my life was changing, my level of joy was so uncommonly delightful that I had close friends share with me that they were waiting for me to have a breakdown. They didn't know how they would have handled the same situation. Instead what happened was, I was so filled with the Holy Spirit, so closely connected to my Inner Spirit, that I began to infect those around me with *love, grace,* and *joy.*

I smiled as I thought about my current situation. I was working diligently... trying to change the world and I didn't quite know how. I had a clear strategic plan and four key pillars. I was self-funding this 'divine calling' through money I had saved, but that was running out. I was now living 'on the edge.' If I thought I was an adventurer before, following the Inner Spirit now was another real test. I was living by example. I knew I had to surrender to the Universe — to do all that I could, and trust God to do the rest.

I should have been stressed out. But that's not how Inner Spirit works. There is a *peace* that comes even in the hard times, when you have no idea where the solution is coming from. There is power in finding *peace* and *joy* in not knowing how the story will end. That's when the 'power' part of the Inner Spirit really kicks in... assuming you remain positive and continue to act as if the outcome that you desire has already been achieved. That is what I believed to be true, and there was no reason for me to believe any different now. I believed. I had *faith*. I smiled with confidence and I just knew everything would be okay.

I have loved my journey of life so much that it almost seems unbelievable. Even though I have had some traumatizing experiences and things haven't all gone as I may have expected, I can honestly share that I always knew that whatever was happening would work out for my good. It was never a question for me. Good things are destined for me, and there is limitless power in that belief. Good News! You are destined for good things, too. You have unlimited power in your Inner Spirit.

"Thoughts become Things" research proves that to be true. Fortunately, the use of Positive Psychology is how the brain naturally works. I have always believed that I was *blessed* and knew I was meant to be a *blessing* to others. I was meant to change the world. Now, at the age of 50, part of my living legacy is to 'bottle this up,' and share this 'belief system' with others.

I discovered my connection to my Inner Spirit as a child, and I continue to nourish the power within to this day. I realize that I still have more work to do. We all do. But, that *is loving the journey of life while living our dreams.* I want all of us to live a life of *joy* and to be intentional about living out our dreams. I offer you the grace and space that allows you to *live your legacy* each day. Believe in yourself. Know that you're not alone. That's what the Inner Spirit does for you. It fills any gaps. It mends any cracks. It heals. It informs. It transforms. It Ignites!

Ignite Action Steps

- Listen. Your Inner Spirit will speak to you as plain as if your creator was speaking through you... from the inside. It will whisper to your heart, share recommendations, provide inklings, and create urges that clarify your next right action. It's an inner knowing, a feeling, and we all have it. Tap into the voice of your Inner Spirit.

- Spend time in nature. Connecting with nature is connecting with the infinite possibilities in the universe. It's a pathway, a gateway to Ignite your Inner Spirit. Being outside is how you go deeper inside.

- Take a moment in nature to just be still and stare intensely at something beautiful… a bird, a flower, a butterfly, or the trees swaying in the wind. Start with just 60 seconds. This is called a 'Bigger Than Me - Moment in Nature™.' When you focus on a single item, with childlike wonder, and allow everything else to just disappear from your mind, you will allow yourself to be taken to a sacred place — that's where your Inner Spirit lives.

• Sit in silence daily — Create a space for your Inner Spirit to guide you, lead you, and instruct you. This is how to love the journey of life no matter what happens.

• To find your Inner Spirit, it's not about looking outside of yourself, nor looking around at your circumstances and then deciding what choice you should make from what you see. Stay inwardly focused and live out your dreams.

• Use the power of your Inner Spirit by looking inside and listening to your heart, and then feeling what you should do because it feels right. Trust that you will just know. It's an *inside job*.

Traci Harrell - United States of America
Founder, It's All Bigger Than Me Ministry
President, It's All Bigger Than Me Consulting
Lead, Bigger Than Me - Success Series™:
Achieving Equity & Inclusion in Systems
President, National Black MBA Association®, Seattle Chapter
Lead, Diversity & Inclusion Champion,
SCORE® Seattle (US Small Business Admin.)
Producer & Host - Bigger Than Me with Traci Harrell
(YouTube Show, Radio & Podcast)
www.ItsAllBiggerThanMe.com

AMY HACKETT-JONES

"In the space beyond other people's opinions, lies a field of inner peace and the truth of what is possible for you."

It is my hope that by reading my story you are inspired to challenge both the status quo and that which you have come to believe about yourself. I encourage you to allow that spark within you to be Ignited so that your strength, courage, and resilience empower you to embrace your innate wisdom.

WHAT CURIOSITY TAUGHT ME

It was 12 PM in Johannesburg, South Africa in February 2006. The sun was high in the sky, bright and intense, shining through the window, as I was pacing to and fro in the house that I had rented, anxious to hear the travel agent's confirmation over the phone. I was hopeful there was still one seat left on a flight from Johannesburg to Cape Town that same day, because there was a chance I'd get to interview President Thabo Mbeki.

I had landed there that morning after a 12-hour flight from London and overheard two nearby businessmen confirming that President Mbeki was going to be at the World Economic Forum in Cape Town the next day. My number one priority was securing an interview with the President.

I had to be there. The success of the project I was working on depended on it. I was increasingly nervous the longer the travel agent kept me on hold. Pacing more fervently, I could feel a bead of sweat form and begin to trickle down my spine, my mind darting, my breath quickening as I contemplated how I could possibly drive through the night across South Africa as a female traveling on my own. I had to be on that plane. There were no other options.

"The last seat on the last flight has just been taken. There are no flights left," she said. I was devastated.

It was a 16-hour drive. Overnight. Across South Africa. I was hesitant, but it is hardwired into my DNA to fulfill the mission that I have accepted, so despite the jetlag setting in, I could see there was nothing else for it… I hired a car and off I went.

The long, hot day turned into a cold, clear, crisp evening, the moon was full and the stars were sparkling. I could see the velvety expanse of the night's sky so clearly. I was excited and a little apprehensive too, at the long road ahead of me, in the black of night, across this vast, desolate landscape.

The further I drove and the later it got, the radio stations started playing slower, softer music, which was sending me to sleep. I rolled down the windows and let the cool night air do what it could to keep me awake, as it whistled through my hair. The rhythmic noise of the wind became my drumbeat as I sang my heart out to just about anything I could think of.

When it was time to fill up with fuel, I bought some coffee, but the edge it provided wore off pretty quickly. I was tired and apprehensive as I pulled into the next pitstop. It didn't feel safe to stop and snooze for a while so I bought the largest Red Bull™ in the store. Necessary, I felt, if I were to arrive in one piece and accomplish my mission: an interview with the man who would open the doors to a new global opportunity.

As I was driving, I had so much time to think. My mind turned to the place it often went to: the fateful day of my accident seven years earlier and those ominous words from the doctor, "You'll never run again".

I'd been skiing in the French Alps during university. Midway through the vacation, I had an accident in which I crushed and fractured my lumbar vertebrae and broke my right hip in three places.

On that fateful day, the snow had started to become slushy, but I thought I'd go for the last sprint of the day down one of the slopes. You see, I'd always been athletic. I was never going to be a professional athlete, but being athletic was a big part of my self-identity… of who I was and how I showed up in the world. I wasn't a newbie to skiing either. I crouched down with my knees bent, poles horizontal under my arms, skis pointing straight downhill and I went for it, all the way down, full speed ahead, until I needed to turn slightly, ever so slightly. I leaned into the corner, and as I did, I caught an edge and went flying, straight into a pylon. Skis, poles, body strewn across the slope. I was in such a state of shock that the pain and fear didn't set in for some time. The slushy snow I lay upon was slowly melting beneath me the longer I stayed there and I could feel the icy cold starting to seep through my ski suit.

Two skiers stopped to help me up, but I couldn't move. One stayed with me and the other went down for help. I was scooped up by the paramedics onto the blood wagon. After five days in a French hospital, a flight to London on a stretcher, and an ambulance ride home, the doctor, who knew I was due to be running the London Marathon a couple of weeks later said, "You'll never run again." Indignant, I thought to myself: "Well, you might as well chop off my legs then."

At that moment, life wasn't worth living if I couldn't run. Running was my freedom, my meditation, my solace, my clarity. My everything. I had been running for as long as I could remember and crossing the finish line of the London Marathon was a lifelong aspiration I craved to achieve. I'd never run that distance before.

Instead, I spent six months in bed, and even spent my 21st birthday propped up against my pillows. I had to learn to walk again with a walking frame, crutches, and later, a back brace for many more months while back at university. Yoga didn't cut it for me. I painfully felt the loss of the thrill I had received from running. I felt so out of shape and I had no muscle mass anymore. It was as though a part of me had died inside and I mourned that part for some time; it was a dark, cold grip around my spirit.

Through the years I replayed those two moments, over and over again in my mind… the life-altering accident and the life-robbing prognosis the doctors gave me. "WHY?!" I often cried to myself. The answer didn't come, and didn't come, and didn't come.

Three years after the accident, I still hadn't recovered enough to run the Marathon, but I finished my studies and graduated from university. I then found a job that paid me to travel the world and interview Heads of State, mostly those from third world countries. I traveled non-stop, and during that time, I continued to believe what the doctors had told me. I didn't question them.

Their words would circle in my mind repeatedly, taunting me, as if they were some sort of bully in the school playground. "You'll never run again!" The power of those four words, delivered so confidently to me by the experts who 'knew best', was immense. I believed them. The only question I held onto was, "Why me?"

Years of compartmentalizing these thoughts had taught me to move on quickly and focus on the task at hand. Getting to that interview. After a long, long, long drive, I arrived in Cape Town early the next morning, too early to check into the hotel. I was exhausted but wired from all the Red Bull. I sat for a while in the lobby, preparing my questions for the interview. I wasn't nervous. But I was restless. I felt the need to move my body and stretch my legs. I changed in the lobby restroom, thinking I'd go for a walk. As I went outside, the streets were quiet. Eerie, in fact. There was not a soul in sight.

All the hours in the car led me to plenty of questioning. I finally exhausted myself of the "you'll nevers…" and the "whys?" and turned them into curious "what ifs…?" — which felt imminently more engaging and empowering. Right there and then, I thought to myself, "What if I tried jogging around the block? I mean, it's just one block. It's not far." This was the first time in seven years that the idea had even had the chance of presenting itself to me; it had been drowned out for so long by the "you'll nevers…" and the "you can'ts." I put one foot in front of the other, and before I knew it, I had jogged, very gingerly around the block. I stopped and thought: "What if… I could do one more?"

Life stood still for a moment. I drew a deep breath in and as I did, I felt a sense of inner peace wash over me.

I jogged two blocks… then three. Then four. Then five. When I got to five, I came alive. I could taste the freedom already, and the cool ocean breeze on my skin was the only invitation I needed. I could feel the thrill that I thought I had lost forever. "What if I could run a few more?"

I kept running. Suddenly, the spectacular vista of Table Mountain was to my left and the sun was rising majestically over the Atlantic Ocean to my right. Joy returned to my heart, I felt as light as a feather, exhilarated, excited. I started laughing to myself, just like a kid in a candy store, and then I remembered the movie, Forrest Gump and the famous words: "Run Forrest! Run!"… and so I did. I ran, and ran, and ran. I lost all sense of time, distance, and pain. I didn't care. I was running, and that was all that mattered.

I had heard of a powerful energy that exists at Cape Point, where the Atlantic and the Indian Oceans meet. I felt drawn toward it. I had no idea how far it was. I didn't care. I just kept running. The sun was rising, I could feel it kiss my cheeks, and continue to stir something in me, as if it were giving me a benevolent nod in agreement, an encouraging, "Yes! You've got this!"

The road ahead of me was long and winding. Somehow, I just wasn't phased by it. On the contrary, I was deeply moved. As I continued to put one foot in front of the other, I felt held; embraced. I was living an intense moment of presence and knew that I was returning home to myself. My inner spirit was being reignited with every step I took. I was reminded of how sport strengthens the soul and of how I used to feel. The magic of running had returned. The happy high; the endorphins, the oxytocin flooding through my veins. I was in the zone once more, it was as if the world around me disappeared and I became one with that moment.

I reached Cape Point and stood in awe at the spectacle in front of me. The power and the energy of the two oceans meeting was immense. Humbled, I got down on my knees and kissed the earth beneath my feet. "Thank you, thank you, thank you" I said, as tears of joy rolled down my cheeks.

I stayed there for a long while, overwhelmed with emotion, both in amazement and awe. It felt as if time had stood still and yet I had been running for several hours. I was unsure how to process what had just happened, when my body started to seize up and I felt a desperate need for water! I spotted a couple walking toward me and asked them what the time was. "Midday," they responded. The conference began in a couple of hours. I asked how far it was back to Cape Town, they said, "40 miles."

"How many?!" I was shocked at how far I had come and how long I must have been running for. I wondered how I was going to get back. The couple were going to Simon's Town (about half way) and were kind enough to drive me there. They offered me some water and a sandwich that I devoured gratefully.

From Simon's Town I took a taxi back to Cape Town. In the taxi, the adrenalin and the endorphins of the run were wearing off. The aches and pains were beginning to set in. So, too, was the awareness of what I had just accomplished.

Until that moment, I realized, I had no idea what I was truly capable of. Everything shifted for me. Absolutely everything.

I arrived in Cape Town, showered, changed, hydrated, refueled, and made my way to the World Economic Forum as quickly as I could. Interviewing the President was then a piece of cake... it felt like a sideshow to the morning I'd just had.

It was inner peace that I arrived at, during my epic all-night drive and all-morning run, which enabled me to shift what I had long held true. During that journey, letting go of the "you'll nevers..." impelled me to create space beyond other peoples' thoughts and opinions allowing the curious "what ifs...?" to emerge. Only then was I able to let go of what others perceived to be true for me, and toy with the idea of possibility instead. I trusted my inner spirit for the first time in a very long time, if not for the first time ever. It gave me the space to breathe, to be, to speak, and I actually listened.

In a world that champions haste over patience, force over compassion, and power over goodwill, the term "inner peace" can turn some people away. This is ironic to me, considering I have come to know inner peace to be the most powerful tool I have. Inner peace is a consistent state of consciousness during which I am fully aware of my thoughts and emotions and how they might be shaping my perception of the world around me. More than that — *I am aware that I am aware of it.*

I am able to take a step back, objectively survey all the elements of a situation and come to a conclusion that is free from ego, bias, judgment, criticism, or misinterpretation.

Inner peace allows me to disarm myself from the frustrations, anger, fear, and insecurities that might otherwise mar my decisions. It frees me up, so I become present to what is happening both inside and outside myself allowing the ripple effect to impact my thoughts, words, and deeds both internally and externally. Inner peace brings inner power. It is in fact my superpower. I have come to see that when I am at peace, I speak powerfully to people — often without saying a word.

Inner peace gives me the ability to thrive in all conditions. I no longer immediately turn outside myself for solutions to my problems. I pause. And in that pause, I turn my attention quietly inside and tune into my inner spirit for insights. Instead of problems, I look for opportunities to go beyond my comfort zone and dare to think new thoughts, ask new, empowering questions, and seek more peaceful, effective solutions.

When I have inner solace as my personal guiding light, I arrive at stillness; I become a pure presence with a clear purpose. I am more able to find the courage to speak what some may see as uncomfortable truths. By making a commitment to my inner connection, no matter what happens, or how fierce the storm of life is in any given moment, I become the lighthouse of reason, collaboration, and solution-based dialogue.

I know who I am and why I am here. No one is able to "press my buttons." Peace, personal power, and an inspired purpose have become my way of being in the world. Peace within myself is my path as well as my goal, and my greatest advantage.

Three years after I reignited my passion for running, while I was living in Panama, I competed in my first triathlon and came second to the European Champion.

What becomes possible for all of us lies beyond that space of other people's opinions. It is in that field of inner knowing and when confronted with raw honest truth, we awaken to what we truly are capable of. Just think what you might be capable of if you were curious enough to believe that there is no such thing as impossible? When and how often do you find yourself listening to other peoples' "you'll nevers," "can'ts," and "shouldn'ts"? If you could play with some curious "what ifs" — what might they be? Where might they lead you? What might become possible for you that seems impossible now?

Ignite Action Steps

- Commit to inner peace as your guiding light and your greatest advantage. The moment you commit wholeheartedly, providence moves too; the universe conspires with you to open doors, present opportunities and connections, and supports you in breaking through perceived limitations.

- Challenge yourself and those around you to question the status quo — immerse yourself in new perspectives to imagine new possibilities.

- Ask better questions — the power of the answers you seek lies in the curious, empowering nature of the questions you ask of yourself. Stop listening to the naysayers and start asking, "What if…?"

Amy Hackett-Jones – United Kingdom
Peace Whisperer | Coach | Healer | Speaker | Author
www.amyhackettjones.com
� *@amyhackettjones*
📷 *@amyhackettjones*

Brent Martin

"You'll only know what the other side looks like if you go to the edge!"

My wish is to inspire you to listen to your inner voice and fully realize that you are perfect the way you are! There is nothing to fix. Your unique life path to living simple and free is not about *having*, it's about *being*.

Empty Beer Bottles and Stale Cigarettes

The first thought I had was, "I'm awake! Woohoo, it's party time!" With all my unleashed 7-year-old energy, I jumped from the top of my bunk bed to land gingerly on the cold concrete floor. I could hardly contain my excitement. I listened intently as I ran up the steep wooden stairs hoping to hear music and the sounds of high heels dancing, but all I heard was cold silence.

I peeked over the top of the stairs. The colored New Year's Eve streamers and empty beer bottles laid lifeless on the shag carpet. The smell of stale cigarettes hung thick in the air. My heart skipped a beat. I ran into the living room. The morning winter sun pierced through the frosty windows, casting an intense light on the aftermath of the party. The silence was deafening. Nooooo, this can't be happening! "Hello?!" I cried out.

I rushed into my parents' bedroom only to see them passed out on their bed My dad groaned as I came close, "The party's over Brent, go back to bed." By now it was starting to sink in. I went barefoot to the front door of our house, large stinging tears rolling down my cold cheeks as I gazed out over the massive snow drifts. My tired brain struggled to comprehend, but as the seconds went by it dawned on me that I had in fact slept through the extravagant party my parents had been planning for months. The new year had arrived without me.

I slouched down onto the shag carpet and let out a whimpering cry as the sadness and pain in my heavy heart was unleashed. How could this have happened to me? What did I do wrong? Did someone not want me to be there?

I was a high-energy and curious young boy, building forts in the forest, fishing in the river behind our house, or playing kick the can with new friends. It didn't really matter as long as my body was in action and I was connecting with something or someone.

It was extremely important for me to be loved and feel included. Subconsciously, I was constantly asking myself the question, "Do they like me and want to play with me?" My thoughts and actions had me do whatever it took to fit in and be included.

I believe every human being first experiences the world through the eyes of their early childhood. Any shame, hurt, abandonment, or grief we experience is carried with us for the rest of our lives, whether we like it or not. I may never know why I didn't wake up that New Year's Eve, but it doesn't really matter now. Being interested in feeling and healing those wounds from the past is likely the most potent work I can do to rekindle the innocence, love, and joy that is at my core. Freeing ourselves of life's traumas can take us on an adventurous and often a challenging journey of being fully present and fulfilling life's goals! Ultimately this freedom will be the source of one of my most treasured gifts that I will carry with me for the rest of my life.

My journey of adventure continued though my teenage years, living fast and full-on, pushing myself to the corners of being uncomfortable, knowing there was always something new to experience. I was forever striving to be noticed, loved, and not be left out. This feeling continuously pushed me to my limits which led me to winning the first ever Canadian Mountain Bike Championship at age 23.

As race day approached, severe tendonitis in my wrist swelled and my confidence slumped. I didn't know if I could ride, but my fierce competitive spirit and the pressure to at least show up was something I could not resist. I carried the yellow 'leaders' jersey through the first three stages and into the final cross-country race. The pain in my wrist and the fatigue in my legs disappeared as I still had to complete two laps over the most technical trails on the mountain. Halfway through the last lap and in fourth place, an energy came over me with an effortless ability to negotiate the terrain. I pushed past the pain, and passed the favored riders ahead.

I was in what I now know as a deep *flow state*. I was completely present in my body and experiencing an indescribable high-performance zone. The challenge of the trail, the competition, and the supportive cheers from the trail's edge were fueling my desire to go faster. The flow I was experiencing was new and utterly exhilarating.

Twelve months later, at the end of a year-long solo traveling adventure, I received a letter from my father. It was before the internet and email so getting a letter from home was a rare and special moment. I had just docked in Phuket after sailing up the west coast of Thailand. I was perched on a bench outside the post office, and with anticipation, I began reading every word of the letter as if my dad were present, standing strong in front of me. After his update on life back home, he got to the crux of the letter. It read, "Everything is great, and would you like to work in the family business?"

My heart was set on continuing the carefree and adventurous mountain life I had left behind a year earlier, so the question came as a huge surprise. But that recurring need to be wanted and accepted ran deep. I called Dad and told him I'd give it a six-month trial.

Six months turned into 25 years. The ensuing roller-coaster ride of wins and losses ended up shaping who I became for virtually my entire adult career. Focusing on the demands and complexities of running a company, while trying to keep myself connected to my family was extremely challenging. Looking from the outside, I had it all: the perfect family, a beautiful and loving wife, healthy children, and a business that was expanding while taking me on monthly trips globally. I was having the time of my life… or at least that was how it appeared!

Behind my emotional curtain it was a different story. The business was suffering, and so was I. I was perpetually overwhelmed, trying to make sense of it all and figure out what I should do. My wife and children said disapprovingly, "You're always away!" Even when I was home, I was not present, constantly thinking about what I needed to do and beating myself up for not doing it better.

The recurring narrative of, "One day when I get this done, it will be much better," went around and around like a broken record in my mind and in many conversations with my wife. This went on for years until the years turned into a decade. All I knew how to do was work harder for longer hours, take more courses, and read all the latest business self-help books. I was never satiated.

I was at my wits end when my buddy Oop invited me to join his business group. It was a big step for me, but I joined because I had run out of ideas on how to have my company be successful. Rather than trying to figure it out on my own, I was invited to lean on other great minds. I'd never been involved in a group where the sharing and brotherly support was so strong.

We were on one of our annual retreats and I had just completed a business presentation. One at a time, my colleagues gave their feedback. The last person to speak was our mentor, Jim. He was held in high regard, like an elder of sorts, for his sage-like advice. Everyone sat up at attention to listen closely to his valuable words of wisdom. I waited anxiously. Without hesitating, he simply announced with all the clarity, simplicity, and respect that I could have asked for, *"Brent, you're incompetent!"*

It was like a dagger in my heart. Anger boiled up, the heat in my body spiked, and the sweat surfaced on my forehead. I thought to myself, "Screw you, Jim! Do you have any idea how hard I am working? What I've had to deal with? How could you!" In that defining moment, I was back to being that 7-year-old boy digging his bare toes into that shag carpet covered in empty beer bottles that smelled of stale cigarettes and wondering why the party had gone on without me.

Returning home, I was overwhelmed with frustration, feeling the weight of the world on my shoulders. I often cried alone, feeling so stressed, helpless, and tired. Sleepless nights left their marks on me, signs of an unhealthy businessman who was really effective at covering up his true emotions. Jim's comments constantly sat festering in the background, impacting virtually every meeting and decision I had to make. The business was such a huge part of my life and with that not working, the rest of my life became excruciating.

With my stress levels out of control and no end in sight, I turned to my sister for support with running the business. Thankfully, she was excited and ready to take on the post of CEO. One of the true bonuses of family businesses is the level of trust that exists, and I am forever grateful to my sister for taking the lead and allowing me to breathe again!

The reality of not being the lead guy who had all the responsibility hit me like a freight train. Overnight, I was no longer running a business with over 100 staff and thousands of customers depending on me and my team to perform. The void was immensely painful. I had sacrificed all that my heart and soul could provide, trying to look good and prove I could do it, but I had failed miserably at being CEO and I didn't know who I was anymore. I was adrift and without purpose. Little did I know that the rudderless feeling of being lost was in actuality a blank slate being prepared for a whole new life to be written on it.

As difficult as it was back then, I have now learned that our best and most rewarding experiences come *after* a struggle. Always keeping that vision and possibility alive is what keeps me moving forward one day at a time. It took me a while to accept that belief as I continued on my personal exploration, hitting a few more bumps along the way.

An extended sabbatical took me on a family adventure to New Zealand, Australia, and Thailand, where I was truly able to disrupt the unsustainable track I was on and begin to discover a greater sense of calmness and peace of mind. This launched my healing process. It was important for me to find ways of returning to the deep *flow state* that I had experienced in the mountain bike race many years before.

After a year of being disconnected from the company, I returned with a refreshed outlook on the business. Viewing the business from this new place allowed me to confidently and clearly see the areas that were not working. My warrior archetype was in full regalia again as I knew I had only one chance to win this battle or we would lose everything. However, I was less concerned about what other people thought of me. I knew deep down what was needed to lift the company out of its current slump. I put everything on the line, mortgaging my family home and buying my sister out so that I had full ownership and responsibility of the company. I knew it would take an extraordinary effort to turn the company around and I was not sure how to do it, but my gut was telling me to go for it.

Two years later, I accepted a very healthy deal for the company that allowed me to pay off all our debt and have the freedom to create the exhilarating new chapter in my life. My Inner Spirit was a key ingredient in creating this new flow in life.

Creating breaks can seem incredibly difficult in our current realities. Our society is in such a crisis of thinking we need to stay busy working on ourselves, our businesses, our fitness, or else our fundamental survival is at stake. When we commit to taking breaks, a new space is created, and healing and creativity emerge so life can begin to alter.

I now live everyday, aware of my needs to be loved, wanted, and admired. Yet, I choose to move in the direction that I am authentically and completely passionate about instead of being driven by these past conditional needs!

I am now able to pause before I make a decision and choose powerful outcomes that are in alignment with who I am, versus who I think I should be to impress others. I can now come back to my center, maintaining calmness while discovering my 'true self.'

I hope my story has inspired you to listen to your inner voice and help you find the courage to take action. Your unique pathway to living a life that is unimaginably simple and free is not about *having*, it's about *being*. Fully realize that you are perfect the way you are. There is nothing to fix.

*P.S. As a result of my journey and doing what I truly love, Backcountry Enlightenment (BE) and its core offering XCamp have emerged naturally in my life. XCamp leads intimate tribes of like-minded go-getters into a backcountry setting, far from our distracted digital lives, where we bring together adventure sports and spiritual experiences grounded in flow science, neuroscience, and mindfulness practices. Our mission is to **"Stoke your Soul and Awaken your Spirit!"***

IGNITE ACTION STEPS

Morning Practice.

Start your day with a morning practice that leaves you grounded, positive, and in perfect flow. Create your own ritual location — a space you feel great in. Meditation, yoga, and breathwork will all anchor you in a deep sense of gratitude, leaving you a more loving and present person.

Connect with Nature.

Your well-being craves a connection with nature. Period. Getting outside is easy and free, even if only for a few minutes a day. Simply disconnect from the digital distractions and breathe in some fresh air, go barefoot, raise your heart rate, or simply feel your body and the sensations that arise. Remember this feeling and come back to it throughout your day.

You are not alone.

I highly recommend creating partnerships and teams to hold you accountable, learn from, and share your transformational journeys together. This can be in the form of hiring a professional life coach or joining a group that inspires you to share a regular mindfulness practice.

You have two roads you can travel. One is to be a creator and one is to be a consumer. Being a creator is where love, joy, and fun lives in our experiences. It's about giving. Being a consumer is where sadness, anxiety, and frustration reside and this is more about wanting. So try giving, being curious, exploring new places, and going to the edge of what you believe so you can see what the other side looks like. It's most often wonderful! We only have one life! Namaste.

Brent Martin – Canada
XCamp Founder & Director of Mischief
www.XCamp.ca

CAT FLOWERS

"Once our inner spirit is ignited, we go through a series of deaths and rebirths, birthing ourselves closer and closer to who we truly are."

My intention is for the reader to be inspired to pursue their own healing and their purpose. Once one pursues healing and healthier relationships, it reflects outward. Your outer relationships reflect your inner relationship. I desire for you to be your own best friend and supportive advocate. As we pursue connecting with love, loving ourselves, and pursuing self-care, our whole life begins to transform.

THE OUTER REFLECTS THE INNER

I'm 27 years old, curled up on the bed in my tiny partitioned section of a studio apartment in Park Slope, Brooklyn, New York. On the other side of the dividing wall, I can hear my musician roommate on the phone discussing the music project she's working on. I smell of falafel even though I'd taken off my work uniform sweatshirt. I was scraping by to pay my $800 a month rent with my job handing out falafel samples for a fast-food vegetarian restaurant in the middle of Times Square. This is not what I had envisioned myself doing after I finished my nine years of college complete with my Masters of Arts. But, since I was new to New York City and wanted to be self-sufficient, I decided I'd do the job so I could stay. This allowed me to keep my other part-time work teaching dance, which I was thankful to do as it was my goal, even if it was only three classes a week to 3- and 4-year-olds and not nearly enough to pay my bills.

I was crying and trying to stay quiet as I didn't want my roommate to hear me. My mind was spinning with all kinds of thoughts, especially about my confusing relationship with Alexander, the guy I was dating. There was a part of me that wanted to give up, just sink into my bed. I felt like there was a dark, gaping hole inside me. I often felt like I didn't have energy, and there was a sadness even behind my smiles. However, the energy of the city and the hustle kept me going. I also felt a high from the sexual connection with Alexander, but like a drug, there was a drop and the high would be fleeting. The relationship was not healthy in many ways, but it fit my desire for self-discovery. There seemed to be a battle inside me and, though I was seeking to listen to the true me, I wasn't sure who that was yet.

My lack of clarity was coming out in my relationship with Alexander. It was undefined, which is not what I wanted. Deep down I wanted us to be in a loving, committed relationship. We were having sex but had no commitment. This was tearing me up inside, but I didn't know how to voice it. I didn't feel like I could relax with him, but I was fascinated and mesmerized by what we had. I was exploring my sexuality and, at the time, I thought I was maybe okay with open relationships and multiple partners. I was hypersexual and I would later come to realize that I was not balanced within, and my desires were not genuine but coming from my inner wounding.

Alexander and I met in grad school in Chicago, when we were in the Interdisciplinary Arts MA program. He had a charismatic personality. He was a painter and visual artist, and he used to work in the film industry in Hollywood. He was tall, dark, handsome, and about 15 years older than me. I would always forget his exact age because he didn't talk about age. I never imagined myself dating someone so much older than me, but our connection felt like it transcended our ages. I was inspired by him and intrigued by what he shared with me. He was so intelligent and could talk for hours about all kinds of interesting subjects like spirituality, quantum theory, art, the film industry, Kung Fu, sexuality, history, and hidden things happening in the world. I learned so much being around him, and it coincided with that period of my life where I was questioning all my beliefs. He encouraged me to open my mind to new ways of seeing things. He was the most confident person I knew. He would be brutally honest and talk about things other people wouldn't. He would say things that mattered to me and see the deeper parts of me. I loved that — I craved *real*. I was so tired of people pretending around me, and tired of me pretending myself. Despite our deep connection, I never totally relaxed with Alexander or felt like I had enough space for myself.

As inspiring as Alexander was, he also had a really mean side. I remember one time he said, "You were cute until you cut your hair." I felt so sad and disappointed that he had objectified me — reducing my beauty to my hair. Immediately, I could feel my body close in to protect myself; I could feel my heart hurt. He would talk about how he liked skinny girls and encouraged me to lose weight even though I was already at a healthy weight. He had a bad temper where he would sometimes throw and break things and call me names such as '*idiot.*' He had an inflated sense of self-importance. He could be manipulative and would belittle me when we got into arguments. It was toxic, I often felt awful and scared. I always felt like I was walking on eggshells, but his charm and his loving side would eventually lure me back in. The relationship felt unescapable.

I was married to my college sweetheart when I met Alexander. I had met my husband our freshman year at a Christian college in Tennessee near where I grew up. It was very much in our culture to marry right after college, and I was greatly influenced to not have sex outside of marriage. I wanted to have sex, but I didn't want to be sinning. We really loved each other and getting married felt right at the time. I didn't want to wait until after we finished college, so we married right after our junior year. Four years later, we moved to Chicago for my MA program.

Chicago introduced me to a new culture where I was exposed to different kinds of people and different ways of thinking. My mind was opened. I began questioning my beliefs and I could no longer pretend that I didn't have questions, especially about my religious beliefs and sexuality. One question I asked myself was, "How could these kind, amazing people I was meeting from all over the world be going to hell just because they believed in God in a different way?" I couldn't believe it anymore and couldn't keep lying to myself. I was questioning my marriage. Something felt dead in it and I didn't know how to fix it. I didn't understand myself, how to be balanced within, or to communicate in a healthy way to repair my marriage.

At the end of my first year in Chicago, I was looking at everything differently and I had a big choice to make. In the end, I chose to leave my marriage. Although the breakup was due to many complex reasons, I unfortunately approached the end of our relationship in a very hurtful way by cheating on my husband with Alexander instead of being honest with him. At the time, I didn't know how to handle what was going on internally or externally. It was too painful for me to be honest with my husband as I couldn't be fully honest with myself. I had not developed enough awareness and my dishonesty created a mess. I left a life of acceptance, comfort, and a family I loved dearly to pursue the unknown and get answers to my questions. It was probably the hardest thing I ever did.

A year later, I finished my Masters and was deciding between moving to Los Angeles or New York. I wanted to live in big cities and keep exploring myself, and the vibrance of a city inspired me. I had felt drawn to New York for a long time and Alexander's choosing to move there influenced me, as we were seeing each other. However, right before I arrived, he broke things off and made a point to tell me not to move there for him.

I was constantly doubting myself and often doubted if I'd made the right choice to leave my marriage. I missed my ex who had been my best friend for eight years. I was lonely. Life was much harder than the ideals I had imagined when I chose to pursue life on my own. Curling up in my covers in the apartment in Brooklyn, I wanted to escape from my painful emotions, as I felt like a sharp knife was digging into my heart, mixed with a shaky feeling, keeping me glued to the bed even though the door was wide open.

That was my low point and it was from there that I started to see how, if I didn't want to feel so depressed, I was in need of some inner healing. I realized I was addicted to the adrenaline, the drama, the excitement, even the sadness. My meditation practice was starting to affect my state of awareness. I realized I am not my thoughts or feelings; I am the observer. I cried out to God — Prime Source Creator, as I often did when I hit a low and didn't know what to do, *"Please help me! I want to be living in your love!"* I was beginning to change how I felt about myself, and realize I was more than this and the self that I was expressing.

That week I had had enough. I believed in myself and in life a little more. I was sick of my own behavior and how down I felt. I complained to Alexander that I didn't have the energy to do much and how I thought it was because of the medication I was prescribed to help balance my mood. It was the next thing he said that got me thinking, "You don't really need that medicine they prescribe you, you need some emotional healing, to heal that imbalance." That was something I knew deep down, but I had been too scared to believe it. Strangely, at the time, I put more trust in him than I did myself. Hearing from him gave me the confidence I needed to trust my own inner voice. For so long, I had waited for something outside of myself to fix what was wrong, like there was someone or something that would rescue me from the mess I felt within me. That week I heard my inner voice urging me to change. I began to realize I was connected to the Love that heals, and that Love was within me. I was capable of more, I was my inner spirit, the soul that lives within. That week, my inner spirit was ignited and it allowed me to connect with Love and my true self. No matter how deep it was buried within me, it was there and I could no longer ignore it.

I decided that I would trust, that I would heal, and that I deserved the support to restore my mind, emotions, body, and spirit. I wanted to live from my center and live in balance with who I truly was. I decided I could no longer wait for a savior to come and rescue me, and I could not depend on someone else to fix what was going on inside of me, to heal me, or to care. I realized I had to be my own advocate. I had to become my best friend. I finally believed I had that power within me. This newfound belief and connection to my inner spirit inspired me to take action for my own self-care. I started looking for the right kind of support, as I knew I couldn't do it alone. I searched the internet reading reviews and bios about the different health practitioners and calling around until I eventually found the one I wanted. I had a peaceful feeling in my chest when I read the naturopathic doctor's website and made my first appointment. She helped me enormously and I eagerly anticipated every meeting. When she looked at me, I could see the kindness and genuine care in her eyes. Her presence had a peace and center to it that I craved within myself. She had an openness and was not judgmental, and I felt an unconditional motherly-like love, yet she also felt like a mentor. When I was with her, she wanted to hear about my life, and I was beginning to realize how it all connected. She helped me understand that my emotional state was intertwined to my physical symptoms. With her encouragement, I pursued natural and spiritual ways to support my health, starting with supplements, nutrition, and homeopathy.

I also found a therapist that I liked and trusted. I liked her philosophy, and she was easy to talk to and felt warm and accepting. It was special to me that she also was a dancer and artist like me, so we could relate on that level. I felt comfortable and cared for, having both of these people in my life. This was key in supporting me to go deeper into my healing process and to understanding clearly how my behaviors and emotional state were connected to what was going on internally. I saw my wounding and where I needed more understanding within. I recognized where I needed more compassion and how to care for myself.

Slowly, I was waking up to myself and to love more and more. I began to hear my inner spirit more clearly. I was starting a healthy relationship with myself, beginning to really love myself. I became committed to my self-care. However, It would take years to fully leave some of my old behaviors behind. Once our inner spirit is ignited, we go through a series of deaths and rebirths, birthing ourselves closer and closer to who we truly are. A death was happening, and it took a grieving and adjustment period to cope with the part of me that I was letting go of. Eventually I just could not do the things I did before. As I began to fall more and more in love with myself, with God, and with life,

I realized my true nature is *love*. I was continually refining myself. Really, Love would save me. Loving myself and the love I felt from the Creator led to me finding my inner balance and helping me find the natural state of who I am — my joy, my peace.

It took me rebelling against how I grew up and exploring my own way, before coming to my center. I wanted to be authentic in my expression. I was unclear on what was authentically me or not. When I grew up, my sexuality had been shamed, which I had repressed in some ways. I did not feel like I could express my sexuality fully or honor it as a natural part of me. I had to heal, but in my 'empowerment' I was giving power to the part of me that wasn't balanced within. Instead I would justify myself, saying this is the part of me that was judged and shut down, but really this was just the other side of the misbalance. What I really craved was a fully embodied, fully alive, loving relationship with myself, with God, and with others.

Eventually my healing led me to a crossroads. I had recently been visiting Los Angeles and I was feeling drawn there. A big part of me was ready to move on from New York — I was feeling my chapter there was coming to a close. I was over the hustle and concrete jungle of New York. Plus, things had finally ended with Alexander. I knew our on-off relationship that had held me for four years was finally over. While I was grieving, I also felt a sigh of relief, a freedom I hadn't felt in a long time. I was ready to move on and have space for myself away from him. I was starting to feel more confident and fall even more in love with myself. I was finally walking away from unhealthy relationships and I was creating healthy boundaries. I was getting into my own groove. My prayer life was also coming alive, as I was conversing with the Creator more.

My Inner voice had been getting louder, and I could feel it wasn't right to stay in New York City. Leaving was a hard choice, as I had an opportunity to stay in New York and direct my first full-length dance show in a festival that, after much work, I had recently been accepted into. However, I was learning to trust my inner spirit's voice, and I could feel my gut telling me it was time to leave New York and go to Los Angeles. After much debate in my mind, I chose to trust my intuition and chose to move to Los Angeles.

I've learned that sometimes there are changes in life's direction and we have to be keen to hear the voice of our soul — that voice that has no words and speaks in whispers. When we quiet the inner chatter, it becomes louder and louder, clearer and clearer. And wow am I so glad I listened! I met my beloved and now fiance a few months after I moved to Los Angeles. If I had not come at that time, I may have never met him. I can see how committing to my self-care and falling in love with myself and with Life has transformed my life and my relationships. I am now in a loving, healthy, and supportive partnership. We have a commitment to our union with the Prime Source Creator and we pursue our union within. We are committed to following our purpose. We realize our union with each other is a reflection of our union with Love. We both know we are partners in our growth and healing, and we are continually refining, working on healthy communication and caring for ourselves and each other with compassion.

I am thankful and at peace with my relationship with the Creator. This goes beyond any relationship with another. The true reflection of the transformation that has occurred as my inner spirit has been ignited is that I have forgiven myself and others. I let go of the anger I had and forgave the people who hurt me. The motto of, "Forgive them for they know not what they do," has become true for me. I now have a peace that I have not experienced since the purity of my childhood. My inner child and adult have been healing. I have found that gracious love is always available to us when we reach out. This love amazes me. I truly want to pursue purity and living authentically. I feel Spirit directing my life and I am in awe of the miracles of life all around us.

Passing the wisdom I have learned to you, I'd like to share... Be your own advocate and your own best friend. Pursue your own healing, and follow your true purpose. If you don't know what your purpose is, ask your Inner Spirit. Once you pursue healing your life, the peace you feel will ripple both inward and outward. Your loving relationship with *Self* will reflect in all your relationships.

IGNITE ACTION STEPS

- Look for a support person to talk to, such as a Therapist, Life Coach, or Mentor.
- Work on your health by exercising, practicing peace, and eating nutritiously.
- Meditate — noticing your thoughts shows you are not your thoughts; you are an observer of your thoughts.
- Focusing on the breath can support calmness and bring you back to your center.
- Choose healthy relationships — the ones who fully honor you.

Cat Flowers – United States of America
Dance Teacher, Artist, Childcare Provider, and Life Coach
www.catflowerslove.com

Katrina Roads

"Live like Love is your superpower."

My wish is to stir your heart to leap into your unlived life. Live like someone left the gate open and set you free! My hope is to invoke curiosity about a special Love, and then to be encouraged to explore being loved in a supernatural way. Love is the ultimate pattern-interrupt. There is a divine love that will transform your own inner self-love. I invite you to dare to know how loved you are.

My Brush With Death Taught Me to Love Anyway

Before I came into the hospital, I was literally two days away from death. I had no proper diagnosis for what was wrong with me. My husband had driven me to emergency the previous night. I woke up from a six-hour life-saving surgery and was having the most confrontational conversation of my life.

"I told you," the doctor said.

"Told me what?" I questioned. He hadn't told me anything.

I looked at the faces of the four interns following him, like puppies hanging on his every word, and the color in their faces drained. They looked shocked waiting for the sentence he was about to deliver, wishing they were not there right then.

"What?" I asked. He looked suddenly uncomfortable.

He looked at me and knew I didn't know. I looked at him and saw that he knew that I didn't know. *Awkward.* With the team-in-training around him, he would have to deliver the unpleasant news. The world stopped for a moment. I couldn't take it in. I was in overload, still dazed from the surgery and in aching pain.

In his detached bedside manner, Dr D. bluntly stated, "You have cancer."

For a moment I couldn't breathe. My disbelief was palpable. The uncomfortable silence hung. The interns visibly shrunk in stature, looked down at the ground, and fidgeted.

"What do you mean I've got cancer?"

"I told you," he said, "I told your husband."

"Like, what kind of cancer?" I blurted out.

That was the first time I'd met him. And I wanted it to be the last. Here I was in a hospital ward with six strangers, thin cloth curtain walls, for all to hear. Zero privacy. Zero compassion from Dr D. His delivery was cold, like he was annoyed with me. He oozed, "How could you not know?" I didn't recall anyone telling me anything.

After almost six hours of life-saving surgery, my abdomen sliced open like unzipping a jacket, I was now hooked up to nine tubes in places no tubes should go. Tubes attached to machines that go beep, an automatic opiate pain relief button, oxygen tubes in my nose, and three drain tubes poking out of my swollen belly attached to a loathsome colostomy bag.

At no point, before my surgery, had anyone even hinted at this cancer diagnosis or suggested it as a possibility. All I could think was that after everything that happened in the past 24 hours, the past nine months, how could no one have even hinted this might be an outcome? It was an emotional grenade.

Seeing my genuine shock, Dr D. changed his attitude and left me with an encouraging parting comment — something everyone wants to hear, "We got it all." And with that message, he smiled. I felt his inner confidence, his pride in his handiwork as a surgeon, and the truth of it chimed through me. He got it *all*. There's *no* tumor left in my chopped up, broken, battered, emaciated 47 kilogram body.

Russell, my husband, was sitting by my hospital bed all the while. I turned to him.

"Did you know?"

He replied that he did, and that he thought I knew! It felt like it was too much for me to take in.

It turns out I had a tennis ball-sized adenocarcinoma in my colon, causing a full bowel obstruction. The cancerous tumor filled up a section of my bowel, poked a tentacle or two through the bowel wall perforating it, and wrapped itself around 10 centimeters of my small intestine creating a tangled mess. The surgeons removed 30 centimeters of large colon and 10 centimeters of the small, leaving me with a stoma bag which I jokingly called my 'tummy butt.'

It was only in this awkward meeting with Dr D. that I learned I had stage IV terminal bowel cancer. At only 47, bowel cancer was considered unusual. With a 9-year-old son, I was too young for this. All I could think was, how the *%#@ could I not have known that I was dying? The tears began to flow, uncensored emotion welled up in me. All I could think about was that I had come so dangerously close to losing my life. That caused me to surrender, and in that moment, my life flashed before my eyes, faster than any human slideshow. Memory after memory, image after image came at me in a barrage. Each one flooding in a life review of powerful, previously unfelt feelings. Pictures of the kind of daughter, friend, sister, mother, and wife I had been. I saw how I had pushed people away. I relived my life, those hateful feelings toward myself that revealed how much I had hurt others in the name of love, or sometimes purely out of my own hurtful feelings of rejection.

All this awakening happened in a blink. It didn't occur in a judgmental or recriminative way — it was the opposite. From the moment of surrender, for the entire time, what I felt more than anything else was Love. My heart and my physical body felt comforted in an embrace of supernatural Love. The tender care and pure acceptance overtook me and so did the grief. I cried, sobbed, and mourned. The hurt began to flow out of me and the love poured into me at the same time.

It was the beginning of an emotional, spiritual, and mental healing along with powerful, reviving revelations. A deep understanding that denial had brought me to that point was revealed. I understood that the hate and anger that was directed toward me as a child brought me there. The deep dissatisfactions that I felt in return had brought me there, along with the idea that I was unfixable, bad, the subconscious pretending I was okay… all had brought me here.

Like a grub's journey to a butterfly, my state after that first encounter with Love marked the beginning of becoming chemical soup; alchemical metamorphosis began. If you open up the caterpillar cocoon and peek inside, all you'll see is soup. The process, the magic, the transformation is hidden to the naked eye. I was beginning to know what compassion was, learning what acceptance of me could really feel like. I wanted all that self-hate out. In becoming super vulnerable, emotional release began the healing process.

Some days after my radical surgery, wandering the hospital corridors one night, driven crazy by all of the beeping hospital noises, I unexpectedly found quiet respite in the hospital chapel. A carved wooden door had caught my curiosity, so I opened it and found an empty, quiet room. In the serenity, sadness swelled, my emotional dam burst again, and I reached out for the Love experience that I had in my hospital bed. The barriers around my heart dropped away. The floodgates of grief rushed open. I let the pain at how I felt about myself, the hurt and grief at the state of my life, the brokenness of my body, and my lack — how sick I had become before I sought real help — flow unhindered out of me.

In desperation, I silently reached out and inquired of the Love, are you there? As my heart opened, my own love emanated from my chest. Again I could feel the 'outside' Love meet me, enveloping me, holding me in its parental arms. Wet tears flowed. If I could have laid on the floor and surrendered to sobbing, I would have. But it was too awkward and painful being attached to drain tubes and IV gadgets. So I sat on a hard chair and emotionally surrendered to release the grief and hurt even more. The deep, almost silent convulsive sobs rolled like waves over me. With every wrack of my body, I could feel the pain, hate, and hurt emptying out. Literally leaving me forever. I felt lighter, unburdened, and exhausted.

Do you know the story of the little Dutch boy with his finger in the dike? He kept his finger in a hole in the dike dam wall to prevent it from bursting. That had been me. All my adult life, I had been holding it up, stopping it from cracking open. Silently. Subconsciously. Desperately afraid that if I took my finger out, there wouldn't be a trickle but a bursting open of the emotional dam that would rip me apart. Obliterate me. It would be a violent ending. My fears and beliefs about how bad I was would be too much to bear. No one could find out. I would drown in a sea of my own hurt, despair, self-hatred, shame, and unworthiness.

But the opposite happened. My finger was pulled out of that dam wall by a detonator named stage IV terminal cancer. Instead of drowning, I was lifted up, rising and carried, and given life-saving CPR by a love I didn't know existed. What I had dammed up were lies and untruths about me that I believed were true — only because the people who raised me said so. Because the people who had raised *them* said so to them. It's the generational hand-me-down. We all live with false notions about ourselves that are damaging (like you're bad, you don't deserve good things, you're not enough, not as smart as her, not nice like him, something is wrong with you, it's your fault…).

I let go of that inner poison. It was like watching a movie of my life, complete with understanding and compassion, yet facing up to my effect on others.

It was acknowledging, releasing, and healing — all in a matter of minutes. It was honest, raw, real, and the end result was liberating. I realized I had never surrendered before, I always had controlled. I grieved for the unsatisfactory life I had lived and for the future I nearly didn't get to have.

In that quiet chapel, the sweet irony was that a God I didn't believe in came to me in my darkest hours and deepest need and unexpectedly loved me back to life. For the first time, I knew I was Loved purely and simply because I exist. My delightful discovery was there is an 'inside love' and an 'inner spirit' that originates from within us to give to ourselves and others. I call that self-love.

In the vulnerability of surrendering in hospital, I discovered there is an "outside love" too. I can only name that Love as God. My experience of the Love was gentle and soft, not harsh. Kind and compassionate, not cruel. Accepting — not punishing.

If the colon cancer had a voice, it said to me, "Katrina, you hate your guts." But the Love showed me I was worth loving. With this Love present, no fear was too overpowering and no emotion too big for me to face.

The result was I stopped being needy, especially toward our son and my husband. It was liberating to choose to live with them and enjoy them, but not need them in an unhealthy dependence. A bonus was that I lost my feelings of discontent. Deep in my spirit, my very being settled, like mud in a glass, leaving the clear water above.

Some people undergo a Near Death Experience (NDE) which resolves their fears of death or they experience a profound and transforming love. Such a love is mind-altering, life-changing, and it repositions their values and aligns their passion and purpose. I experienced all this while barely alive. I nearly died, but didn't. Therefore, I'd like to share three key heart-opening messages I heard during my *Ignite* moment.

The first message I heard was '*Love Anyway.*' Love like you want to be loved. I experienced a deep understanding of human motives and our core underlying needs. As I felt so completely accepted for all that I was, I knew how to accept another. A forgiveness released me from the shame and guilt over many hurtful things I had said and done to those I claimed to love.

The healing effect was so cathartic that, from my hospital bed, I telephoned my sisters, mum, and some friends. From the depths of my vulnerable heart, I told them how sorry I was that I had hurt them. It was extraordinarily restoring for all of us. I understood in an entirely new way how much our personal relationships matter. On the other side was the knowing that our connections to one another is what gives meaning to life.

The second heart-opening communication was the realization that I had a *'Life Unlived.'* It was like the words were dropped into me and the knowledge exploded inside of me. I'd nearly lost my life and had faced imminent death, but now, I had to face living. It was living I had been truly afraid of all along. Suddenly, I understood that there was an entire life filled with my own purpose, waiting just for me, with my husband and son alongside, but not center stage. I felt connected with my reason to live and was elated that I wasn't meant to be living in the shadow of anyone. It felt so appealing to know I had a purpose outside of mothering, being a wife, or pleasing people! Crazy as that sounds, to connect with the truth that 'my life is for me' set me free. I saw how my purpose is not to make other people happy — my purpose is to show them how to do it themselves. My gift is to feel comfortable as me and to let my love of life radiate outward.

The third gift that thrills me daily is *'Natural Gratefulness.'* It settled upon me and occurs naturally without any effort to generate it. I feel grateful for everything: for the healing power in my body and the captivating minutiae of life. I feel grateful for simple things like making nourishing food for my family; waking up our son; playing with our fluffy dog; the feeling of my feet on our squeaky Aussie, Sunshine Coast sand; the warm air on my skin and the joy of singing; I absolutely love it all. I feel alive!

Since my brush with death, I carry within me a solid sense that the universe we live in is fundamentally good. That Love ignited a spark that can never be extinguished.

Now, I'm all clear of cancer. By surrendering that fateful day in 2013, when I let go of control, a synchronicity occurred that still astounds me today. Previously I'd distrusted doctors and hospitals. However, the dream surgery team was on that day, the nursing team's experience was *par excellence*, and I was cared for superbly over the 23 days I spent in hospital. Everything in my life flowed like *wow*.

I'll let you in on a secret. More than self-love, there is a Love Trio and we need all three. There is your personal love to give, then there's the love you receive from someone else. Thirdly, there is The Love — God's love — to receive, although God belongs as number one. That love is so profoundly different to that of humans, as it comes with no expectations or conditions. Humans don't love unconditionally. God does. True spirituality is of the spirit; the spirit of Love merging with your inner spirit. The Love of God releases your need for others to make you okay. Self-love is important, powerful, and much needed. Yet there is another love worth your curiosity. I encourage you to let it into your life. It's transformative. It will Ignite your love for yourself and others to heights unknown. Love is your superpower!

If you too have a *Life Unlived* that you feel beckoning, take some time to pay attention and tune in. Allow its voice. Don't wait until a crisis occurs or you're on your sick bed to restore relationships, heal inner hurts, or live any dream your heart nudges you toward. My wish for you is to Ignite your spark so that you can fan your inner flame into an inferno of inner fulfillment. My desire is for you to discover in your life how you are relentlessly, ridiculously, and remarkably loved.

IGNITE ACTION STEPS

I invite you, if you feel you have a Life Unlived, to take a moment to sit undisturbed and visualize, imagine, and explore. Where are you living your life for others? If your talents, abilities, or desires were voices that could speak, what would they say to you? What proverbial bricks in the backpack of your life do you need to surrender? Don't wait. All you're doing is delaying fulfillment, pleasure, joy, and contentment, along with deep and meaningful connections with quality people. Your gifts are yours. Only you can unbox, unwrap, take them out, develop, enjoy, and become you.

Do one further exploration: What ideas or beliefs about The Love or God hold you back from being curious about a god that loves? Have you had religious experiences that have hurt you in a way that led you to turn from spirituality? Have you felt unwilling to connect? When you let go of preconceived barriers, you encounter Love.

Katrina Roads – Australia
B.Sc, Cl.Hyp, Advanced Rapid Transformational Therapist (ARTT).
www.katrinaroads.com
@katsrapidlytransform

DR. SUSANA SEBESTYEN
HB.Sc., O.D. F.A.A.O., P.V.T., C.E.D.H., P.N.1.

"Change the journey as you change your dreams!"

My message to the reader is that your dreams are shaped by your journey and your journey is shaped by your dreams. You may identify a journey before you realize a firm goal or a dream, and that's okay. Follow your heart and trust that eventually you will find your passion, even if you take detours while searching. The experience you gain makes you stronger and helps you achieve success.

ImPOSSIBLE ME

As far back as I can remember, as early as 4 years old, I struggled with my vision and as a result, my self-esteem. I would look in the mirror and wonder why my right eye was not looking in the same direction as the left. My mother would often pass by the mirror and say "Oh you're doing it again Suziiiii. You do that when you want to impress people." The moment she would say that, my right eye would straighten. "That's it, see, you can make your eyes straight and you don't have to try to impress people along the way. Don't worry, they will see you for who you are." My mom's reminder to focus helped me become conscious. It didn't take long for me to learn that it's not necessary to impress people on the outside, but rather prove my worth with my actions.

My brother, who was a year older than me, gave my parents a lot of grief. He was very smart, but alway seemed up to mischief. My parents found out that he stole watermelons from the garden nearby and that he ripped out our neighbor's roses, among many other mischievous acts. As he got older, he always seemed to hook up with the wrong friends and stay out late, waltzing in the house like nothing happened.

The math teacher we shared at school loved us both, but she was frustrated by my brother's lack of motivation to excel academically. Hearing her talk about his mental abilities motivated me a great deal. She was amazed at how fast he could solve complex problems and was frustrated by why it took me forever to get the same result. She seemed to want to merge his smarts with my motivation. That awakened the competitiveness in me, but I kept it a secret. I created imaginary competitions, and when I won, I felt invigorated. If somebody realized my abilities, it was a bonus.

My determination to show my best translated to me developing my role as a motherly big sister. My younger sister was born when I was 7. I proudly held her in my arms, took care of her, and tried to teach her everything I knew. My mom trusted me and encouraged my closeness to her. My brother's troubles, along with his intellect and my responsible demeanor, helped solidify my parent's 'big plan' for the future of the entire family. I was in the dark about these plans for much of my childhood.

I struggled tremendously to be perfect. I needed my glasses to see, but I hated them because they were hideous, adding to my low self-esteem in regards to my wandering eye. I learned years later that they were very special glasses, from a behavioral ophthalmologist. The complexity of the prescription meant that even the color of each lens was slightly different, to help with the light sensitivity in my lazy eye. But my mom taught me to control my eye movements on demand. Even during my eye exams, I would naively try to straighten my right eye to hide my disability so the doctor wouldn't give me a 'multiplex' prescription. I needed them to do my homework though, so I got smart. I always lost them in a place that only I knew and then I pretended like I didn't know where they were. That way when I needed them I could reach for them, and when I didn't, well I could just pretend I lost them. In hindsight, now I'm pretty sure Mom knew my tactics. My aunt, who was an optician in Germany, would make me glasses and bring them as a gift when visiting us in Romania. The problem was, she always picked them out without me ever trying them on, and she never chose the most fashionable frames. Back then, I thought she didn't like me much, but later I realized that it was probably a cost issue for her and my parents.

Living in Romania in the early 80s was no fun for my family. I didn't really know this as a child because I had everything I needed. Given the circumstances, my parents were well-to-do. My father had a Master's degree in Tool and Die, and that was a big deal. He was very well-liked as a big boss at the internationally known Victoria watch factory in Arad. This helped tremendously when it came to supplying the essentials for our family, at a time when even bread was hard to come by. He also had jobs on the side. My mom was a technician at the same factory, but her bigger passion was her own business as a seamstress. She used to make clothes for the entire neighborhood.

We traveled for nearly a month every year of my childhood, which was an opportunity most of my friends didn't have. I recall each trip to the Black Sea and through the mountains, crossing over the Transfăgărășan roadway and through Transylvania back home. My dad always tinkered with his baby blue Skoda™. We packed up the Skoda every summer to the brink, such that with all five of us and the luggage, it was just about scraping the ground. I remember we could hardly wait to get to the Black Sea to roll our bodies in the fresh smooth sand, waiting for the waves to reach out to us so we could taste the intense salty water.

My parents always dreamed of a better life outside of Romania, and they knew that escaping the Ceaușescu regime would be just as dangerous as our future if we stayed. My mom always worried about my brother's crazy adventurous side, suspecting of his plans to escape the country, just like my uncle had done years prior. This meant a good chance of getting caught at the border, which at best would leave him in jail, but at worst would leave him shot and dead.

When I was 4, my uncle cleverly disguised his escape by going on a fishing trip, from which he never returned home. It took months to find out he wasn't dead. My aunt followed years later with my cousins to Germany, reuniting the family as my uncle proved he was of German descent. When I was a teenager, my uncle encouraged my parents to apply for a visitor visa in Germany, with a solid promise to return home. That meant leaving us kids behind, alone, in the family home.

The night my parents called me and my brother into the kitchen to have a long chat changed everything. We were 15, 14, and 7 years old. They told us their plans to leave for Germany without us children. They were not coming back. The plan was to reunite later, outside of Romania.

I sank into the chair in despair not knowing what questions to ask, not knowing what was to come, what their decision meant for us kids. I was in full shock, catatonic. How were we going to survive just the three of us, so young? We weren't prepared. My parents explained that we kids were the security blanket for the government, the commitment to return home, otherwise they wouldn't have been able to get their passports. They didn't have much of a choice. My brain was filled with the fear of being left for an undetermined amount of time without parental supervision, but also with the curiosity of how we would embrace independence. I was afraid about my brother being crazy, authoritative, and irresponsible, especially considering his past. I worried about how I was going to make my sister listen to me, and how I would live with myself if something happened to her.

When I looked my parents in the eyes the day they left, I had no idea if I would ever see them again. I felt lost, and with a huge responsibility put upon my shoulders to deliver on a promise to get along with my brother, and to help in the upbringing of my sister, without a clear end date.

The next year involved a lot of crying, desperation, anxiety, lack of sleep, and fear of the unknown. We learned to cook, clean, do laundry, handle money, and do repairs around the house, all without the luxury of today's technology in our pockets to look things up. We learned to communicate with each other, and we became closer than ever. My brother and I formed the bond of a lifetime, and both of us became parental figures in my sister's life, while also having a lot of fun.

It was almost a year before mom and dad, from Germany, managed to apply for our passports on the basis of family reunion under compassionate terms, and we lost our family home in exchange. My sister, now 8, was too young to qualify for an individual passport. But my brother, who was now 16, was no longer considered a child in Romania, and therefore could not qualify for the reunion or even an exit visa. And since my sister had to be added to my brother's adult passport profile, I was left the only one to potentially be able to leave the country, being still just under 16.

My uncle came to our rescue by contacting a friend to drive from Germany to smuggle me out of the country. They were the most frightening and awakening two days of my life. Although I had a passport, I didn't have an exit visa from Romania, and no entry visa for any of the countries ahead of us. I had no idea if I would be turned back from the border and not be able to reunite with my parents. At the same time, our sibling bond had become so strong that I couldn't see a future without my brother and sister.

I made it to Germany on a bright sunny day. And given the success of my arrival, my uncle decided that he would himself try to use his two boys' passports to attempt to smuggle my siblings out of the country. He departed Germany three weeks later under the guise of a new fishing journey. He traveled with nothing more than his fishing gear and three passports. He drove to Romania, picked up my siblings, and told them to act as if they were his children. Thank God my sister was a tomboy. She had to stay cuddled up in the back of the car, pretending to sleep the entire way, so nobody would ask questions. They cleared the Romanian and Yugoslavian border in the middle of the night, so it was hard for the officers to question the 'kids" identities. But it was daytime when they arrived close to the German border, so he directed my brother to get out of the car and walk the same path he himself took many years before on his previous 'fishing' trip. He reassured my brother the end of the path would be the 'brighter side'.

The family was reunited that day, and it was one of the happiest days of my life. I gladly idealized my endless future possibilities, now totally different from 'a job in the watch factory,' one my dad would have helped secure for me back home.

Since we were Hungarians from Romania, we were not liked in Germany, and gaining a German citizenship was near impossible. We didn't even get approved to attend school for a year. Thankfully, my dad's occupation was preferential in Canada, and he landed a good job in Toronto. With this, our landed immigrant status was approved, despite none of us knowing a word of English.

When we arrived in Canada, I was petrified of not being able to speak the language. To add to that, I was dumped into the tail end of Grade 11, rather than the start of Grade nine, having missed that time in school while we were in Germany. Then, my mom made me a life-changing promise — if I pulled through Grade 11 despite my fears, she would buy me contact lenses. It was an incredible pledge for her to make, since my contact lenses were very expensive in the 80s. And let me tell you, we arrived in Canada with nothing. Even the Skoda ended up in a museum in Germany.

Each of the kids and my dad had a piece of luggage on entry, but my mom's bag was lost. This was utter despair for her. She would say to me, "I arrived here with less than you did, all I had was the clothing I was wearing. If I'm able to rise out of that, you can buckle down and study hard. You don't need to be perfect, just pass". My mom's desire for me to be on track with school and my dream to have contact lenses converged to motivate me to excel academically.

My journey to graduation was shaped by these dreams. I learned fluent English within three months. I got the top grade in 'English as a Second Language' class, as well as Grade 11 Advanced English. In June of that year, my English teacher pulled me aside, asking me if my career choice would be an English teacher. When I expressed that my strengths were math and science, she gave me a personality-based occupation survey to fill out. When we reviewed the results, I saw nothing else except the word OPTOMETRY. That was it for me. I knew where my future was headed. My mom stood by my side, watching me shape my journey, being my backbone along the way.

My mother's promise and my hard work had converged to help me realize my dream. I was intrigued by the complexity of my vision issues. With each of many visits to the optometrist, along with mounting questions, the 'doctor' environment and my new vision paved the entry to my career in Optometry.

The Optometry that I practice today is immensely different from the Optometry that I learned in school. It involves a combination of allopathic medicine specializing in ocular surface disease, along with a largely behavioral component involving vision therapy and neuro-optometry. As an integrative practitioner, I incorporate natural medicine, homeopathy, nutrition, and energy medicine into my daily practice.

What I considered a disability became a gift. It allowed me to find my future and *see* my path. I learned that every negative can become a positive. Every door that closes makes another one open. Taking risks forces you to make changes, ones that can ultimately change your life.

I was guided with the support of others along with determination and my inner strength. All those dreams helped to shape my personality, build integrity, and empowered me to embrace new adventures. The fear of change should not stall you, but rather nudge you to want to explore. And the fun part is that the journey doesn't end.

I've had a number of Ignite moments over the years. Some were more apparent at the time than others, and some changed my journey's course. My message to everyone out there is to stay open to change and look for those moments that can help shape your identity.

If you don't know what you want in life early on, don't worry... Follow your heart, embrace change, and trust your inner voice.

Ignite Action Steps

Listen to your Inner spirit, trust that those Ignite moments will eventually guide you in the right direction. Detours are scary, but can be life-changing.

Keep dreaming, keep thinking and analyzing. Although you may fear detours at first, take a nudge or advice, grab an opportunity, and stretch your limits to embrace the unknown.

Strive for change. The comfort of being in the same place will leave you in the same place, while others stream ahead.

When you think you've reached your goal, you will see another reveal itself. One goal in life isn't satisfying — we need many. We just have to manage them so they don't become overwhelming. Baby steps are essential to success.

Dr. Susana Sebestyen – Canada
HB.Sc., O.D. F.A.A.O., P.V.T., C.E.D.H., P.N.1.
Doctor of Optometry & Optometric Clinical Homeopathy,
Vision Therapist & Precision Nutrition Coach
iexam.ca

Chris Plough

"Curiosity is a seed of liberation, allow it to grow."

I want to help you know yourself and learn to trust your inner voice. We have multiple voices that consciously and unconsciously drive us. They can be confusing and some lead us away from ourselves. Your inner voice is your Intuition — listen to it and you will live your life well. It will guide you to places that you wouldn't expect — yet exactly where you need to be.

Revelation in the Gobi Desert

I am alone for the first time in 42 days. Lying on the floor in the back of *Volga*, a hulk of an ambulance spray painted in fluorescent rainbow colors. The engine has seized, and I'm stuck on the only paved road I've seen for weeks in this desolate landscape within the Gobi Desert of central Mongolia. My friends have left. Dan is gone. Steve is gone. For the first time since we began this adventure, almost six weeks ago, I am surrounded by my own silence. It is suffocating.

I smell the scent of the desert after it rains. I've known it most of my life. It tickles a deep part of my brain. I'm brought back to a memory of standing in the New Mexico desert when I was a teenager. Just outside of my parent's double-wide mobile home...

"No. I'm not going there." I sit up and scramble out the back door of the ambulance. The sun is moving high in the sky. I look down the long stretch of open, barren road — nothing. I peer around Volga in the other direction

— nothing. All I see is the vastness and the mirage waves on the horizon as the desert begins to heat up.

I slam my hand against the side of Volga and shout. "Fuck!" My thoughts begin to spiral. I feel myself looking for someone to blame. "How did I end up here? Why am I alone?"

The victim in me surfaces.

And, somehow, I immediately knew… Because I chose this. After nearly 10,000 miles and several days of crawling through broken gravel roads, we found this stretch of asphalt. In my excitement, I pushed the pedal down and cruised this pristine stretch of open road. Flying along at highway speeds! Running with the windows down. Feeling the wind blowing across my face. I had this sense that *everything* was going to be okay. That all of the challenges and the obstacles we had encountered throughout the UK, Europe, Russia, and Mongolia would be worth it. We were going to make it! There would be a crowd of people cheering us on as we…

BANG! I slammed back into reality. The engine misfired and then stopped. I remembered that the radiator had been leaking for days. Now, with the weather warming back up… Shit.

I coasted Volga to the side of the road. Maybe it wasn't bad. Maybe she just overheated. Pour some water in the radiator — pee in it if we have to. We'll be back on the road. Come on! By this point we had overcome incredible odds. The front suspension had broken and was held in place by nylon straps and spare bars from our gurneys. We lost our brakes over a thousand miles ago. There was the electrical fire that destroyed the starter and killed the headlights. The frame cracked when we fell down a ditch in the dark and slammed into a runoff pipe. A door had fallen off. The windshield was shattered like a spiderweb. Then there was that bumpy Russian road where the left rear wheel literally flew off! After all that, there was no way we were going to give up!

"Are you fucking kidding me, 9700 miles in and now we're stuck?" The engine was seized. Steve got out, yelled, and slammed the driver mirror in rage. I simply accepted the facts. Hmm, a change of roles. Last week, I was screaming up a storm and he was the voice of reason. I reached that point of overload, where all I could do was resign, knowing there was nothing we could do but move forward.

In a turn of luck, a vintage Land Cruiser™ approached and without thinking, we jumped up and flagged it down. Immediately we decided that Steve would be the one to jump into the truck packed with strangers, and I would stay with Volga and our gear. He would find a way to get us the remaining 250 miles to the finish line in the final city, Ulaanbaatar. I felt torn between my obligation to watch over the gear and my determination to make it to the end. The truth, though, was deeper than that. That quiet voice inside spoke and I, not fully knowing why, simply listened and stayed.

I walked around our unkillable yet broken friend. Gliding my hand across her side. She carried us and sheltered us for weeks. I couldn't leave her here in the desert... Yet, how long would it take Steve to find help. Hours? Days? Without a phone or network, all I could do was stay there and wait.

My stomach rumbled. I stepped back inside and sat on the floor beside the gurneys. I liked the floor — and had taken to sleeping on it weeks ago, just after we entered the Czech Republic. The gurneys were padded, but the floor was longer and I could stretch out. I pulled down one of my duffel bags and reached in for some local mystery meat snacks that we had scored at our last stop. After my belly was filled, I laid down and pulled an old T-shirt over my eyes to block out the light.

I began to reflect on the last few days and how Dan left. It was unexpected. I appreciated all of the times he had helped me. How useful his Boy Scout knowledge and sense of "do-it" had been. I also thought of how he quit. A few days before, he decided to leave and headed for the airport, to make it home before his classes started. I loved him like a brother, but felt betrayed and couldn't understand how he could leave when we were so close to the end. Stranded here, I wondered if he was right to leave.

Shaking myself awake, I stretched, walked around Volga to the shade, plopped down into the dirt, and leaned against her side. I remembered the choice I made four years ago. The choice to quit a safe and secure job, working with a team of people who were like family. Yet how boring and unfulfilling each day felt after we were acquired by a large billion-dollar corporation. Going from leading a rockstar team to being a cog in a bloated machine. I once spent an entire day ignoring email and surfing the web. No one noticed. No one cared. And that was the day I heard that quiet voice. I knew I had to leave... but I had no idea what to do.

With the bright-eyed naivete of a 29-year-old, I quit. No real plan. I cashed out my 401k and decided I was a consultant. I knew technology like the back of my hand. Yet I knew nothing about business plans, networking, sales, marketing, or accounting... but I was inspired and determined!

My saving grace was that I had a stellar reputation from the start-up I had left. Consulting with a large company selling logistics software, my skills became in demand. I was often the only one who could solve the technology problems that many of their customers were having. Soon I was being flown around the world to fix things. The UK. Sweden. Singapore. Australia. All across the US. I couldn't keep up.

There were also many parts of the software that I had no idea how to configure. I needed help. The business grew dramatically after I partnered with my friend and colleague, Sam, so that we could run our company together. He knew how to configure and use the software, and I knew how to to install and optimize it. The best of both worlds. More importantly, he understood processes, procedures, and deadlines, while I was a by-the-seat-of-my-pants and envision-the-future guy.

Together, we grew. The first year ate up my savings. The second put us in the low six figures. The third in the high six. The fourth, in seven. Now, we had a dozen friends working for the company and I began to design our first hosting infrastructure. Everything was going straight up!

And then… it happened. Friday morning after Christmas, there was an early phone call. I was tired and grumpy. As soon as I answered and heard my grandmother's voice… my heart sank. It was about my parents. I went numb. I barely heard her speak. The next few weeks were a blur. Each time my emotions came up, I told myself, "Not now."

Soon enough, I was back in Philly and focused on work. After all, I had this company that depended on me. We were growing and I was so close to living my dreams. I went heads-down for months, working 60, 70, 80-hour weeks. Waking up in the middle of the night to solve problems. I began to sleepwalk through life. I traveled, laughed, and took funny photos in all the hotels. I convinced myself I was having fun too.

Then the economy tanked and the recession began. I wouldn't admit defeat. I began to work even more. I stopped exercising. I stopped hanging out with my friends. Nearly everything I ate came from a convenience store. Payroll made my stomach churn. I sunk every penny I had into the business so that I wouldn't have to fire my friends. I couldn't look like a failure. Unwilling to ask for help, I was going to pull us through with sheer willpower.

I began to spiral. Downward. At night, I would take my motorcycle out recklessly — jumping railroad tracks and riding into oncoming traffic. One night I totaled it and limped away with a fractured ankle. I laughed it off. My friends thought I was adventurous, but I knew the truth. I had stopped caring about my life.

A few months later, at a Halloween party that my dear friend Zita was throwing, a seed was planted. Another friend, Bob, told me about the Mongol

Rally, where these crazy folks drove insane vehicles all the way from Bristol, United Kingdom to Ulaanbaatar, Mongolia. I laughed it off. Yet, my inner voice wouldn't let it go. Soon enough, I was convinced that one way or another it was happening. I recruited Steve and Dan to come along and spent the next nine months preparing my company to run without me. This time I was able to ask my team for help, and was amazed and relieved at how well they stepped up to the challenge.

That is how I ended up here — sitting against a fluorescent ambulance, alone, on the other side of the world. It was getting late and I knew from experience how cold the desert could get. I stood up and walked through the back door. Reaching into my duffel bag to grab a long-sleeved shirt. And that's when my hand grazed it. That cold and angular piece of glass that I had been avoiding this whole time. I had stuffed it away, in the bottom of the bag, and banished it to the back of my mind. I knew it was there and yet I had tried to forget about it. Until now. Through all of the challenges, the blowouts, getting lost, breaking down — it was what I had really come for.

I wrapped my hand around this precious memory and pulled it out. Beams of light prismed through the glass and cast rainbows on the floor. I ran my fingers over the etched letters, "In Loving Memory of Rob and Louise Plough." I allowed myself to look deeply into the photo of my parents embedded within. I remembered the day my sister gave it to me and thinking then that they looked like ghosts, trapped in glass. Tears welled up in my eyes. I wanted to hold it together... *I* didn't want to break down. I felt my inner voice speak deeply, telling me it was time.

I am ready. This is why I am here. I know what I have to do.

I left Volga, crossed the road, and kept walking. I walked and I walked. Until Volga looked like a toy truck behind me. I came to a mound of dirt that seemed out of place. I knelt before it and closed my eyes. Holding the memorial, I plunged into all the memories that I had locked away. That call from my grandmother. Flying to Montana for my parents' funeral and living in their home for the week with my grandparents, uncles, aunt, sister, and friends. Enjoying their company yet feeling disconnected. Unsure of every step. Moving as if the floor beneath me was crumbling away. Entering the church. Standing before their caskets. Looking at them. Mom first. Then dad. They didn't look like them anymore. They were empty. I didn't know what to feel or how to feel.

Clutching their memorial to my chest, I felt a wave of grief roll through me and I cried. Tears streaming down, no longer held back, falling into the desert dust. I surrendered to my emotions. I sobbed and wailed. I yelled out at the Universe. I felt all of it. Pain, rage, sadness, and hurt. Abandoned, left behind, unprepared, and terrified. Stuffed down for years, pushed away by work and keeping busy. All coming up and all coming through.

I couldn't tell if it had been minutes or hours as my tears waned. I came back to myself and felt a deeper peace. One that I had forgotten. I dug into the soft earth of the mound and laid my parents' glass tribute in the hole. I thought back to the last time I had seen them and their smiles. The spark in their eyes. Unconditional love and support. I spoke some words softly to myself and covered them up. I let them go.

As I stood up, I felt different. I knew that I had experienced an inflection point. A culmination of events from which the trajectory of my life would be forever altered. I decided to aim away from self-destruction and toward a meaningful life. Then I realized that I had no idea how to live such a life. Right there, I promised myself that I would keep exploring until I understood how.

As the sun began to set, casting pink hues across the clouds, Steve returned with something I never would have imagined — a large truck with a 'who-can-fuckin'-believe-it' crane! Steve was a hero. We stood there and watched Volga get picked up by a crane and loaded onto the flatbed. We made it to Ulaanbaatar, and, though everyone else had already finished and gone — Steve and I celebrated.

The decade since that revelation in the Gobi desert has been incredible. Beyond my previous dreams. Some amazing — my company continued to grow into eight figures, giving me the financial freedom to explore. Others were hard — I chose to face many fears, traumas, and uncomfortable truths along the way — yet always worthwhile. Fortunately, I chose not to do it alone. The first step was finding communities where I was accepted as I am and encouraged to continue growing. Ones where I could share my lessons and help others. Relationships that are mutually caring and invested in.

I explored traditional and non-traditional means of understanding myself. Journaling, meditation, psychedelics, adventures, travel, and nature. Plus all the therapies you can imagine — talk therapy, hypnosis, NLP, EMDR, brain scans, group retreats, yoga, physical trauma release, philosophy, spirituality, plant medicines, indiginous rituals, energy work, and more. They each helped me understand myself in different ways. These gave me the tools to understand my conscious and unconscious. To feel decades of emotions that had been repressed. To break out of cycles of depression and suicidal thoughts. To clear away the confusion and noise. To see myself clearly, accept, and integrate. To trust and love myself, then my community, then humanity. To help others do the same. To live a meaningful life. To more clearly hear that voice inside and trust it.

Now I share my experiences to help a sleeping generation wake up and understand themselves, be themselves, listen, and express themselves. As you become curious about yourself, you'll learn to differentiate the voices and patterns that guide you. The inner voice, Intuition, is often quiet and patiently guides you toward experiences and relationships that will help you grow. Be open to hearing your inner voice and know that it will guide you to exactly where you need to be. Trust that it will help you live your life — the one only *you* are capable of living. A fulfilling and meaningful life that is uniquely yours. I wish that for you. Big Love.

IGNITE ACTION STEPS:

Be curious about yourself. Imagine what's possible. Feel it. Allow it, don't judge it. This is how you learn from everything that happens in your life. If you do only this, you will continue to grow and evolve.

Listen to your inner voice. Do whatever helps you tune in. Journaling. Walking. Meditation. Playing with your pet. Driving. Just don't tune out. Don't distract. Give it time. Three minutes, an hour, a day — whatever is right for you.

Find a community where you are accepted as you are. Be exposed to new ideas, continue to grow, and help others with your wisdom and experiences.

Explore different ways of understanding yourself. Stick with the ones that work for you and be willing to try new modalities as you grow and evolve.

Be gentle and patient. Treat yourself as you would treat a loved child. Guide yourself with compassion. Accept your stumbles. Celebrate your wins, including the tiny ones.

Chris Plough – United States of America
I help us know, accept, and be ourselves.
Conscious Pioneer / Chief Soul Officer
https://chrisplough.com

WARRIOR

FRANCIS PICHÉ

"Your breath is sacred; don't waste it.
Live your life fearlessly from the heart and use your voice."

My intention is that you transcend your fear, that you jump into your highest self and discover the unchartered territories like the Viking. No land would have ever been discovered without the 'inner soul' voyage. The wonderful opportunities are on the other side of the turbulent seas of life. My intention is that you feel enlivened by your own soul's voyage and be fully self-expressed with love and power.

AWAKENING THE VIKING WITHIN

I couldn't decide between following my heart's desire and comforting the fear that was telling me to be safe and not *click*. I only have a few minutes to make this decision. I watch the timer ticking away on my laptop counting down as I sit in the hotel lobby after checking out. My heart starts beating faster with the knowledge that I'm running very late and it's now or never to make this decision. I've been on the road for two days heading from Vancouver, Canada to San Diego, USA. I need to decide now, put my laptop away, and get on the road!

I had maxed out the money I had and was under stress concerning my investor visa to work in the USA. But, that's not what is bothering me this morning. I am facing a dilemma. I feel paralyzed between what my mind is saying and what my heart yearns to do. My mind wants to play safe and gain more financial security. My heart wants to follow its call to go to Peru for a sacred Ayahuasca ceremony. The countdown to book an excellent flight deal is about to expire. This message keeps flashing on my screen. My heart is pounding. All I have to do is click the 'Book Now' button. But I can't. My mind is going crazy. My heart's desire seems both compelling and insane, and I don't know what to do.

The thought of going to Peru seems ludicrous. I have already invested *so* much money in my visa, company, and mission. I'm afraid to spend more and increase my debt. Going to Peru feels foolish — it isn't a sound financial decision. My monetary gains are pinned on a phone call that will give me confirmation of a lucrative business transaction that will provide the money I need for this trip. Waiting for this transaction to close has been very stressful. I've held on, because without it, I don't see how I can go to Peru.

The prospect of going to Peru and to do Ayahuasca had captured my heart several months before, and ever since I had been debating it in my mind. I had received intuitive and symbolic messages loud and clear to do Ayahuasca, which is a plant medicine ceremony. I knew in my heart that I had to do it in Peru, a genuine destination for it. The only question in my mind now was, "When should I go?"

Not being able to wait a moment longer, I called my client. She had no new information — the outcome was still uncertain. My chest was full and I could barely breathe. I couldn't take it anymore. Based on all the facts, it was now clear. I just couldn't book the trip. The uncertainty was too prevalent. So I closed my laptop and I decided to get on the road to San Francisco to pick up my friend. All I needed was a quick washroom refresh and I was out of there.

While in the washroom, a flashback suddenly hit me. "Wow, I am about to make exactly the same decision I made 20 years ago," I thought. At that time, I decided to skip a personal trip to Peru. The reason I had decided not to follow my heart was that I chose to kick-off my first career job in a multinational company. I accepted a position in a coveted key strategic program, chosen among a selected group of 36 people across the USA. The future that was painted was alluring. It had a promising career progression leading to management roles. The industry was far from being my favorite. My soul wasn't inspired. Who wants to sell electronic components? But the salary was incredible for a 21-year-old. I told myself, "Selling is selling, right? Doesn't matter what it is in the end if it helps your clients." It would be several years before I realized the cost of prioritizing money over following my heart.

I stayed on the treadmill for four years, by which time I couldn't stand it any longer. The whole time I was sleepwalking, being conditioned to chase the perfect life. Without knowing, I was slowly dying inside. I could feel the spark, radiance, and vitality leaving my soul on a daily basis. I felt enslaved in the materialistic system.

I still vividly remember the day I left that job. I felt I was getting out of jail while my inmates were still inside wishing they had the courage to leave a 'comfortable' job.

My deprived inner self-expression cost me more than I had anticipated. A week after quitting, my fiancé decided to cancel our wedding three months before the planned date, ending an eight-year relationship. It was hard — I hadn't seen it coming and it felt like more change than I could bear. In the subsequent years, I was determined to gain something positive from that experience and embarked on a personal development odyssey where I learned, I grew, I failed, and I succeeded. I became stronger and more spiritual. My Viking soul was leading me on a journey to discover the value of following my heart's desire and I was beginning to see the path more and more.

Discovering our calling often starts with seeing the clues Life has been leaving us all along. It turned out that my path to find the courage to follow my heart's desires had started years ago with a birthday card from my godfather. It read, "Do what you LOVE and CHOOSE what makes your heart come alive, not what will pay you more. Otherwise, you will be POOR all your life." When I reflected on his words, I could see how I had been trading my passion for a paycheck for so long that my 'ignored' heart had poisoned my relationships, self-confidence, and career success. Reading that card was the prompt that made me decide to become an entrepreneur and follow my dream.

The second important moment on that path to put my heart in front of my financial worries was an unforgettable call with my life coach Gary. He asked me if I would accept a challenge to do nothing for three days but focus on the choices I would make if I had only five years to live. What will be my legacy? Who will I become?

As I stood in the hotel washroom, these two events were still reverberating in my psyche. I realized that money was once again my deciding factor — it was going to control my life again. What's the point of living if you live in fear? My senses came back. After feeling so conflicted, I felt my mind clear and align with my heart and my body. I knew what I had to do. Although it seemed illogical financially, I was not about to ignore my heart again! I exited the washroom determined to transcend my fear. I pulled my laptop out of my bag, reconnected to the internet, and went back to the same site. The page was still alive and so was I. I clicked the 'Book now' button and boom! My flight was locked in. I was going to Peru in less than 10 days!

I was naturally anxious to know what would happen to me during my first plant medicine ceremony. I felt like I was in a safe place knowing that the ceremony was conducted by a priest and a shaman and supervised by a doctor and a nurse. My intention for the ceremony was to fully embrace my fears in order to go *beyond* my potential, or as I like to say to be 'transpotential' and ensure going forward that I would always have the faith and courage to follow my heart.

The experience that changed my thinking so much was the conversation that I had with the Goddess Pachamama, also known as the Mother of Earth and Time, and revered by the indigenous people of the Andes. The life-changing message began 90 minutes into the ceremony when I started to interact with the spirit world and humbly receive the wisdom shared by Pachamama. The conversation was similar to listening to a small inner voice, except that I knew the voice wasn't coming from me.

I saw myself going back in time to when I was five years old. I had forgotten about this event. I was at the edge of a diving board about to complete my final exam to graduate from the Level One swimming course. All I had to do was to jump in the water. I was scared. I felt dizzy as I watched the water move before my eyes. I felt paralyzed. I couldn't do it. My legs were shaking and I was frozen.

"Francis, jump," the instructor said. Sensing the height of the diving board, unbalanced and anticipating the brutal impact as my body hit the water, I firmly refused.

"Jump, Francis."

"No."

"You have to jump Francis."

"No, I won't jump."

"If you don't jump Francis, you will fail the course."

I didn't care… and I failed. I didn't want to risk my life.

Viewing the scene with me, Pachamama told me: "You didn't jump, Francis. And it's good. Sometimes, we follow our gut feelings and we don't need to listen to what others say and abide by their decree." And then Pachamama took me by surprise. "By the way, Francis, I own your breath. You don't. You don't get to choose when you have it and when you don't." As she said that, I felt my whole body losing its oxygen as if someone was sucking out the whole content of my lungs. I started to feel deprived really fast and I suffocated. Nearing full air extinction, the oxygen came back with a huge feeling of liberation. And then again, the oxygen left my body. The ebbs and flows continued for a little while. I breathed deep and loud, grunting like a bear. The withdrawal of all my oxygen was frightening. The influx was reassuring when I felt my lungs rising and being filled with oxygen again.

At one point, the cycle stopped. I questioned if I was dreaming or if what was happening with my breathing was a side effect of the psychoactive brew. Then, Pachamama talked again. "I don't think you understood me," she said. "I own your breath." And then the biggest air secession occurred. I was almost completely out of air. I was wheezing intensively. I had to tap out like in a MMA fight. But then, when I finally surrendered, the oxygen came back with abundance. I never had so much appreciation and gratitude for my breath. "Thank you, thank you, thank you," I said. "I am deeply grateful for my breath. You own it. Thank you." And here is where Pachamama gave me the biggest message I ever received in my life, "Great. Now that you know it, don't waste your breath."

Smack! What a message! What a boost of life and courage it gave me to live my life fully as I had taken it so much for granted. Who cares about fear when your life departure could be one breath away? Pachamama proceeded to bring me back to the diving board when I was five years old and she gave me another present. "Remember what I told you about the jump Francis? Sometimes, it's good not to jump — except when you and I know fear is holding you back from jumping and that your heart knows you should jump. It is in those moments that I am asking you to *jump,* Francis." The words reverberated in my head, "Jump, Francis. Jump." I saw myself looking at the pool again, seeing the water moving down below, and I jumped. I acquired the lesson from Pachamama. I felt my past rewired.

In my new state, feeling like I had transcended my fear, Pachamama taught me how to use my voice. To do this, she took me back to an episode of cliff jumping several months before in Croatia. At that time, I participated in an activity where we had to shout a mantra that would transcend our fear of jumping off the cliff. This mantra was supposed to resonate with an archetype that we wanted to reconnect with in our lives. I chose, "I am a Viking!" The reason I chose this incantation was because I felt that I had lost my power and my masculine warrior soul, the soul that can traverse the unforgiving seas of life, unapologetic for his determination and focused on protecting his kingdom and its high standard of integrity.

Pachamama ordered me, "Use your voice, Francis. Proclaim, 'I am a Viking!'" I thought, "Well, I already know that I am a Viking. I already proved it in Croatia. I don't need to yell this." It was silent and there were three others in the room participating in the ceremony. "Excuse me," she said. "Is there a little fear of embarrassment inside you? Is that how a Viking acts? Would a Viking *be* like that?" And then I thought, "All right. I will do it." From deep in my stomach, I roared, "I'm a Viking!" In a matter of thirty seconds, the nurse and the doctor hastily approached me. "Are you all right?" they asked. "Do you need any help?" I smiled, almost laughing, thinking of how the scene looked from their point of view. "No, no, I am good. I am good. Thank you." And Pachamama left me with this message, "See, when you use your voice, I will provide you with all the support you need. Use your voice." What a gift she gave me and it was an honor to receive it.

There is a saying that Pachamama will not give you what you *want* but will give you what you *need*. How powerful it was to get these meaningful reminders: *Don't waste your time. Life is precious. Don't be afraid when your heart knows that you ought to make a leap of faith. Use your gifts and your talents. Life will reward you with assistance to propel you and fulfill your mission along the way.* I've carried these lessons with me ever since. I hear them during my morning meditation sessions, priming me for the day and filling me with courage and reverence for life.

After my retreat in Peru, I felt the change in my attitude and the ways that I felt like a Viking — I felt centered and strong and people noticed and commented on my transformation. For the Warrior, speaking is a cheap currency versus the real action he takes to accomplish his goals. There is no one else to blame. Blaming puts the onus on others. Justifying my misery is depleting my power. Being a Warrior Soul, or a Viking, is to take responsibility for everything in life. It's choosing to be fully committed to my decisions and assuming all the consequences that follow my choices. It's being integral to my mission and serving my tribe.

I grew to understand that a Viking is unapologetic and isn't afraid to be embarrassed or look bad. His vulnerability is also his power. He is living his life fully and completely as he knows he might not be alive tomorrow. Every breath counts. I realized my chance. It was my time to stop playing small. It had looked like I played big, but in reality I was always afraid to do the ultimate jump of using *my* voice to make a global impact with a message of resilience. I realized that the responsibility is solely on *me*. No one to blame anymore. It's *all in* on me. Now I understand that my abundance, my happiness, and my joy come from within *me* and me only. I am the Viking captain of my own ship and I am honoring how I use my breath — I am no longer wasting it. I invite you to do the same dear Warriors and Goddesses because you are worth it and it's our birthright. I know this because I am the one who extinguished my own flame while I still had oxygen left.

What's preventing us from doing anything we want in life? Nothing but fear. We know this truth, yet we don't always transcend it. Why? Fear is not real because it only lives in our imagined future that hasn't happened yet. Fear doesn't exist 'now.' Fear is still present in my life, but I have just gotten better at transcending it. As I've discovered, it takes courage to move through fear and once I understood that my breath is fragile and that all suffering is a self-inflicted creation, I realized how free I am. Today, I choose to follow my heart and I reap my harvest called freedom!

If you wish to fulfill your dreams, the real question for you now is this: If you knew that God, the Universe, or Pachamama was 'breathing you' and you only had five years left to live, who would you become, my dear friend? Use your time. Don't waste it. Express your gifts and reawaken your inner power to serve your community! The world is waiting for you. The time is now!

Ignite Action Steps

Slow down and do nothing for three days. Ask who you would like to become if you only had five years to live. Write down your findings after the three days are complete. They will provide you crisp clarity. Can you describe what you see, hear, smell, taste, and feel? Why is that so important for you? List 10 reasons. This is your conviction — it will support you while you face adversity and setbacks.

Nurture certainty. Imagine the feelings of your future self after accomplishing your dreams. This will eliminate your self-limiting beliefs. What would you tell yourself? Start with, "I remember that..." This process will create certainty.

Cultivate courage. When challenges arise, look at them objectively with equanimity. Remember the impermanence of life. What can you do to elevate your energy and raise your vibration? Forgive yourself and express self-love. Happiness comes from within and lives in the present moment. Remember what formed your conviction. Don't waste your breath, live fearlessly. The time is now!

Francis Piché – Canada
Mindset Coach, Founder & CEO of Resilience Element
www.francispiche.com

WARRIOR

JASON B. FLORES

"Being great is something that is never achieved;
it is constantly ever-evolving."

My wish is for you to understand if you are not willing to risk, then you will have to settle for ordinary. You have nothing to lose if you at least try… and have everything to gain.

IT ALL STARTS WITH ONE FOOT FORWARD

As early as I can remember, I have always been an adventure seeker. As a little boy riding my bike every day, I would seek out every nook and cranny of my small midwestern rural neighborhood. I'd explore the woods on foot with friends in a quest to uncover the perfect space for building forts and bonfires, always with loads of laughter of course. My curious carefree soul has continued through my teenage years and into my present day.

Travel is in my blood; always has been and always will be. With every place I visit, I find I satisfy one piece of my curiosity only to reveal another. I have been blessed to have my passion thus far bring me to see all 50 states by the age of 30 and over 40 countries. From Oman to Scotland, Bali to Brazil, my curiosity continued to drive me to discover how the rest of the world operates. The gamut of various cultural traditions, values, and ways of life absolutely fascinate me, so I am always on the hunt for how to expose myself more and more into those environments.

One adventure flipped my life upside down in a blink of an eye and changed me forever.

Let's flashback to my thirty-first year. My girlfriend and I were traveling by boat in the frigid North Atlantic just off the coast of Iceland. We were gazing up at the sky in huddled, shivering groups of tourists, hoping to get even the slightest glimpse of the mystical glow of the breathtaking Northern Lights. Earlier in the day, we had embarked on an amazing hike and tour through the famous Golden Circle. The sheer natural beauty of the geysers, snow-capped mountains, and jagged ice formations filled my vision and left me with a deep sense of awe. It was already an incredible day and the suspense of waiting to see the sky light up in neon green was going to be the icing on the cake.

Unfortunately, it was an overcast and frosty evening and we began to hang our heads low as the boat returned to shore, huddling deeper into our coats. Then for about 10 seconds, we were able to see a few shimmers of green flashes peek through the clouds and deemed it still somewhat of a success. This venture was a valiant effort as we at least managed to sight the beloved Northern Lights however briefly. Back ashore, we decided to head back to the hotel and turn in as we had another long day ahead — we had tickets to take a dip in the Blue Lagoon before hopping on the nine-hour flight back to reality in the USA. That is where things start to get hazy and I have blanks in time.

I distinctly remember being abruptly awoken from my sleep by an excruciating headache. It was the early morning, around 4 AM. It's unexplainable, but the best analogy is that it felt like someone had hit me in the head with a bat. I woke my girlfriend up and told her I had a ridiculously painful headache. It was atypical of me to get a headache and, concerned, she told me to try to relax as she started to look a few things up on her phone to figure out what might be wrong.

While she did that, I sat on the edge of the bed. Deciding a Tylenol™ might help, I got up and walked over to get some from my bag. Sitting back down on the bed again, I felt dizzy. I wondered if it was because of the headache and hoped the medication would do the trick and help me shake it off. I decided to stand up again, but to my surprise, my right leg would not cooperate. I tried to lift it, but it would not move. A few seconds later my arm likewise refused to move. It felt like my body had become a dead weight. Before I knew it, there were people in the room lifting me out of bed and onto what I could only assume was a stretcher. I laid there in an immobile body, the world around me reduced to a string of objects, lights, and shadows flashing by me as my sight slowly faded. I had absolutely no idea what was happening. Fear, anxiety, and confusion quickly overwhelmed my mind and body.

Next thing I knew, I was at the hospital being asked a series of questions and seeing flashes of white and green running all around me. I laid there feeling helpless, dazed, and confused. There I lay, unable to move… scatterbrained… indescribable emotions. A memory of my mother, a nurse for over 35 years, popped into my head. She had always told me ever since I was in diapers, "Tell me what hurts," – and that's exactly what I did. My head was pounding so hard it felt like someone had implanted a jackhammer into my skull. I blurted out anything and everything I saw and felt in hopes they could use the information to treat me. "I see lights, I see a doorway, I see people running around." It wasn't much, but I was hoping it was better than nothing.

The last thing I remember was a flashback of my entire life — all the people I love, family, and friends. Then all my experiences — childhood tee-ball, basketball, and travels all around the world. And then all the angst and anxiety melted away instantaneously. Among the chaos, confusion, and scariness, a feeling of tranquility, satisfaction, and acceptance suddenly overcame me. I didn't have regrets. I had lived an amazing life in my 31 years here on earth; if this was the end, I was blessed and honored to have met those in my life and have a chance to do what some don't in a lifetime. As my eyes closed and the world around me vanished, I felt I had found my inner peace and tranquility, in case my show curtain had actually dropped.

Two days later, I awoke.

The first sensation I became aware of was the hospital bed. Clustered around me, my loved ones explained I had had emergency brain surgery from a severe bleed known as an arteriovenous malformation (AVM) that paralyzed my entire right side. An AVM is a tangle of abnormal blood vessels connecting arteries and veins in the brain that cycle oxygen-rich blood from the heart to the brain and oxygen-depleted blood back to the lungs and heart. A brain AVM is like a time bomb with an unknown trigger that disrupts this vital process. This rare congenital condition has an estimated 10 in 10,000 who suffer an AVM annually; about half result in a sudden fatal hemorrhage. Their words made no sense. I laid there in the hospital not being able to even add 2+2. In denial, I told myself it was a dream. I tried to get out of bed and collapsed to the floor. Well, so much for a dream.

Despite having my parents at my bedside as I spent the start of the holiday season in an Icelandic hospital, I found myself quickly plunging into a depression as the reality of not being able to walk started to set in. Simple daily rudimentary practices such as going to the bathroom, brushing my teeth, or feeding myself were beyond my ability and I depended on the staff to perform them.

Three weeks later, the day had come to make our way back to the USA. Being immobile, I had to have special transportation to the airport and aboard the plane. That process was everything but conventional — I was wheeled out onto the ramp planeside and loaded onto a lift contraption controlled via a joystick-like something from Atari in the 80s. It was a far cry from how I had walked myself onto a plane on my way to Iceland a few short weeks earlier. Once aboard the aircraft, and successfully transferred to my seat, I needed to try to relax. About four hours into the flight, a problem struck that is forever ingrained in my mind. My catheter leg bag was full and needed to be emptied. Unable to get up from my seat and go to the bathroom, we had to get creative with coffee cups, both my elderly parents kneeling on the floor of the plane trying to finagle how to release the bag contents at 30,000 feet without making a mess. It was an absolute nightmare. "This has to be my rock bottom," I thought.

After successfully completing the journey back to Seattle, I found myself in rehab for the next eight weeks. Little did I know my lowest was yet to come. I worked hard at rehab only to feel like I had hit my ceiling. Recovery was no longer netting out anywhere near what it was the weeks before; it had come to a grinding halt. The reality of this set in and sent me straight into a tailspin. I was so frustrated with what had so instantaneously happened to my life and drove full speed into depression.

One day as I was struggling to maneuver my way out of my shower chair, it hit me: I didn't want to do it anymore. That night, I sat at the dinner table with my parents and flat out stated, "I don't want to live anymore." I felt like a burden. I felt unlovable. I could see their faces change from upbeat to devastated, a sudden grief and fear shining out of their eyes. My body curled up further, my head hanging low between my shoulders. They paused for a moment, turned to me, and their next words changed my life forever. They said, "Jason, we love you so much and are so sorry that we did this to you."

The words blasted through my body with the force of a hurricane. Hearing their confession was leveling. My parents taking the blame for a congenital condition was unacceptable to me. I felt this was mine to bear. I lifted my head and met their gaze head-on. "No," I said. "It's not your fault. It's on me."

And it was. It was up to me how my life would play out going forward. I couldn't change what happened, I could only change everything that would happen in the future with how I acted. This thought snapped me out of my funk and slung shot me on the trajectory to fight and show the world that anything is indeed possible. I haven't looked back since. This is now a key anchor in my life.

The question that fueled me was "What do I truly have to lose?" I thought I had everything: a great job, a beautiful home, but all of it suddenly didn't matter. The things that mattered were moments with my family, friends, loved ones — the invaluable stuff of life. For them, I would do anything, and that is when I learned the greatest gift is to truly be unselfish and give back. Before the 'incident', I had it all wrong. I thought life was about my career and pushing forward. In reality, life is all about those you love and who you are surrounded by. I had *everything* to gain. I had my whole life ahead of me. I realized that I could make an actual impact on other people's lives and help those who may have felt similar to me at one point in *their* lives.

It was a struggle. In the beginning, it was just coping for the first couple of months. Being in a wheelchair rolling around one-handed just trying not to go in circles… a few months later came the cane that constantly fell to the floor every time I leaned it against the sink as I brushed my teeth… then the persistent limp making me wobble as I walked, and relearning to sign my name — now left-handed instead of right. Ironically, a walk in the park seemed like a longshot and I knew it was just the beginning.

One evening, five-months later as I laid awake brainstorming what I could do to keep myself sane, I thought maybe all I needed to do was break this down into palatable steps. And that is exactly what I did: one day at a time, 24 hours, 1440 minutes. That simple formula is what propelled me through every sunrise to sunset. As far as I was concerned, that is all I needed to get through as I fought day in and out. Being in a gym was not foreign to me as I had been athletic, but little did I know that this was the ultimate exercise for my mental strength and inner warrior. I would spend days at the gym giving it my all and each day taught me a new facet of my own human existence and how that connected to others. What I uncovered is...

Humility is constantly evolving and allows us to become the best versions of ourselves.

Initially, I wanted to point the finger. Pawn the blame off. Why did this happen to me? It was all <blank>'s fault. That is a horrible feeling. In reality, there is no one and nothing to blame except for it being inherent to the way of life itself. If I knew that I would spend hours on a boat freezing to see a few brief seconds of a faint shimmer of light, would I have done it? Not at all. While it didn't turn out as expected, I made the best of it. I found the positive in it, even if it was minuscule (and it felt microscopic some days). I found the learnings from each experience. Always seeing the positive is still and always will be a struggle, but I know it's possible; just keep at it and I'll find it. When I focus on learning, the negative suddenly dissipates and becomes irrelevant.

Release and Bet on Yourself. You are worth it. You have so much to offer.

Ironically, it is often the easiest and clearest path that is the hardest to embark on. To just 'release' is a notion that on the surface makes logical sense but is the toughest to execute. That stands true for someone like me who has been conditioned to put my head down, keep going, and make things happen…until I looked up at the wall that I often hit and pushed through no longer budged. I was stripped away of options. I had to release, let go of control, and accelerate in the high vibe lane to only witness things start to fall into place like magic. I started with small wins such as waking up and being thankful for a new day, being able to take a breath and get out of bed. I recognized the gratitude for the small things I took for granted and it changed my outlook. For me, the body that was once in a wheelchair is no longer sitting still, but instead, up and moving, doing a 5k race and in the best shape of my life.

Vulnerability and Gratitude are hidden signs of strengths and not weaknesses. They are magic just waiting to be unleashed into every crevice of our lives. I know life requires self-love to truly embrace and accept oneself for who they are — this a key skill. I had to learn to persevere and push forward. Like it or not, what you see is *me* and I love every bit of myself unconditionally just the way I am. I needed to bring light, be positive, and stop beating myself up on negatives — there are no negatives in my eyes now; it's all beauty. The faster I became conscious, the faster I could release all the illusions. To *unlearn* societal conditioning was the hardest; as I didn't want to be someone society dictated me to be. Embodying vulnerability to open up more and exhibit gratitude by giving thanks brought me such unexpected powerful energy, light of positivity, and joy in my life. It gave clarity to my purpose of inspiring others. I know I am already amazing the way *I am* and constantly evolving to something greater.

Today I still don't have it all figured out, not sure that I ever will, and that is just fine as I am human. My right side still has impairments. In my right arm, I can do some large movements such as raising my arm, but I am still unable to write or type and my right leg has a brace to assist in my stability and walking. Nevertheless, it has not stopped me as I walk at least 5 miles a day and continue to globe-trot, clocking in over 150,000 miles in flights to 15 countries in a year. I have ambitious goals ahead: doing Machu Picchu, completing a half marathon, and skydiving. Exactly one year to the day from my AVM, I climbed onto a plane headed back to Iceland, my destination once again that hospital.

This time, I was going in gratitude, and I visited every one of the doctors and medical staff to thank them for saving my life.

I have always found a way to dig deep and make something happen by harnessing my inner drive and will power. This was no easy feat constantly battling my own self mentally, physically, and spiritually. Sure, I have been in the shoes of wanting to run far in the opposite direction, but I learned to make an about face and how taking the path less traveled brings the most reward. People often ask me if I would change my life if I could. I would NOT change a thing for the world; it's made me the man I am today and if anything, I am forever appreciative. I don't want to be a good version of me; I want to be great! And this experience helped me get closer to that ideal. I believe this is something that is never fully achieved but is constantly evolving, and I am determined to keep on being a warrior, to keep continuing forward and forging a path where one may not exist. Truly anything is possible. And for warriors like me, where there's a will, there's a way.

You are also a warrior. Look at obstacles in your life with the lens of the warrior within you. Unleash it. Let its fierce determination and willingness be an authentic guide for your journey forward. We grow and evolve together. We learn from each other through experiences. We are ONE Warrior Soul. Don't settle for ordinary. Risk everything. You have nothing to lose and everything to gain. YOU are worth it!

IGNITE ACTION STEPS

When your warrior self feels unable to face a challenge, know that you are not alone. Do as I did: break this down to palatable steps. One day at a time, 24 hours, 1440 minutes. Make a plan, list the steps to take, and tackle them one foot forward at a time.

Jason B. Flores – United States of America
Tech Product Solutions Executive Leader, Travel/Transportation Industry
Entrepreneur, Co-founder, President and COO – Resilience Element
@typejason Email:jason@jbflores.com

Esther López

"Your thoughts are the seeds for the fruits of your life.
Choose what you plant wisely."

As you think, so you feel, so you act, and so it is your life. The key word is "YOU." You can choose your thoughts and literally create your life. Through my story I will share with you how I did just that, hoping that you too Ignite your Inner Spirit.

From Wheelchair to Bodybuilding Podium

Lying naked in this cold hospital bed, trembling, covered by a green sheet, I'm scared as I wait for my surgery.

I cannot feel or move my right leg, my foot, my toes... For the thousandth time, I touch my leg with my hand and I feel nothing. I try to move my toes, but as usual, they remain still... it is like a quarter of my body is dead... I am just 24, having to get around in a wheelchair, and I need help with the most basic things. What I really want to do is run away... but I cannot even walk.

Before completely losing mobility and ending up here, I tried so many things to stop the pain and recover. I have used both conventional and alternative medicine. I have tried numerous therapies, resisting the suggestion that I should get used to living with pain and limitations. I have spent over four years refusing to believe all those messages, rejecting the idea that my life would be so limited.

But what if they were right? What if surgery doesn't work either?

Hours later, I wake up in the recovery room. I can see other beds around me and hear the beeps of the monitors. I can feel the wound in my back, burning. I quickly touch my leg, my fingers stroking the skin. The skin in my leg reacts to my fingers! I can feel it! I can see my toes moving under the sheet! It is like being alive again, elated, full of the joys of spring. A tear of emotion and gratitude slips down my face.

It has been a long journey. I remember the starting point. I was 20. I was at home, about to go out, when I bent down to pick up the keys that had fallen on the floor. Suddenly, as I moved, I lost feeling in my legs and fell down. I had no sensations in the lower half of my body. I dragged myself across the corridor, crawling on my hands and pulling my legs along the cold tiles, until I got to a phone and called my father. "Dad, I cannot feel my legs!"

That day, we started a long and arduous peregrination of trying to find a solution. I am so grateful for my father's tireless support, as we tried one thing after another. I went through different stages, ups and downs, and eventually recovered feeling in one of my legs, but that was it. The doctors thought I had experienced some kind of physical trauma involving a car, a motorbike, or a horse… but nothing like that had happened. Instead, I believe the root cause was most likely the fact that I looked after my mom as she lay in bed during her long illness. My parents were divorced and, as the older sister, I threw myself into caring for mom. It is amazing how our body holds onto our emotions and continuously carries the load. How strong it is. And, at the same time, how wise… knowing when it is time to release the pressure. I was fine while I was 'needed,' but once my mom passed away, it seems my body decided it was time for me to stop.

The surgery went well and after a few days I started walking. Like Bambi learning to stand up for the first time, trembling and hesitating at every step, with all the messages of limitation bumping around in my head: "You have to be very careful when you move," "Always ask for help," "Remember that even if you walk again, you cannot run, you cannot jump, you cannot move any weight." I did not want to live by all those rules. NO! I was only 24. Could I really accept those limitations?

But I had so many doubts… What if they were right?

Doctors had advised me to focus on doing some light exercises to strengthen the muscles protecting my back, so a couple of months after the surgery I joined a gym. My only experience in a gym up to that point had been some aerobics classes. I had never even been in the fitness room and was not familiar with dumbbells, bars, discs, or any other equipment. But I had been given some basic routines to start with — and I had my determination.

There happened to be a new trainer at the gym — a bodybuilding champion. He would work out while I was doing my workouts and I remember noticing him noticing me.

One day, he came up to me. I was putting back some dumbbells and, in the mirror, I could see him approaching like a big, rocky mountain. My two arms together were smaller than one of his. He stood in front of me, folding his arms across his wide chest and with a deep voice asked, "Have you ever thought about competing in bodybuilding?"

"WHAT?!" I thought that was the most ridiculous thing I had ever heard.

"You have a good physical structure for it, and I have been observing you for a few days. You are very focused, disciplined, and persistent... I think you would be good at bodybuilding," he continued.

"Well... you don't understand... there is a reason I am training like this," I said, and I told my story.

He listened, arms crossed in front of his chest, and replied, "OK. And so what?"

That was the difference that made the difference: "*And so what?*"
What if they were all wrong?

What if I chose NOT to live by those messages of limitation? What if I decided to create a new story for myself? He could not see any handicap or limitation in me. He could only see possibilities. For whatever reason, I decided to believe in him and, in so doing, to believe in myself.

Something inside me sparked. Suddenly, all those dreamy images of me being strong and healthy, independent and free... seemed real! It was a paradigm shift. My Inner Spirit was instantly ignited, and I could feel a vibrating energy running through my body. That created a new mindset, a whole new world of possibilities...

And yes, I rose to the challenge and he became my coach and trainer. At that time, I had no experience whatsoever in bodybuilding, competition, training, or nutrition. ZERO. But I learned... A lot...

From that moment on and during the following months, I worked hard, always focusing on my goal. My goal was not to WIN. Not really... My goal was to earn the right to be on that stage competing.

The hardest thing to do was to refuse to listen to all those people who were saying, "You are crazy," "You should not do it," "You should accept your limitations." It was challenging. But to paraphrase the old proverb, *where there is a why, there is a way*. And the bigger the 'why', the easier the 'how'.

I wanted to prove to myself that I was capable, that I could create a different life from what was expected. I wanted to prove to myself that YES, I *could* do it. I wanted to prove to many that INDEED, it *is* possible.

I set a goal. I was committed. And, like a warrior, I never gave up.

The competitions were just a few months away and there I was. With my unbreakable goal of earning the right to be standing there on that stage, among the competitors, equally eligible. With my big 'why' of proving that it was possible. And, thanks to my trainer, with both a training and a nutrition plan. I was determined.

I used to do my workouts mentally the night before, visualizing each exercise, each set, each repetition. Feeling my muscles contracting and stretching. Feeling my sweat. Relishing my satisfaction after a good workout session, one in which I had given my all.

I would often visualize myself in competition, through all the rounds, smiling and enjoying every second of the experience.

I did everything to visualize myself being strong and healthy, feeling proud of actualizing my goal.

Only 11 months after surgery, my goal of qualifying for a competition became real. I took a four-hour train trip on my own to Madrid for my first competition. I had the support of my father, though he was not really into bodybuilding. I had the total encouragement of my trainer, who believed in me before I even did. He was not allowed to take the day off and come along but his energy was with me. So, there I stood, finally on stage at the Spanish Olympia Championship, with the number 86 pinned to my red bikini, standing next to the rest of the competitors, going through each round, until the moment the judges shared their verdict.

"Third place, number 86."

That was me! It was one of the most exciting moments of my life...

But it was not over. It was not the time to relax, because just two weeks after that, I was on stage again at the IFBB Spanish National Bodybuilding Championship. This time my trainer was with me. We were competing in the Couples discipline and I was competing individually as well.

Couples competition... Third place for us!

Individual competition... Second place for me!

The moment I held that last trophy in my hands, feeling the audience clapping in a standing ovation, I was so proud of my triumph. Not for having reached the podium, but for the journey. Not for the trophy, but for what I had learned.

Among all those in the auditorium, only my trainer and I knew how far I had come. Only we knew that I had been in a wheelchair less than a year before.

Taking my place on those podiums was a great achievement and I learned a lot from the experience. Not only about bodybuilding and competition, training and nutrition. I understood the power of commitment, persistence, and perseverance. Most importantly, I learned how to listen to my true Self and follow my Inner Spirit against all odds. In every fiber of my Being, I felt the pride of setting a goal and not quitting.

Way beyond trophies and recognition, it was a feat of personal growth. An achievement in proving to myself that I *could* do it. An achievement in proving to many that YES, it *is* possible.

I know for sure that had I believed and lived by the limiting messages I was receiving for so long, I would be a different person today. Neither better nor worse. Just a completely different person, with different beliefs, and a different way of thinking and facing life. Most probably with a different professional path.

It took me a long time to understand why what I did worked so well. It took me years to learn that we really do create our lives through our thoughts. Our thoughts fuel our feelings, which then drive our actions and ultimately create our outcomes. I became fascinated with the science behind these facts, and I have been searching and studying this ever since. Years after my competitions, I met one of the most amazing individuals I have ever known, Brian Mayne, the creator of a technique called Goal Mapping, and suddenly it all made sense. So much sense that I went on to train in his techniques and became a Goal Mapping Coach and Practitioner. When you create a Goal Map with this technique, you get a clear picture of your goals, your whys, and your action plan. It acts as a blueprint for your thoughts. It is a subconscious compass, keeping you focused and guiding you to spot the circumstances and situations that will help you achieve your goals. Energy flows where attention goes.

How many times do we live by other people's expectations of what our lives should be, maybe to be liked? How many times do we let others' thoughts and opinions influence our lives, maybe out of a desire to avoid confrontation? How many times do we give up on our dreams or ideas, maybe because we want to fit in? While we are busy pleasing others, our Inner Spirit cries inside us, fading away day by day, dying slowly.

As Napoleon Hill put it so well, *"Whatever the mind of a man can conceive and believe, it can achieve"*. This works both for the positive and for the negative. I am a firm believer that you can make this work in your favor. You can transform your troubles into triumphs. Any limits others set on you are only real if you believe them and allow them to be true. You can turn your dreams into reality. You can stand on the podium of your own life and receive the trophies of your own making. I am living proof of this to be true. And you can be too.

The world needs ignited souls, sparkling spirits, vibrating in balance, and living in integrity with their inner voice.

Ignite Action Steps

Your subconscious mind is a fertile field for the dominant thoughts you plant each day to grow and deliver the fruits of your life. This is what I did to make the process work in my favor and you can use the same approach:

1. Decide what you want. State it as an affirmation, personal and positive, and in present tense. Choose an image that clearly represents your goal.

2. Identify why you want it, stating it as an affirmation. Remember, the bigger the 'why,' the easier the 'how.' Choose an image that connects you with your 'why.'

3. Attach emotion to those images and affirmations. Feel as though you have already achieved your goal.

4. Ideally, have a printed copy of your images and write your affirmations next to them.

5. Spend a few moments each day, first thing in the morning or last thing at night is best, programming your subconscious by saying your affirmations out loud while visualizing your images and feeling your emotions in each cell of your body. See it, say it, feel it.

By doing this, you will be focusing your dominant thoughts, spurring your emotions, and directing your actions toward your goal, helping you to attract and spot the circumstances and opportunities to realize it.

Goal Mapping adds the science behind this and a step-by-step process to create a visual map of your goals, your whys, and your action plan. I now use it in all areas of my life, and you can too. When I work with clients, I often get them to engage in Goal Mapping to transform their lives.

I did not know about Goal Mapping when I was 24, but I instinctively followed the steps above. We are so wise inside… if only we listened within.

I bet you have dreams. I know you have goals. I am positive you have something in your life you want to change… Dare to dream, trust your Inner Spirit, engage with your goals, choose your thoughts wisely, and get ready to be ignited.

Esther López – Spain
Coach & Trainer
Life & Business Coach, Health & Nutrition Coach
Wingwave® Coach, NLP & Hypnosis Master,
Psych-K® and Goal Mapping Practitioner
www.Smart-Change.es
online.goalmapping.com/SmartChange

ALBERT URENA

*"Every man is an embodiment of love; it just
takes a reminder of our tenderness."*

**My intention in sharing this story is to show you that transformation is
possible no matter where you are in life and to awaken in you the spirit of
brotherhood. No matter what challenges come your way, you can be certain that you will overcome them with the support of your fellow warriors.**

WARRIOR LOVE

Loving others and expressing kindness is something we take for granted,
especially us men. We rarely get to experience those feelings and some of us
were raised with the idea that men can't feel and that we have to numb ourselves.
Today, love and kindness have become pillars in my life. Everywhere I go, I
preach a message of oneness and unity. I consider myself to be the peacemaker
who shows up to resolve all conflicts in kindness and harmony. I teach people
to accept who they are and embrace others for who they truly are. Today, I have
a circle of men in which I can be transparent and take my superhero cape off. In
those moments, I feel safe and accepted — I don't have to put a mask on. It is
a group of men who I trust and know I can count on, who support me and push
me to play a bigger role in the world. It wasn't always this way. I wasn't always
the friendly Albert who was surrounded by exemplars. Let me take you back
to a time in my life where I was a totally different person from who I am today.

My family immigrated from the Dominican Republic when I was a little kid. My parents had come to the United States looking for job opportunities and a better way of life. In 1993, when I was four years old, on a cold winter night in Yonkers, New York, my father, Antonio, had been working hard the entire day in the food market, La Bodega, and was ready to clock out and come home to us. He was eager to spend time with his newborn baby of nine months, that being my little brother, Jose. With that excitement in his mind, suddenly a man walked in the door. My father turned around and recognized his friend from our neighborhood, a guy he used to drink beers and play dominoes with every weekend. My father smiled and greeted him when the man pulled out a gun and pointed it at my father, demanding money.

My father thought his friend was playing around and told him to put the gun away. The man, desperate for money, lacking compassion, pulled the trigger, killing my father with one single shot to the head.

That moment changed my life forever and the lives of my entire family, immediate and extended. All this led me to a promise I made myself, that I would be a warrior and take care of my mom, sister, and newborn little brother. It was now 'us against the world.'

I grew up with hate in my heart and with a desire for vengeance that consumed every cell in my body. People told me that I was operating under a victim consciousness, reacting to everything with defensiveness. Detention and juvenile centers were my second home. In school, I got into problems at a young age, there were kids who attempted to bully me, and I always got into fights. Even if I was smaller than my opponent, there was no way in hell I would be disrespected. Once in high school, my rebellious spirit took over. Experts say our teenage years are the most crucial in determining our futures — unfortunately most of us are not looking that far ahead.

During my sophomore year in 2005, I was 15 years old, attending high school in the Sunshine State of Florida in the United States. I felt a deep void inside of me, and I craved connection with a tribe of young men who I could identify with and express the emotions of anger and hate I was feeling. I didn't find that with my circle of classmates.

I found it with a group of people in a street gang. Once I joined the gang, I had a sense of being unstoppable and untouchable. That did wonders for my self-esteem. My popularity quickly grew in high school, and I became known for being the crazy small Dominican kid who likes to fight. Being a gang member clearly had its perks, for suddenly almost everyone respected me and all the hottest 'mommies' wanted to date me. I got involved with many girls, looking to fill that void in my heart with sex and drugs.

Skipping classes, talking back to teachers, walking out of class, starting food fights, scratching people's cars with keys, smoking weed inside the school bathroom — these were all things I thought made me cool, a warrior among the students, and not a loser.

As a Latino Warrior, I couldn't be scared of taking risks, including colliding with rival gangs, skipping school, and getting arrested by the police. Little did I know I was taking a risk that would start a chain-reaction of chaos when I got into a red car with my friend Angel. That small action sparked a 'beef' that would have major consequences for my entire group of friends. It seemed harmless — I was accompanying Angel to a girl's house, a girl he was flirting with. The driver turned out to be her boyfriend who, filled with jealousy, drove that car, with us in it, into the trunk of a tree. The driver started to fight with his girlfriend — the target of my friend's flirtation — and we took the opportunity to get away.

A few days later, I attended a beautiful night of celebration. My friend Sabrina had just turned 15 and we were doing her 'Quinceañera', which is the Hispanic version for the Sweet 16, at a club her family had rented. She was gorgeous, wearing a long crystal dress, with her blonde hair wrapped up with a crystal hair clip. She looked like Cinderella, straight out of a Disney animation. Everyone was having a great time. I remember sitting on a high back chair in the middle of the party, also nicely dressed, as I got suited up for the occasion. I had my girl next to me, who also was looking stunning with a cobalt blue dress and her beautiful brunette hair. That was when a guy approached me to whisper in my ear, "Junior is outside with his friends and they are looking for you and for Angel." I felt invaded — how could he show up and ruin this beautiful night?

I immediately told my best friend and the word spread in a matter of seconds. We walked outside and *boom* a major fight broke out. Suddenly, the Sweet 15 party had turned into a classic ballroom brawl. Sabrina was crying asking me, "Why Albert? Why did you have to ruin my party?" I felt heartbroken for her but, instead of taking responsibility, my resentment took over. I blamed it on Junior for coming over with his unwanted friends. My excuse was, "We just defended ourselves." It took years for Sabrina to forgive me; I'm surprised she even did. It took even more years for me to forgive myself.

The next day, after long hours of classes, the bell rang and it was time to go home. I was walking with some buddies from school to the bus stop and we boarded the city bus. I received a text message warning me that Junior was following our bus in a green SUV full of guys out to get me. As we got to my stop, one of my buddies started panicking and told me to run home. I looked at him straight in the eye and said, "I ain't running from nobody!" Filled with pride, I crossed the street and waited for the green SUV to pull up. Six guys got out of the car. The baddest looking guy came up to my face and asked me if we had 'jumped' his boy and I replied that he'd come looking for it.

When I felt a punch strike me in the head, I grabbed the guy by his rosary and started punching him in the face and did my best to defend myself against my attackers. I got stomped in the head so hard, it left the signature of the boots 'Timberland' in my cranium. I was later told that the ambulance arrived after the neighbors called the police and I was taken to the hospital.

I can still remember the look of disappointment on my mother's face when she learned that I had been in a fight. I felt like a bad son and I worried that I was putting my mother through the same pain she had felt with my father. Something I do cherish from that time in the hospital is that many of my Warrior brothers came to see me. They really showed they cared for me and were there through it all.

The following day, I got another text warning me that Junior and his friends were going back to our school and this time they were looking for my best friend, Angel. I immediately got up from my bed and put my gold bandana on my forehead, ignoring my black eye and all the bruises on my body. I made some calls and walked over to my high school. The entire McDonald's™ plaza was full of people; some were there just to watch but most of them were there to fight and support us. My entire crew showed up. I couldn't believe how many people were there to watch my back. It felt golden at the time as I felt I wasn't alone anymore.

I stood with the masses of people in the plaza, just waiting for the attackers to show up. I noticed this girl Maria, who knew both of us well, calling Junior on the phone. She was telling him not to come because there were too many people and he was going to get hurt. I got so angry and yelled at her, "Why are you giving him a heads up?" "Because he's my friend," she replied. "You didn't give me a warning!" I continued to yell. "I wasn't there!" she said. "If I were there, I would have warned you too!"

Due to the warning, they didn't show up. Later that night, I was home sitting outside my apartment in the staircase when I got a call; my Warrior brothers were in a car chasing Junior and his friends. My crew was being shot at and they had started shooting back in retaliation. The gunfight ensued until the driver was hit and the car in front stopped moving. Our enemies were injured. My friends attempted to get away, and then were cornered and stopped by the police. Two guys got hit; everyone was detained and many were quickly arrested.

Fear is part of human nature and that fear pushed one of the members to 'snitch' and say who had shot the gun. That was the beginning of the end of our tribe.

Our leader, Macho, got convicted of a felony, and went to prison for fifteen years, and it was all because of my stupid 'beef.' I lived with regret throughout the following years, thinking to myself that I was the one who needed to be locked up, not him. Guilt took over me, especially when other members of the gang started getting arrested, and some got deported to their native countries. I couldn't grasp how so many *small* decisions had created such a huge mess and ruined the lives of so many families.

Not long after that, one of my tribe brothers, Craig, was playing basketball when out of nowhere he had a heart attack and passed away. That was it for me. I realized something needed to change in my life, for at 16 years old, jail, deportations, shootings, and death, was the reality surrounding me. I realized that life is valuable and that the wrong choices could ruin your life forever.

It was at Craig's funeral, where us 'criminals' — teenagers involved in gangs and drugs — were holding our hands together in prayer, some of us crying, all of us being transparent for the first time, no one showing their 'tough' side. Something amazing happened in that moment for me. I received the insight that every man is the embodiment of love; it just takes a reminder of our tenderness. I felt love in my life for the first time in so long in place of just feeling anger and resentment.

All of these events led me to seek God. My girlfriend at that time had just converted into Christianity and even though I was raised Roman Catholic, I was eager for change. One night I accepted an invitation to a local church named Torre Fuerte — 'Strong Tower.' When the pastor, Luis Carmona, was preaching, I felt grounded in the Now. It felt as if no one else was there, just me and God, speaking through the pastor. At the end of the service he made a call to accept Jesus Christ as your personal Lord and Savior. Inspired, and in tears, I raised my hand and walked up to the front. The pastor prayed for me. That was when I was born again, with a renewed sense of purpose in life.

In the Christian church, I got involved with a group of men and young adults, changing the people I surrounded myself with. Slowly but surely I began healing from within, learning to accept those guys that weren't considered the 'cool' kids. Learning to hug others. Learning to say, "I love you" to my friends. Praying. Sitting in silence practicing mindfulness. My spiritual growth began there as I started devouring books. I read the entire Bible and got interested in other philosophical books. Attending several spiritual retreats was like soul cleansing, purging all the low vibrations of emotions that were stuck. That's when I shifted from hate and anger to love and became a Praying Warrior.

No matter the mistakes we have made in the past, no matter the hate we have felt, no matter how violent we have been, every person is good deep inside. I know this to be true in my soul. We all do what we think is best according to the perception we have at that moment. Therefore, forgive yourself and forgive those who have hurt you.

I identify myself now as spiritual, not religious; embracing other ideas and accepting that we all look at life from different angles. We are evolving from an ego-centric mindset, that perception of *me versus you* and an e*thno-centric mindset*, that perspective of us versus them, into a new level of consciousness. This new consciousness is described by philosopher Ken Wilber of 'World-Centrism' as seeing each other as One and 'Cosmo-Centrism,' which is the reality of being one with God and everything that exists.

I am grateful to announce that almost 15 years later, my warrior brother Macho got released from prison after serving his sentence and demonstrating good behavior. Throughout the entire period, we kept in contact and I believe that communication played an important role in both of our transformations. Inside, he studied Islam and Christianity. He got in touch with his higher self and, now that he's free, he's dedicating his time to unite men through music.

This is the time to heal the heart of the wounded warriors: engage in brotherly love, open up to those around us and share our truth, share our most intimate secrets, tell people we love them and start giving hugs. This is what it means to be a man in the 21st century.

It was by Divine Grace that I was able to get out of the violent world of street gangs and heal my heart from all the hate and resentment that poisoned my soul. Transformation is possible no matter where you are in life. That is why I am now committed to spreading a message of unity among us, of brotherly love. No matter where you're from, no matter the color of your skin, no matter your religion or sexual orientation, I am committed to share my story so you can be the loving warrior that you are.

Despite the challenges that come our way, we can overcome them, because we are not alone. We have a circle of Warriors supporting one another and there's nothing that will stop us! As men, we are all Warriors; we are all fighting for something we believe in and that's what keeps us going. That love within us is what sparks the flame of life in our hearts. In the middle of the most extreme situations, we can find peace and harmony knowing we are not alone. That's what I like to call Warrior Love.

Ignite Action Steps

1. Ask yourself this empowering question: "What if I saw every person as redeemable today?" (I want to thank David P. Wichman, author of *Every Grain of Sand* for this question.)

2. Forgive yourself for the choices you have made in the past.

3. Forgive those who have hurt you.

4. Let go of your old identity; you're no longer living in the past.

5. Engage in a men's circle and share with authenticity.

6. Say "I love you" to your male friends and family members. Hug them, too; you'll like it ;)

7. Connect with your higher Self through prayer and meditation.

8. Get involved in a spiritual community.

Albert Urena – United States of America
Transformational Leader
alberturena.com

WARRIOR

JONATHAN V REECE

"Be a student of life, for life."

My intention for sharing this story is to encourage you to call upon the warrior within and become the man you are meant to be. Discovering who you were created to be is a lifelong journey, a road with many obstacles. The lack of a positive male role model or mentor in your life, as is my story, is only a fork in your road. Your journey to manhood can still be victorious. There is wisdom and mentorship accessible to you. Go out, find it, make it your own, and apply it. Learn to love learning and be a student of life.

SEARCHING FOR A MENTOR

The absence or the presence of inadequate or incompetent male role models playing the central character of man, father, and husband has a far-reaching effect on any young person, but especially young boys. These effects are often not realized, seen, nor felt until many years later when that boy becomes a young man and is thrust onto the stage to play those same roles. Being called upon to portray these ideals has been a recurring challenge throughout my adulthood, given my ill preparation. I have had to call upon my warrior within to summon the wisdom, courage, and strength to step into each of these roles when life and duty calls.

As a young boy, I had very little access to my father or even a father figure. I come from a family of fourteen children, three of those children out of wedlock, coupled with seven divorces — yes, seven! With two divorces for my mother and five for my father, it was very hard for me to ascertain a true sense of what a man, father, or husband should be and how one should act. This narrative sounds much more daunting than is the actual case for me as I was isolated from most of it by distance and time. There are 35 years separating the 14 children and I was number six in birth order with two older sisters and three older brothers, but still no male guidance. As with most young boys, I had no idea how this was impacting my growth and development as a young man.

I grew up in a single mother household with up to three siblings living with us at any given time until I turned 10. After that, the household stabilized with my mother, older sister, younger brother, and I as the core of our home with an occasional short stay from my eldest sister when she was in the in-between — between the next job or relationship. Most of my younger pre-ten years are not much remembered, probably out of psychological repression as a protective measure.

Fortunately for me, my father was still around but was two hours away. My only opportunities to see him were periodic weekends and a longer, lengthy stay during the summer months when I had respite from school. My memories of that time are fond but my exposure to him was rare. Limited by the presence of numerous women — four marriages and three divorces all before I turned 11. The dynamics were constantly changing. Fridays after school, once a month, is when he would pick me up for our weekend together. Most scheduled Fridays he would show, but some he would not, nor would he call. I remember sitting in the front yard for hours on these occasions, periodically walking to the end of the drive with tears rolling down my cheeks, praying for his car to appear at the end of the street. It never did. Luckily, I had the strong and stable home of my mother for some sense of normalcy and stability.

I do have good memories of days with my father filled with boating, fishing, skiing, and church. My father was an avid fisherman and owned his own boat. Our summer weekends together were mostly spent on the lake. Some days we would bring in loads of rainbow trout, walleye pike, sunfish, bluegill, and sometimes even a catfish. I can't remember a day when we did not at least catch dinner. We would bring the fish back home for preparation. He taught me, by the age of seven, how to expertly clean and debone each of those fish except the catfish. I would watch him clean those since the skin was so tough, they would always prove a challenge for me. I loved learning from him. His method, maybe unorthodox, was to score the neck, nail the head of the catfish to the tree right outside the back door, take his pliers and peel the skin off the back of the fish, and cut the skin off with the tail fin. This would leave us with a nice clean catfish for dinner. I enjoyed our many fish dinners together. These weekends of fishing continued until I was 10 and his third wife was ready to deliver me a new baby brother.

As new siblings began to arrive, my time with him became even more limited and ultimately ceased once he moved to Texas, a five-hour flight from me in Michigan. I learned through my teens and early adulthood that it was mostly a blessing that I didn't grow up in the same house as my father. My mother — intelligent, strong, and stable as she was — tried to protect my love for my father and never spoke an ill word about him in front of me. She instructed my older siblings to do the same. But, as siblings do, over time, they shared the stories of the physical and mental abuse that they and my mother were subjected to by my father. I was far too young at the time of my mother's divorce from my father to ever experience this. To my recollection he was never physical with me and only spanked me once as a young boy, but the stories my siblings told rang true and over time solidified the need for me to find a male role model outside of my family.

As I grew, the stories became more believable as his marriages fell apart and more stories were shared. I began to see my father as the antithesis of a male role model. He was an example of the type of man I did not want to emulate. For this, I can now thank him. As my father's eldest son, that was my experience. My younger siblings who got to live with him may have experienced him differently. Each of us had our own unique relationship with him and for that I am thankful.

In my teens, subconsciously, I began to search out strong male role models and leaders. I had a propensity to gravitate toward the fathers of my close friends, teachers, coaches, and older mentors. One of my best friends, CK, lived six houses down and was three years older than I. I spent many days with him and his father doing projects around their home. Building two wooden decks on the back of their house and popping a sliding glass door in their back TV room, bought from the classifieds that morning, are two of my favorite memories. Spending time with him, his family, coaches, Boy Scouts, and other male bonding opportunities that my mother generously provided became my examples of manhood, fatherhood, and what a good husband looked like.

The complexity of my family structure began to impact me more as a young man and into adulthood. I started to realize how different my experience had been. Having older siblings in their thirties and younger siblings in diapers started out as a good conversation piece but then turned into a lengthy monologue of how it all came about. I did feel unique to have such an interesting story. Although, needless to say, I was still searching for a strong male role model or mentor in my life. I realized the older you get the harder it is to find that person.

For me, college was my Ignite Moment and a fork in the road to manhood. The summer after freshman year, I took a position with Southwestern Publishing Company that turned out to be the ultimate growth step for me. The position was selling books door-to-door. During my first summer, the training they provided, before we hit the 'bookfield', introduced me to the world of personal development. Without knowing it, I was being exposed to countless new mentors and role models. I began to read the writings of Dale Carnegie, Napoleon Hill, Og Mandino, and Zig Ziglar. I had read the Bible for years, but the words from these men were different, more pragmatic, more practical. Their writings opened my eyes to a whole new level of understanding of manhood, self-worth, and self-discipline. These authors provided a framework, guidance, and the male role models that I needed.

Working for Southwestern Publishing teamed me with male leaders whose sole responsibility was to mentor us to be successful in the 'bookfield' and as young men. The mentorship was not only in selling, but in leadership and systems. I grew tremendously that first year. It was not easy. It was truly painful at times. I was lonely, often isolated for days, knowing no one other than my teammates. We were assigned a territory and expected to work on our own. I had to step up and be a man of my word, be a warrior, and navigate the system to meet my daily and weekly goals.

One thing I became very familiar with on the 'bookfield' is rejection. Rejection becomes your companion since it is with you all day every day and is usually waiting to greet you behind the front door of the very next house. We would joke that we all heard the words 'not interested' so often that it became one word to our ears, 'nonstred.' — expecting to hear it but delighted and sometimes surprised when we received the opposite and were welcomed into a home.

It was my second summer and my team and I set up base to work the towns in and around Morgantown, WV. West Virginia is known as one of the poorest states in the United States which added to our challenge of door-to-door sales. What my 20-year-old self initially failed to realize is that those folks had great pride and wanted more for their children. I was selling guidebooks to assist their children with each subject in school to help them excel and get into college. Remember, this was pre-internet, search engine, and cell phone days; books were cool back then.

I remember one very warm and humid July day. I had heard 'nonstred' so often, I thought it was the only term left in the English language. I had been shot down repeatedly all day long and the sun was quickly setting. You don't knock on doors after dark in the 'Hollers' as you might get a 'shotgun greeting.' I drove up to what was going to be my final door, according to my paper map, just outside Kingwood, WV.

There was no driveway and I could not see the house immediately, so I parked on the street. As I opened the car door, I could faintly see the house in the distance at the bottom of a 30-foot hill. As I made my way down the hill on foot, the sun seemed to be setting more rapidly behind the tall trees. Standing in front of the home now, I could see it was a modest one room home that also included a couple of corrugated steel bedroom additions protruding from each side like wings. Off to the right, in the distant woods, I could see the outhouse, which was still common in these parts. I knocked on the door fully expecting to hear the only word I had heard all day. To my surprise, the mother welcomed me into the living area to see what I had to share with them. As I stepped in, onto the dirt floor, I noticed one lightbulb hanging from the ceiling. This provided just enough light for me to take my place on the empty seat, which appeared to be the front bench seat from an old Chevy with seat belt receptacles still intact. The mother asked one of the children to turn off the black and white television with protruding rabbit ears full of aluminum foil. As I began my script, the mother and three children became engaged. I placed the first book onto the tractor tire and plywood coffee table in front of me and the children grabbed it and began to turn the pages vigorously. I pulled the second and third books out of my bag and just handed them over, so each child had one. The mother began to tear up explaining she had not seen her children interested in anything pertaining to school in a long time. She wanted more for her kids than their current situation allowed, and she knew the only way was getting them a good education. She immediately rose from her lawn chair in the living room and disappeared into the kitchen. She returned with an envelope full of cash and asked what it would take to have these books for her children. She laid down the money on the plywood in front of me as the tears flowed from her eyes.

As I left the home that evening I felt victorious. Not because I made a sale but because I believed the books I left would change those kids' lives forever. I realized that persistence, perseverance, and self-discipline pays off not just for me, but for those I encounter. If I had given up early or not even gone out that day, those children would not have the opportunity to excel at school and hopefully go off to college and change their family tree. To me, that was the victory that day.

Whether I failed or was victorious in meeting my daily goal, the true victory and growth was getting up the next morning and doing it all again. There were many days I failed epically. This is where I learned internal fortitude. I had to overcome fear, doubt, and sometimes despair to continue. I had people counting on me. My manager, my teammates, my family were all expecting me to be a success. To be a success, I must hit my goals. My goal was to be successful enough to come back the following year to lead a team of my own, which I did. This set my life as a young man on a new trajectory.

I was onto something. I realized that I needed to stop searching outside of myself for that one person, the mentor. That one person is me. I must create that person from all the wisdom I have that is already accessible. I must become the man I want to be. I must be both a student of life and of *manhood* if I was to be successful. I knew this was to be a lifelong journey and I was excited for the endless possibilities.

The desire for a strong male mentor has not escaped me throughout my adulthood. There have been many surrogates, both current and past, that I am thankful for. I realized I could not do this by myself; instead I must be willing to do the work on my own. We grow when we press ourselves past our physical and mental limits. This I can do. Whether from a living mentor or words on a page from one of these and many other great authors, I must take and apply that wisdom to become the man and warrior I want to be. It has been and will be a lifelong journey that has no end until I come to mine. I am always trying to be a better man, husband, father, brother, friend, and all the other myriad roles we men play in our adult lives. I have become a student of life, *for* life.

Today, I can proudly say that I have been married one time, to the same beautiful and amazing woman for 20 years and counting, with one handsome, bright, and talented teenage son. I use these books, the wisdom of these authors and mentors both past and present. Most importantly, I do the work. I take that learning and apply it to my life, my thoughts and my actions daily. I realize I will not be able to teach my son everything he needs to know about manhood before he is off on his own creating his own life; however, I try every single day to be the best role model I can be. The most important thing to me is to be the best example of a man, husband, and father that I am capable of being right now. I try to teach him how to become his own warrior, to learn, and to love to learn. To be a student of life, *for* life.

At times I have failed in each of my life's roles, probably more than I would want or care to admit. I know that I will continue to fail in the future, for that is the way I learn. My goal is to not dwell on a failure but to admit it, seek enlightenment from words or mentors, do the self-work required to overcome and be victorious next time around. I want to encourage each of you men to do the same.

We will all fail at times in the roles we play in life as men. When this happens, be encouraged that this is a learning opportunity for you to grow into the warrior and man you want to become. Do not dwell on the failure but admit it, seek knowledge, and do whatever work you must to overcome and be victorious next time. Do not search for that one person. The person does not exist. That one person is you. You can create that person from the wisdom that is already accessible to you. You can transform yourself into the man you want to be. You need to be a student of life and of manhood if you are to be a success. This journey of manhood is a lifelong one. *Be a student of life, For Life!*

IGNITE ACTION STEPS

- **Recognize** that you will fail. We all fail; I have failed many times. Take ownership of your failures, face them, dissect them to understand exactly what, how, and who you failed. It could be your spouse or significant other, your children, your parents, your siblings, or it could be you just failed yourself. Whatever the failure is, own it, study it, and understand it to recognize it next time.
- **Seek out wisdom** and knowledge of how to address and overcome that specific failure. Ask a mentor or do research on the topic to find mentors in books, chapters, articles, or on pages on which you can draw wisdom from to bring change into your life.
- **Apply** — Now comes the hard part. Apply it. Choose a method. It could be reading and taking notes, talking with a friend, journaling, or meditation. Find the way that resonates in your soul. When you find your soul method, that will bring real change over time. This is learning how to love to learn.
- **Practice** — Make it a lifelong practice to work on yourself. No one else can. Many will go through life from day to day and their trajectory will be controlled by their successes and failures like the wind. You can change it. You can control your trajectory. You must learn how to love to learn in your own way. Most importantly, you must be a student of life, for life.

Jonathan V Reece – United States of America
Mortgage Finance Guru / RE Investor / World Traveler / Stoic Philosopher /
Author / Entrepreneur / Teacher / Lover of Life / Voracious Learner / World Changer
www.JonathanVReece.com

Jeffrey C. Sorensen

"Our true freedom lies within our greatest struggles."

My hope in sharing my story with you is that you may remember how strong and powerful you truly are. My intention is to remind you that you are not a victim of life; everything that happens in your life is an opportunity for growth. Your most challenging moments provide you with an opportunity to remember who you truly are. You, my friend, are a warrior.

Finding Freedom Within

This is the story of how I learned that I could survive anything.

Before everything changed, mornings on the beach were my most cherished time of the day. Every night before I fell asleep, I would smile knowing I would spend the first hours of my day walking with my feet in the sand, my two canine companions Karmen and Karmella beside me — splashing in the waves. There was nothing I enjoyed more than to wake up in the morning just before sunrise and head out of the house barefoot to the beach just across the street. I was happy, but life was hectic in those days. Spending that time in the morning watching the spectacular sunrises, squadrons of pelicans, and the flocks of herons, lifted my spirits and released my worries into the fresh sea breeze. I would often return to those memories in the challenges that would soon come.

So much had changed since I first arrived three years before, in the bustling port city of Mazatlan, Mexico. Life had been an uphill battle for so long, but now my restaurant was finally doing well and I was even dating again for the first time in years. The one thing that had stayed constant through all of this was my draw to the ocean, her soothing ebb and flow lulling my stress and easing my sorrow and loss. I was finally inching out of survival mode. I felt like I could breathe for the first time. Strangely though, over the past few weeks, I had a new and unsettling feeling that something didn't seem quite right.

Since I had returned to Mazatlan after spending some time at home in Western Canada earlier that fall, I felt out of place, like I didn't belong in that chapter of my life anymore. I couldn't quite figure out how to make a change or even what change I needed to make. When I was back in Canada, I had remarked to several friends, "I feel like I'm not going to see you again for a long time." If only I had known.

Karmen and Karmella had become my family. Karmen with her floppy ears and sweet temperament meant so much to me — she had been like a guardian to me through so much change — through my years of addiction and through the struggle of my recovery. She had arrived in my life as a pup just as I was falling into the sweet, warm grip of opiate addiction. She was always by my side, from the days and nights spent scoring drugs in the alleys of the Downtown Eastside in Vancouver, to the weeks I spent lying on my kitchen floor detoxing from pills, to my suicide run across Canada and through the US on my way to Mexico to find true healing. I loved that dog more than I had loved any human in my life. She felt like my best friend, a confidant, a wise old teacher who taught me so much. It is a beautiful thing to connect so deeply to an animal of another species, to feel their thoughts, their pain, their love and devotion.

Karmella with her burning, golden eyes was more challenging. She was a Mexican street dog I had picked up when I first arrived in Mazatlan. She was tenacious and confrontational, like a different species. Although another dog was the last thing I needed as I struggled to let go of the last of my addictions, having those two constant companions probably saved my life. They gave me a reason to live, a reason not to take my life as I battled with the loneliness and grief of having lost everything I had worked so hard for, only to wind up living in an RV trailer on the beach in Mazatlan.

Yoga had provided the lifeline that helped to pull me out of addiction. I found the practice shortly after I arrived in Mazatlan and dove in headfirst. I started the process of relearning how to breathe, how to move with my breath, and as a result, how to flow with life. I began teaching shortly after I started practicing at the request of one of my instructors. I loved sharing with others something that had been so transformative in my own life. I had finally completed my yoga teacher training after teaching unofficially for almost three years. It seemed like everything was coming together in some ways and in others it just didn't feel quite right.

I had no idea how 'not right' my life was about to become, but a couple of weeks later when I found myself in a concrete, cinder block room sitting across from a lawyer, with a cold, hard metal table between us, my suspicions started to ground themselves in my reality.. He told me that my sentence would be between 10 and 25 years. I laughed at him. I thought he was joking. He wasn't.

At that point, I had been put in a solitary cell — for my own safety I was told. I was okay with that. My brief stay in 'La Sala' upon my arrival at CERESO Mexicali was beyond comprehension of the normal constructs of the human mind. It was a holding room with row upon row of bunks, six bunks high, four bunks wide, two or three men to a bunk — many of them addicts brought straight in off the street for minor drug offences — mixed with men who had committed every sort of crime imaginable. To a white guy who spoke very little Spanish, it was a terrifying hell on earth — an insane asylum, filthy, crawling with cockroaches, both human and insect.

To be whisked off to a private cell seemed like a blessing. Although the cell was filthy and barren with the exception of a metal bunk, a sink, a hole in the floor, and some bits of trash and discarded items strewn about, I was thankful to be away from the madness of La Sala — for the first few days anyway. Still in my street clothes, I felt ridiculous in my North Face™ vest, plaid shirt and designer jeans. I spent the first day cleaning the cell with a splash of Pine Sol left in a bottle I had found discarded in a corner. I had also discovered some remnants of a couple of bars of soap scattered around. I squished them together into something I could clean myself with and I washed a scrap of blanket that had been forgotten on the top bunk that served as both my blanket and a yoga mat. I spent the early part of each morning as I would anywhere in the world, deep in my practice of meditation, yoga, and breath. I would return to my breathing throughout the day as my mind attempted to run away with the devastating thoughts of the new reality I was locked in. I envisioned being back with my dogs on the golden sand, playing in the waves as they crashed upon the pristine beach.

It was unbelievable how quickly I forgot about the outside world, how challenging it was to retrieve those visions as time went on. Soon, the only world I knew and could remember revolved around my cell, *Celda 220*. I was terrified to be removed from the safety of my temporary cell. The loneliness was crushing, but it felt so much safer than the alternative. I hadn't actually been able to see inside what would become my permanent home, but I could see down the hallway as I was ushered to and from my current solitary cell. The number of men, who funneled past me as they were ushered outdoors to a dusty cement playing field with a chain link fence known as 'campo' once a week, simply did not match the size of the space they emerged from. There were hundreds of men, streaming out from a row of cells that was only a hundred feet long.

The men who filed out one by one were like the Mexicans of the movies — *cholos* they called them. Mustachioed with tattooed faces and drawling singsong voices, all of them were curious to catch a peek of the white guy in the cell at the end of the hall. It seemed as though they took great pleasure in being as obnoxious and offensive as possible — that was the general way of being, I would soon find out. It was like an unwritten contract between inmates, that everyone would digress into their crudest, most ignorant behavior.

At night, men from all the cells in the hall would sing corridos together, howling their allegiance to the legendary *El Chapo, La Santa Muerta, the Malo Verde* -- bastardized gods born from the fusion of Catholicism, indigenous beliefs, and the Mexican drug culture. The songs would start about 9 PM and build in fervor for hours until the singers were scolded by the guards to stop at lights out. I would cover my head with my arms and pray to be released. I was still imagining that I would go free soon — I was deep in my denial at that point.

New prisoners were delivered to their permanent cells once a week and, for the long term prisoners, it was prime time entertainment to watch the newbies ushered in, to shout obscenities and be as lewd and threatening as possible. When I arrived, everyone knew who I was, they had seen "La Canadadiense" on TV and couldn't wait to hear the story of how I had landed myself in this hellish little world.

My first steps into the 11' x 11' cell were incredibly intense and nearly over-whelming. I felt the room spin as the 30 other men in the cell crowded around me like dogs sniffing each other as they greeted me, sizing me up, speaking in Spanish and broken English. All I could do was breathe and feel the intensity of the emotions as they arose. Fear, anxiety, and anger washed through me. I felt like lashing out to create space around me, but it seemed like a bad idea. As overwhelmed as I felt, I had a strange sense, a deep understanding that I was exactly where I was supposed to be in that moment. I could feel this was a test, an exam of sorts. I prayed to God that I would pass.

The first days were tough settling into the cell and, even more so, the cus-toms. It was a world ruled by dysfunctional egos and an animalistic hierarchy. There was no rhyme or reason to the rules, they didn't need to make sense, it was just the way it was. My Spanish was poor, most of it was words I needed to know for the restaurant — little of that applied here — my limited Spanish led to many misunderstandings, scuffles, and all-out fights in my first days, weeks, and months. I struggled to maintain my composure as I laid on a thin blanket on the concrete floor at night, cockroaches running across my face. Stories I had read in the book *Four Thousand Days* of cockroaches laying eggs in the ears of Thai prisoners drifted through my mind. At times I felt like imploding. I wished I could — to just vanish into nothing and escape the nightmare that had become my life. In jail, sleep was my only reprieve, but the crushing reality of waking up in a cage everyday quickly shattered any sense of peace.

Almost immediately upon arriving in my newest cell, I started to figure out how I could do my yoga practice in the midst of the chaos. I needed to find a way to center myself, or I knew I would definitely be there for the 10-25 years my lawyer had implied. I knew if I wanted to find a way out of prison, I first needed to be okay with where I was, and in order to be okay, I needed to stretch, I needed to breathe, and I needed to focus my mind. Somehow, I needed to find a way to do that in a ridiculously overcrowded cell.

There was a very systematic progression of sleeping positions as one joined the cell. Newbies started sleeping next to the bathroom on the water-soaked floor outside the shower. From there they progressed, flipping head to foot, toward the door of the cell. The next step was to move up onto 'la tabla', a 'second story' — a metal framework precariously welded onto the top bunk, covered in scraps of plywood. Finally, if one stayed long enough, they would get one of the six metal bunks. Men were packed in the cell like sardines in a concrete can, so tight that there was literally nowhere to step on the floor at night; one had to crawl along the edge of the bunks to get from the front of the cell to the bathroom in the back.

I realized the only place I was going to be able to do my morning yoga practice was by staying next to the bathroom. For over a year, to hold on to that spot, I forewent my opportunity to move through the progression and slept on the soggy floor. This way, I could awaken in the morning before everyone else and sit, meditate, and breathe. During these times, I breathed my freedom, I visualized it, and affirmed it with every breath. After breakfast would arrive, everyone would go back to sleep, except for me. That was when I would take my scrap of blanket, lie it down on the floor, and flow through my yoga practice. These practices kept me alive. They kept me calm; they gave me peace and helped the waves of grief, sorrow, anger, and despair to flow through.

Once a week we would get taken outside for nearly an hour, into 'el campo,' the concrete playing field surrounded by a dusty dirt track. While we were there, we could talk on the phones if we had a phone card and if we could find a phone that worked. Vivian, one of the women who had worked at my restaurant, had taken my dogs when I didn't come back to Mazatlan. It was on a Monday morning when I called her that she told me Karmen had been killed. Karmen had been hit over the head with a shovel by the owner of a dog that Karmen had attacked. Hearing the news, a jolt of pain and anguish ripped through my body like a bolt of electricity. I thought I might crumple as the strength in my legs gave way. I couldn't breathe. As the guards called us to line up to return to the cell, I knew I couldn't show my pain to anyone. In the animalistic hierarchy we lived in, that weakness would be pounced upon like hyenas ripping apart a carcass in the wild. I did my best to let the pain wash through me as I settled back into the cell. I breathed with it; I felt it deeply. The pain, the guilt, the shame, the anger, and the loss. I sat quietly and stoically by myself for days as I processed. I didn't want to talk to anybody, look at anybody, or explain to anybody what was going on.

I realized what I was feeling was the essence of the human experience. I understood that this is why we are here — to feel this range of emotions and to experience them deeply. There is a beauty in this depth of feeling and in the surrender. I understood that it was truly a blessing and an incredible gift to love someone so much that it broke my heart to lose her. I learned that grief is the other side of the coin of joy — when I accepted that, my suffering eased. I realized that I no longer needed to suffer. I finally saw my suffering as a choice and a perspective. In this I found my freedom and I knew from that moment on I could manage anything that life threw at me. At that point, I dove even deeper into my practice and I connected to something inside me that was limitless, strong, and pure. I renewed my obsession with my freedom. I breathed it, drank it, ate it, spoke it, and visualized it as I went to bed that night and every night to come.

Eighteen long months later, my freedom came. The guards finally came to the door one day and said the words I had been whispering everyday into my own ear, "Jeffrey, ya te vas." I was finally free, to where I didn't know, and I didn't care. I was free.

Like any challenging situation, we often think the situation is the challenge. Often that is only the beginning, the repercussions are when we are truly tested. After spending six years in Mexico, the last two immersed in a Mexican jail, returning home to Canada seemed like moving to a strange foreign country. The culture seemed unusual, the people cold and distant.

I wondered at times whether I had it in me to start again. In those moments I remembered back to sitting on the floor of my cell and remembered how hard I had fought for freedom. I seldom entertained the doubts for more than a moment before ushering them back out the door. I simply couldn't allow them to inhabit my mind and I knew if I was going to make it, I needed not only to put one foot in front of the other, I needed to run.

There is a part of us that always tells us that we cannot manage what we are experiencing. The truth is that we can always manage what life gives us; however, sometimes, it will take everything we have, and a little bit more. This is how we grow. We are powerful beings, capable of so much more than we believe. Remember this, no matter how challenging life gets, you will rise — and be stronger for it.

IGNITE ACTION STEPS

1. Find a piece of paper and a pen. Write down all the challenging situations you have lived through. Recognize the strength it took you to persevere through them. Our true strength lies not in the size of our muscles or our bank account, but in the depth of our connection to the power that lies within us.

2. Create a daily practice. Feel your body, move your body, feel your breath, feel your emotions as they arise. Feel them deeply, do not run — this is what we are here for. These emotions are born of you — love them and let them go.

3. Learn to be okay where you are. Be grateful for what you have. Write it down. Talk about it. The first step to moving on is being okay with where we are right now.

4. What do you really want in your life? Whatever it is, visualize it, breathe with it, speak it, feel it, and regardless of what anybody tells you, *believe with every ounce of your being that it will come true!*

Jeffrey C. Sorensen - Canada
Founder - breathARMY
www.breatharmy.com

WARRIOR

SANTIAGO RAFAEL PASCUAL

"You will find yourself in problems; in problems you will find Yourself."

In my near-death experiences and reality-disrupting events, I've found the biggest treasures. My intent is to share these realizations that lead to the embodiment of my Spiritual Warrior. By facing adversity and my own weaknesses, I learned to prevent misery in my life and dance through my challenges gracefully.

THE SPIRITUAL WARRIOR DANCING THROUGH THE STORMS OF THE EGO

My reality of the world was shattered when I was only 10 years old. On my usual three-block walk home from my English classes, in the gray streets of Buenos Aires, I got mobbed. Crime was rising in this alienated city. I came across two boys no older nor bigger than me. They were scavenging the trash, as many people did at that time, in search of something of value. I saw them spot me and instantly my instinct knew I had to act fast and be smart. They started chasing me. I ran as fast as I could. I still remember this scene in slow motion: when I looked over my shoulder, they were there, running at full speed, as if they, too, were running for their lives.

Suddenly, when I was just meters from my home, I crashed into a car that was stuck in traffic. It was rush hour; the street was full of cars. I remember hitting the vehicle strongly, crashing into it, as a cry for help, hoping someone would get out to rescue me.

To my surprise, no one came out. Dozens of people were around, yet no one seemed to realize that these were not my friends and we were not playing. I was stunned and in shock, I couldn't believe this was happening and no one was standing up to them for me. I also remember measuring the boys and thinking to myself: These guys are not bigger than me. How can it be that I'm so vulnerable?

The helplessness sensation and the disappointment in all the careless people is an imprint that I vividly can remember. While they were pulling my sweater, demanding I hand it over, and my bag, I couldn't move.

Until — what felt like an eternity later — two older boys came to ask what was going on and scared them off. The young thieves fled.

These older guys told me they didn't react sooner because they believed we were playing. Only when they realized what was happening did they intervene. They walked me home where I stayed for a week. The shock was so strong that I fell sick in bed with cold chills and was puking for many days. I felt weak and I didn't want to venture out into the dangerous world again.

With time, I gained confidence and learned how to avoid and prevent problems — how to move smarter. Nevertheless, I kept engaging in many dangerous situations during my early teen ages. I didn't want anything to prevent me from doing what I wanted.

Contemplating in hindsight, this was a repeated pattern: I looked for extreme situations to find my limits. I remember at 3 years old, I jumped into a lake even though my parents told me not to because they thought I didn't know how to swim. To prove them wrong, I jumped in while they were sleeping… only to find out that they may be right: I may *know* how to swim, but not for long enough to not get tired and drown. Fortunately, my father woke up and came for me before I could no longer sustain myself floating.

At 5 years old, I was playing superheroes with my cousin against the older kids in the kindergarten. It was my cousin and I against five older kids. There were no rules, in a sense. We were 5 years old and no one had taught us the rules of how to fight, so there were many low blows and tricky, sneaky tactics to really hurt our opponents. We proved that we could take them down. It was, in our minds, a great victory.

I started going outside the 'safe zone' from an early age, but then it became more extreme in my teen years. I was 12 when I went to hard core punk rock concerts during the dangerous nights of Buenos Aires. That was not a place for a kid. Most people were taller and bigger than me. I felt asphyxiated by the compressed massive crowd. I couldn't breathe. The open spaces were for 'pogo' — very violent expressions where people kicked and punched each other; many wore spikes on their clothing for this. I learned that those who won were those who acted with that aggressive expression. I emulated the ones who could sustain being in that 'eye of the storm' with awareness of the dangers; this gave me freedom. That freedom helped me develop a strong personality and a willingness to expose myself to unsafe environments.

My parents sent me to a religious and strict school and it was hard for me to fit in. I was the black sheep, easily spotted and targeted. I made no real effort to blend in. I had long hair and that triggered many of the people there. I questioned the content that was being taught and the dogma that was subliminally fed. This was a repellent to friends at school and an attractor to the bullies. My disruptive presence threatened them all. Everywhere I went, the bullies came to 'measure the alpha' and put everyone in their place. Most of the time, I had to use my wit and intelligence to disengage, and this included bluffing.

I could give the appearance of strength and security in civilized places, but there were real dangers where I lived, and at times, I had to move alone. The freedom to do the things I wanted required passing through to the other side of those dangers. That's why I decided to learn how to fight.

I went to kickboxing training for two years and it changed me. Suddenly, I had extreme confidence — the confidence I lacked when those two kids tried to mob me. My way of moving and the way I wielded myself — my presence — changed. Now I was not only defiant, I emanated respect. And when I didn't, I made sure they reconsidered.

When I was 15, I moved to another city and entered a new high school. The first week of school was my birthday and I invited everyone to my party. They loved me for my charm and my organizing skills. Many of the 'weirdos' who were bullied came under 'my wing.' I became dominant as their ally and guardian. My birthday event was emblematic for the hierarchy of the school; all classes came and this became a ground for factions to resolve conflicts. The two biggest bullies of the school started a fight in my living room. They broke a window. I separated them and expelled them from my house.

I was in a position of making them accountable. Nobody believed they would pay. They said: "You won't get money from them." On Monday, I met each of them and demanded they pay for the window. They looked me up and down, and as I came from a place of sense, they agreed. It was a milestone for my class. They saw me as a peaceful hero. I knew this was possible because of the confidence of knowing how to fight (if I had to), my intellect, and the innate sense of presence I now embodied.

I kept training my fighting skills. The dojo where I trained was very aggressive. To get the first belt, we had to have black eyes and broken ribs. Once, in one training round, I got a fissure in my ribs. I cannot describe the sensation of wanting to puke the pain out while feeling asphyxiated… I thought I was dying.

With time, I felt weak in the dojo, but strong in school. I started mocking and teasing my friends… and accidentally made their lips bleed sometimes. I realized I had become the bully… I had crossed the line and I was abusing my power. My boosted ego wanted me to prove myself, but attacking friends to prove hierarchy made me see I was hurting them and myself emotionally, also. I felt ashamed and stupid.

And then… I fell in love with a girl. This made me use all my energy for making music and love. My confidence and my capacity of protection remained with me, as well as my capacity of influencing, dealing, and ruling wherever I went. Later in life, I understood that this was a sublimation of my energy and power, the maturation of archetypes in myself necessary for my integrity.

When I entered college, I tried to hold on to the way I related to my friends and girlfriend, but maturation set us on different paths. I wanted to keep the same system and ways of being, but this led to a period of decadence and numbness. Being the cool guy, the alpha guy, was not as rewarding as before. The world was bigger, many were playing that game, and no one really cared, so I stopped caring. I no longer knew where I fit or where I belonged anymore. This led to misery.

Addictions emerged in me; mainly to the things that I was stuck in: Parties, games and substances that numbed my feelings. This was followed by lack of motivation and willpower. Loneliness, obesity, arthritis, depression… My life became unbearable. I couldn't even sleep from the discomfort of being in my body. My downfall kept going.

I started looking for extremes again. I had many near-death experiences in this quest for feeling alive. I didn't seem to react, to awaken. I was numbed to life. I stopped caring if I was putting myself — and sometimes others — in danger. Life was hell. Nothing mattered.

My pain and heartbreak were well-hidden on the exterior while internally I was at war. I was in torment for my very being, for my willpower, and for feeling alive again. While in this swamp of existence, at a hip-hop party, I saw a dancer. It was like a rapture that captured me. It disrupted everything I knew. It got me out of myself. There was something there that was *so important* that all the rest of the things in my life faded away. I knew that if I followed that light, there was a way out of the swamp. It was an inner certainty that there was something real in this magic that I had just witnessed, and I had to figure it out. Dancing showed me a light that I was compelled to follow.

I connected with the dancing world and with more sensitive people who knew how to channel emotions through healthy movement. All of a sudden, I had to leave behind my old system in order to do the training, performances, and competitions with my dancing team. I had both motive and purpose. I could enjoy music and my body. I could express myself in a new language and connect deeper with others. I fell in love again.

While I was expanding myself and my gifts began to shine, my ego also expanded and took over. I set up big events, traveled, and gained lots of experience. I became the Ambassador of World of Dance in South America; no one ever had a title like that over a continent. I felt greatness. I felt powerful. And again, I got used to it. To make it happen, I put all my life savings into it. I borrowed money from others. I was under so much stress to keep up, while trying to still be *me,* that I stretched too thin. I felt like a fireman constantly putting out a sequence of never-ending fires. It grew so big that it became an untamable monster. It consumed me; took over my life, finances, health, and relationships. The cost of being there was so high. I collapsed.

Spirituality and Self-help became my raft. I had many spiritual awakenings during this time that guided and helped discover my true *Being.* Then I received an Akashic Records Reading. What it showed was assertive and liberating. I just had to move on — something that was very hard for my inflated ego, as I was clinging to the past and what I had achieved.

As my spiritual connection developed, the paths in my life became clearer. I arrived at a high level of enlightenment and freedom of being. I had strong revelations about the Multiverse and all the beings at play. A whole new level, a whole new perspective on the game of life opened up. But the problems didn't end. They became more complex and subtle. Now I entered a territory where there was always someone more intelligent or powerful than me... The rules of the game were very different. I had to learn them, so I met with great masters, teachers, and shamans to comprehend them better.

Having contact with advanced intelligences that are behind the curtains of normal perception has disrupted my reality many times. On several occasions, I have had to face Demons and Evil forces that were hidden in myself and others. Like when I was in a cave under a tree, having a shamanic lesson on the root and destination of our power, the devil showed up in my visions. I recognized the devil, and in facing him, I was not scared. A messianic figure representing good appeared alongside. They both told me: Power is neutral. The way you use it is the direction you will give it. Ever since that moment, I grew in power and comprehension of the Universal forces.

The most humbling lesson my ego had in this new realm was during my Akashic Records Initiation. This was a reconnective journey, an activation of my channel, and a soul retrieval where I was shown the recurring patterns in my life. During the initiation, we journey deeply through intimate parts of ourselves. When I was in front of the main guardians of the Records, my 'All-mighty' personality showed up in arrogance and I was willing to destroy the guardian that was in my way. In the very instant that I 'destroyed' it, everything froze. I was taught that these *beings* are immortal and cannot be defeated. They were testing me and the ways I behaved.

I was humbled by this lesson: It's not about how powerful I am. It's about how I behave — how I use my power wisely and respectfully for what is sacred. It's a lesson that I will never forget.

Life, with the challenges and opportunities it brings, keeps teaching me every day. These gifts, this power, and the spiritual connections that have been given to me are to be used with ethics and honor. This comprehension and the integration of the wisdom of hundreds of Akashic Records openings elevated me to the point that I could receive the Mastery title and co-create a strong lineage of Akashic Consultants. I'm blessed for meeting and reconnecting with this soul family. We are constantly growing and improving our soul connection while in service for the healing, remembrance, and harmony of the world and the multiverse.

Today, I'm fulfilled. I can always handle the challenges before me. I've learned that all problems are an opportunity to find ourselves. This is the main goal of the Oracle archetype within: To Know Ourselves.

Having the Akashic Guidance, the Initiatic teachings, and the honorability codes has been an Amulet to overcome every obstacle while not getting stuck. It is the way to sustain the fulfilled states of being. We all have a Path, we will get lost and overwhelmed many times. What we can do is face — in a different way — the problem, the challenge, the hell-like scenario we may find ourselves in. Remembering our Spiritual Warrior within, we will be able to gracefully traverse any challenge, and in that test, we will find a great treasure: Ourselves.

IGNITE ACTION STEPS

- Identify where you are in life. You are on a Path, you are on a Way somewhere.

- Is your conscious, Heroic, Highest self leading you?

- This Path will have Quests and you will be faced with monsters, big trials, or, as we call it in the initiatic teachings: Sphinxes. Learn to identify them. If you can't approach your problems from an overview, look from a higher perspective. Take a look at the references I've shared in the resources section of this book.

- Once you know where You are in your Path and what the Sphinxes and patterns are that usually trap you, you can Initiate your Heroic Path (or reengage with more awareness). For this, the definition of your Treasure, the Result you want to reach or gain in life, will create a Quest.

- It's always useful to have Allies and the Oracle that brings Amulets. A trustworthy Oracle can provide higher perspective, reference, and Amulets for the Way. This story may be one of those Amulets you are receiving; to go deeper check the references at the end of this book. There you can connect with an Oracle, preferably with an Akashic Record Consultant with the honorability codes.

- Remember that your Quest to Your Treasure has already started. The attitude and awareness of each step will make the difference to your Arrival. All the initiatic paths will lead you to the Greatest Treasure. Have you Discovered it yet?

Santiago Rafael Pascual – Argentina
Master in Akashic Records,
Life Artist Formation Associated in Manifestation Director
www.LAFAM.org

Michael Tyler

"Truth Revealed is Truth Instilled."

May your perception become more clear. May your truth be revealed. Take the brave journey of self discovery for, in it, you will find the Warrior of Truth. In Truth there is the freedom to become the warrior you were always meant to be. Journey with me in the next few pages, and you may discover the answers for yourself. When the limits are stripped away, the truth is all that remains. What is revealed to you was always there.

Battle for Veritas

I awoke one winter morning feeling a dull ache in my chest. It had been my only companion for the last 3 months. I was roughly disappointed that I was still alive. There were these gnawing questions in the back of my mind: Is this all there is? And if it is, why? Do I really need to be here? Is freedom really attainable? What is the truth of our reality? And overarching all of it, I couldn't escape one single question: If I don't have a destiny, what the fuck am I doing here? The questions were like a whisper that then progressed into a roar that I could not ignore. The pain grew until I was fed up and got out of bed. I was angry; could barely think straight. This war, this battle within me, had been going on for three whole months and I needed answers.

I had reached the point where I was either going to continue on the path I was on and lose myself, or face the truth and start down the road of self discovery... the place where I would let go of who I once was and allow for expansion of my soul, proving what I had always known to be true about myself, my world, and begin to act in accordance with it. I had no awareness of this at the time; I was just fucking over it.

Many times when truth is revealed to us, it comes at a price, but that price is what instills it within us. It tattoos it onto our souls. This was my dark night of the soul. The moment when I couldn't tell myself one more lie as to who I was, what I believed, or that I was ok. And...I was definitely not 'ok.'

From the outside looking in, everything was good. I had a career I loved as a firefighter and paramedic, a new truck in the driveway, and a condo by the bay that I enjoyed with my 2 beautiful children. By all appearances, I had a good life. Yet my life felt empty. Like nothing I ever did was unique, important, or good enough. I distracted myself with my career, my kids, and going out with friends. Nothing helped.

For several weeks I had asked out loud to God and to myself, "Why am I here? What is my reason to keep breathing?" There was silence on the line. The pain in my chest was unbearable. I sat on the end of my bed, looked up and begged God to send me a sign. I told him I knew I wasn't supposed to test him, but I had reached the end. I thought, "There has to be a better way." So I came up with a plan to leave it in God's hands. It was apparent I had lost faith in myself.

I set the timer for 5 minutes. I told God, "If you're listening, I need a sign for the reason I am here. Give me a reason to keep breathing." I honestly didn't know if I would. I looked at myself in the mirror with disgust. I had hit bottom. I hated myself and felt unworthy of my life. Of course none of this was true, but my perception was clouded and I couldn't see my way ahead.

Then a miracle happened. The phone rang. It was my 10-year-old son calling me with exactly 2:22 left on the timer. Startled, I smiled and looked up toward the sky. I picked up the phone and heard his young voice on the other end, "Hey Dad, are you coming to pick us up today from school?" I choked back the urge to cry and told him yes. I was happy, sad, and relieved. I told him we would all go to dinner that evening and that I loved him very much. I dropped the phone and slid off the end of the bed onto my knees. I began sobbing with agony, my stomach convulsing as if I were going to vomit, unable to hold in one more painful emotion.

It was the beginning of 'the shift.' I realized that I was worthy of my life. I focused on my children that day; after all, they were my God-given purpose. If for nothing else, they were enough.

The next morning, I headed to work and I received another sign from the

Universe, this time from a loyal fire-fighting brother at the station. That fateful day when he walked up to me, I realized that I had, somehow, in all my doing, fighting, loving, and sacrificing constantly, forgotten who I was. I no longer knew what I believed in. Add to the fact that I was not enjoying my life; more importantly I did not know my true self-worth. I felt that my true self was out there, (the truth about my environment, myself, my place in the Universe... everything), but I had no idea how I was going to find it.

My fire brother walked up to me and said quite simply, "Hey bud, noticed you have been down lately and wanted to give you this book. Now keep an open mind; it's pretty deep stuff." The title read *The Secret*. I smirked at him and took the book, skeptical, but at the same time, I couldn't deny the timing. Just the day before I had asked God for answers and now here was a friend handing me this book. His intuition had led him to reach out to me, something I never would have expected. A blessing indeed.

To my delight the book was a page turner. Answer after answer flowed to me. I looked up from the book with a new perspective of the world. I had been looking at my life all wrong. *The Secret* had confirmed what I had always felt to be true. It was like I was seeing the world before me for the very first time. The 'code' that I grew up with came back to me. "A man is what he believes."

I was the first born son to loving parents. My parents divorced by the time I was 5 and shortly after, my mother remarried. Soon after I graduated high school, I started working in construction. And then 9/11 happened. I eagerly joined the US NAVY's Submarine Service, ready to prove my worth and see what I was made of. The 'code' had been reinforced my whole life and activated me to take action; it had been there all along. *A man is what he believes and fights for what he believes in.*

Having stepped away from my childhood and my parents' religious beliefs, I had no idea who I was at that point, but I figured a war would be the environment to close the gap, so to speak. I moved up the ranks quickly and served honorably. I became a father, a husband, and left the Navy at the end of my enlistment and became a firefighter and eventually a paramedic as well.

Many truths we hold dear in our world depend largely on our own point of view. I had my belief system put through a 'god gauntlet' and out the other side came a new perspective. My mind's eye had been opened. There was no going back through the gauntlet so I could be in the darkness of self-doubt and personal pain. My warrior had been awakened once more and the war had begun for the rights to my soul. I was excited.

It is said the most important thing a warrior can take into battle is a reason *why*. First why: fatherhood. I was a father to a 7-year-old daughter and 10-year-old son, but I needed to Love myself so I had something to offer my children other than sacrificial love. You can't give away what you don't have. As I loved myself, so I would love my children: my second why.

It is also said you need to know 'thy enemy.' In this case, the enemy was my ego, the falsehoods of my environment and upbringing, and my old belief system.

I needed to educate myself on a *new* perspective. I added a gratitude list to my morning routine and started becoming more aware of how I talked to myself. I started correcting my negative self talk with 'I am' affirmations along with many other techniques. I began a custom exercise routine and began small 10-minute guided meditations. I resumed reading the Bible again along with everything from Doctor Wayne Dyer. I discovered the Bhagavad Gita, the book, *The Way of the Peaceful Warrior,* and *The Wisdom of Florence Scovel Shinn.* I ingested as much information as possible.

When you show the Universe that you're listening and exercise faith in yourself, the Universe returns it with truth. What you put out comes back.

Truth: You are never alone.

Tim and Allyson were a couple I had been long time friends with. I opened my home to them for 2 months while they transitioned down to Florida. Having their company in my home was truly a blessing. Unbeknownst to him, Tim was a great coach over those two months. He was always encouraging, educating me on finances, took me to his networking events, shared his insight and formula for success. Tim and Allyson were yet another sign from the Universe that I was definitely not alone in my battles.

Truth: Generosity is a great way to raise your vibration and bring in abundance. When you battle *against the darkness*, generosity is a powerful act.

I listened to podcasts and read books. Living my life with my rapidly changing mind set, I was meeting resistance. Why? The answer: my perception of Love was narrow. I believed that all love was sacrifice which is what I had been raised to believe. It was the only love I knew and it was KILLING ME. If all you do is give and never receive, then love equals sacrifice and that isn't love. The root of my pain was not fear; it was love distorted.

Truth: To feel your existence is the very definition of being alive. To feel divine love through your soul is to unequivocally know thy SELF.

I learned the true meaning of love through meditation, discipline, education, affirmations, and the arts. I was loving my life and began to feel ownership over it.

You can know a truth but unless you experience what it feels like, it is not instilled as a belief. Once I believed I was worthy of love and that I *am* love, I began attracting different people into my life. Serendipitous moments began happening all around me. I began finding answers to questions that I didn't even know to ask. Through this education of self, along with my awareness of my environment ever increasing, I realized the emotion behind my thoughts, words, and deeds was the power to my freedom.

Truth: Love and the fear of love being taken away is the power behind everything in our existence.

We bring the fear into our lives by thinking that love is in limited supply. *God is Love.* The very essence of what we create in our Universe is what we put love toward; or you don't.

I Corinthians 13:4-8 tells us, "love is patient, love is kind..." It does not dishonor others, it is not self-seeking, it is not easily angered, it keeps no record of wrongs. Love does not delight in evil but rejoices with the truth. It always protects, always trusts, always hopes, and always perseveres.

I became Love and became the Warrior of Truth.

Little by little, with the help of friends, I was learning to maintain my code. I was learning that resistance from people in my life as I shifted was to be expected. I had to resist being surprised by it and hold fast to my truths. To maintain my path. I was in a battle and with any battle there are casualties. I had to arm myself with the confidence that I was the expert on *me*.

When seeking the truth to any subject, I went through a process I called, "why ask why." I kept asking myself *why, why, why.* I applied this technique to my inner battle when it came to my thoughts, words, emotions, deeds.

So why seek truth? Why go through the process of removing limits we have spent our lives believing in? Why question ourselves, our reality, our beliefs? These are the questions on the journey to uncovering the *authentic self.*

The discovery of truth in all ways and forms brings about freedom, love, and fulfillment in life. It determines the foundation of the warrior belief system, our code, our rationale, our conscience. When you know what you are willing to live, to fight, and to die for your code will determine what kind of warrior you will be. Don't spend your life following someone else's beliefs, code, or truths.

Question your truths, your beliefs about why you feel, think, act, or believe anything. Be honest with yourself. If you don't like the answer that comes up, seek to educate yourself about what is universally true.

Resistance activates your warrior soul. Arm your inner warrior with love, discipline, and most of all, belief. Believe that no matter what the environment is giving you, you will prevail.

Continue to improve your code and feed your warrior soul adventure, love, and unvarnished awareness. Look through the lens of curiosity. Win the battle by asking why. Take responsibility for everything in your life. Exercise gratitude. Share new discoveries with those who are like-minded. Give into love more than fear to make the choices in the way that *you* think, *you* feel, and *you* act.

The answers to who you are and the truth about our Universe is within. Let your soul have a place to roar! Allow your warrior to be unleashed.

IGNITE ACTION STEPS

"There's a peace only to be found on the other side of war. If that war should come I will fight it!"
— Sir Sean Connery as King Arthur.

"Rather than love, than money, than fame, give me truth."
— H.D. Thoreau

"Truth is the beginning of every good thing, both in heaven and on earth; and he who would be blessed and happy should be from the first a partaker of truth, for then he can be trusted."
— Plato

The one practice I arm myself with is meditation. It has been the single most valuable asset to me in seeking truth, freeing myself of limits, building inner strength, being ever present, and envisioning my future.

Start with guided meditation and eventually create your own custom practice. Follow the steps below to get your inner process going.

Choose your meditation place free from fear; *peaceful*. I recommend instrumental music or playing frequencies that allow you to clear your mind.

Get into a comfortable position. If lying down, I recommend you place your hands over your abdomen area to ensure the highest connection possible.

Breathe deep and focus on nothing else but your breathing in and out. When you breathe out, let out the primordial sound *"OhM."* It will deepen your body connection with your soul self. Breathing is the essence of our physical connection to our environment. So breathe.

Once the mind is still, you are in your power. You can ask yourself a question about anything and receive an answer. Voice your gratitude for your life. Forgive someone or yourself. Or simply BE. There are no limits.

Finally allow yourself to be free. Truth needs to be freed in order to thrive. Therefore truth will always set you free.

Continue to sharpen the sword of meditation. Devise your own custom way of meditation on your journey of faith, trust, and loving thy self: the way of a true warrior.

The truth you seek will find you. It will be instilled in your heart, mind, and soul. The warrior within will be awakened with the spirit of freedom, truth, love, and firm foundation of self. Prove your newly discovered truths by living them fearlessly. Faith is the process, wisdom is doing, and knowing is accomplished by setting into action that which you feel in your heart to be true. When you meet resistance, be the rock of truth in a river of fear. Strengthen your heart with love. Ground yourself in truth. And you will know what is to be ALIVE, to be free.

Michael Tyler – United States of America
Firefighter / Paramedic / A.R.E. Certified Meditation Guide

WARRIOR

BRIAN SCHRIEBER

"The accomplishment of your dreams lies in the conviction of your decision."

My story was written to inspire you to walk away with the confidence to pursue a goal that you never thought possible and capture the dream of a lifetime.

SPRINTING TO AN IRONMAN

One day, a friend gave me a free entry to a triathlon. I was at work, focused on the ordinary day-to-day tasks on my to-do list, when my phone rang and it was him saying, "Hey, I have this free entry to the triathlon. Do you want it?" I was taken aback. I had run mud runs, 5K, and 10K races before, and I always did like adventuring, but a triathlon? The idea of it sounded like a new adventure that was more than a little intimidating. I knew I could swim, bike, and run, but I had never considered tackling all three in a single event and there was something about the idea that caught my imagination. It was totally in line with the types of adventures I liked doing. And it was free. I hesitated only half a second before telling him "Yes," I was happy to try it.

I did not have much of a background in running, besides running track in high school for a couple years, and to me, high school track was more of a social event since I was usually one of the slowest on the team — likely because everyone else practiced more intensely and much longer than I did.

The race was only a few months away, but it didn't occur to me to train for it beyond what I usually did for fitness. When race day arrived, I was a bundle of nerves. There were far fewer competitors than I was used to in the 5K and 10K events I usually did. Right off the start, I realized that while I *could* swim, I was not an experienced swimmer. The same applied to biking and running. I had done it, but I was far from an expert. I completed the two legs of the race, and thought it was fun but tiring. Nearing the end of the third leg, after swimming 600 meters, biking 12 miles, and while running the final 5K, I felt like I was dragging a bowling ball behind me that grew heavier with every step. I just wanted to stop and walk it off.

After running a second triathlon a year later, I learned there were various distance levels of triathlons to compete in. At the end of my sprint triathlon races, I was exhausted. I distinctly remember being in my bedroom contemplating the distances involved in an Ironman™; a 2.4 mile swim then riding 112 miles on a bike and after THAT you run a MARATHON??? Forget that, no way, that was never going to happen. I was fairly convinced that that goal would never eventuate.

I kept running in shorter races, sharing the starting line with people who were huge in racing and were competing on the world stage. It was fun and exhilarating, and I saw some progress in my race times, but I was becoming bored with sprint triathlons. I needed a bigger challenge. I signed up for an olympic distance of a one-mile swim, 24.8 mile bike, and 10K run: the Wildflower Triathlon in southern California. In this event, I had to learn a hard lesson.

For my previous races, diet and how to eat right were not as important. I did very little training and gave even less thought to what I ate. But during the Wildflower Triathlon, while on the bike, I developed a cramp under my ribs on my left side. I thought it was something you power though. As the bike portion came closer to the end, the pain got worse. By the time I reached the second transition, the pain became excruciating and it was very difficult for me to run. With the crowd cheering me on, I tried to keep going without making the pain look obvious. I ran with a slight limp which became worse with each step. After I rounded the first corner, out of sight of the crowd, I started to walk, relieved that I could hide my embarrassment of having to slow down. I tried to continue for a portion but could not make it. I knew I could run through the pain as long as I had a goal to get to. Then I would stop to walk again for a short distance.

About half a mile into the run was a box of energy gel packs for racers to take. I grabbed two packs and kept walking. My running pace had slowed to a measly 13-minute mile. I sucked down one gel pack and the excruciating pain that I had beneath my ribs immediately went away! I MEAN GONE! I couldn't believe the pain vanished so fast. I drank some water to wash down the gel and started running at a 6:26 (six minute twenty-six second mile) pace. I could not believe the speed I saw on my watch. I kept that pace for the remainder of the race. I finished Wildflower and knew: I was adding gel packs to my training.

With every race that followed, I learned new techniques and I was able to increase distance in all three areas — realizing I *can* do this. I knew I would need to ramp up my training. I decided to train for a half Ironman and go on a two-year training regimen to complete the full Ironman. I found some training schedules for Olympic, half, and full Ironmans. At first, I used an Olympic schedule that I found online. That schedule worked well, but the half Ironman workout calendar I used next was awful. I knew I had to train harder for the full, so I took the hardest Ironman schedule I could find and increased all the training day distances by 125 percent. It was a really bold move, but it felt right. Making up my own outline and dissecting my performance after each race to incorporate my lessons learned became exciting. I saw it was possible and I knew that I would complete the full ironman because I made my own schedule. After a few short weeks, I was obsessed with this new goal.

I knew there was no going back. It was not hope or even belief; I knew without a doubt that I would make it across that finish line. There was nothing anyone could say to deter me. Not even the doctors telling me how unhealthy it was to put my body under such heightened distress could stop me. Nothing. I had built up so much momentum toward this vision that it was impossible for me to lose. Or so I thought.

After completing my next half Ironman race on a 96-degree Fahrenheit day, I was feeling accomplished. I was proud of how far I had come and that I was not giving up. That is, until I had to run more miles. On some days in my training, I had to run 15 miles. Once I passed 12 miles or so, my knee braces that I wore were not cutting out the knee pain I had. I surmounted blisters on my feet by applying petroleum jelly on them and kept running. I relieved the cramping by buying a foam roller to massage my legs, but this knee pain just was not going away. I knew I couldn't complete the marathon portion with so many miles of excruciating pain. I was not ready to throw in the towel. There had to be something that could help me get through it. I was losing momentum fast. I felt desperate and driven to find a solution.

I heard about the benefits of alkaline water and bought an alkaline machine to make my own H2O. I saw a dramatic difference in my training. Not only did my knee pain completely go away, but I ended up running at a faster pace, for a longer distance, on the same path, at the same temperature. I could now toss my knee brace since I didn't need it any longer. It was a relief to find this one solution that made such a big difference.

After an intense workout, doing 50 percent more than I normally do on my bike, I collapsed on the living room floor, shaking. It was terrifying to my fiancée who dashed to grab the phone, frantically about to dial 911 as I told her, "I'm fine," unable to stand or stop shaking. After some convincing, she relented and helped me to the Epsom salt bath she had drawn for me.

'Bonking' refers to the slow train wreck that comes from overexercising. Bonking is where a person exerts themself to a point that they basically collapse. The legs turn to jelly, you feel very weak, you have uncontrolled cramping and dizziness, and begin shaking. The glycogen reserves in your body are depleted and you have low blood glucose. The good part about this is the body knows this might happen again and prepares for it by raising your level of performance. Bonking happened to me several more times along my journey, but this made me a better endurance athlete.

I was squeezing every free minute of the day that I could to train. I really had become obsessed with crossing that finish line. Fitting in time with friends, family, work, and my fiancée was no easy task, but it got done. I believe I became a better scheduler the more I had to arrange my day around training.

There was one week in my training that was harder than all the rest. That was my hell week. I knew I had to train harder and for a longer distance to compete in the full Ironman. I made one section of the schedule to really push myself. I knew it would be tough; the final leg of hell week was *really* going to hurt. The weekend started off on Saturday as I rode 130 miles, ate, showered, slept, and got up five hours later at 6 AM to run 26.2 miles and swim 5000 meters. The marathon I had scheduled for this day was the Malibu Marathon in California. The race started out great, but I started to burn out when I ran out of alkaline water in my hydration bag at mile 22. I struggled those last four miles, crossed the finish line, sat down under one of the tent canopies, and felt an uneasiness as the world around me started to spin. My adrenaline wore off and a fog settled over my brain. The feeling of discomfort was different than the other times I had 'bonked'.

I remember the paramedics asking me if I wanted to go to the hospital. I didn't think I needed to, but I had never felt that way before. I decided to go just to be safe. They put me on a stretcher and wheeled me off into the ambulance. I felt extremely embarrassed to be leaving on a stretcher with all the other athletes standing around, some of whom were my friends. In the ambulance, they gave me an IV and after a test or two at the hospital, they said I was free to go, telling me to take it easy. I felt as if I had let myself down by not completing my hardest weekend. I wanted to go jump in the pool to do the swim and complete my 5000 meters for the day, but I talked myself out of drowning.

The day of the full Ironman, I woke up before my alarm clock. As soon as I became conscious, my eyes snapped wide open and I felt the excitement in the pit of my stomach. My nerves were on edge, but I had this sense of aliveness that was not adrenaline but a genuine awareness of my body's ability. I got out of bed to go sit on the balcony of my hotel room, overlooking the shore of where I would be swimming in a few short hours. I quietly listened to the wind moving in the trees, and with this calm happiness, I *knew* I was ready. I knew my inner determination had gotten me there.

As the sun rose, I walked my bike to the swim-bike transition and set up my space. Part of the morning routine was to inflate my tires but one valve was not working! It was 45 minutes before the start of the race and the last bus was about to leave for the start line. The tire was 40 percent of what it should be, and the nerves started to swell in my stomach. Nothing I tried was working. After a few more tries, somehow the valve gave way and air went into the tire. Phew!

Arriving at the start line, I swam out to the marker buoys in the water and waited for the cannon. Looking at the shore, seeing the adoring friends and families of the athletes anticipating the excitement of the day, my adrenaline rose. I treaded water, surrounded by my fellow competitors, realizing then what it was that I was about to do. The countdown started. The athletes counted down along with it in strong, confident voices, shouting with such conviction. BOOM! An eruption of cheering followed the sound of the starting cannon. That moment was the most memorable part of the race. All the preparation, setbacks, training, bonking, blood, sweat, and tears to prepare for this day was over. My two-year journey came down to this one day. It was like Christmas morning and I got to open the gift I had been waiting so patiently for!

The swim was the most beautiful 2.4 miles of swimming I had ever swam in my life, but the bike had a few fun moments in store for me. I was around 30 miles in when I realized the handlebars had begun to drift. The bike was riding straight but somehow the handlebars twisted clockwise. I realized I had not tightened the handlebars. With each mile, it got worse and worse. Soon enough the handlebars were 30 degrees off. I stopped to fix it and luckily the aid station had the tool I needed. I reached the bike-run transition and jumped off my bike, handing it to the race team member to secure while I grabbed my other gear, put on my running belt with water and gel packs, and began the marathon portion. About 10 to 15 miles in I started to feel winded and overheated, but as luck would have it, it started to rain. Not just a little but a lot! I loved it!

I came down the finish line runway and was high-fiving all the spectators as I ran toward the colorful finish line arches. Two years of preparation had built up to this single day and I was elated. I finished the run with my infamous cartwheel, and just like that, I had completed my dream.

Three years prior to race day, if you told me I would have the title of an Ironman, I would not have believed you. I did not know a soul who had done anything that was so physically demanding. I had to conjure up an insurmountable amount of self-motivation to be able to finish it. I had surprised myself that I'd achieved what I had set out to do. It made me realize that if I pursue my lofty desires and follow them though to the end, I can do anything. Not giving up and staying on the path of the things that I truly had a passion for was my biggest 'AHA.'

Hearing about what I did had inspired other friends and family to complete an Ironman. I didn't know I had become such an inspiration to others. This was a pretty fulfilling feeling, hearing feedback about what others are changing in their lives and how they are pushing further than they normally would have. This makes my accomplishment feel even more rewarding.

A month after the race, my sister called me and said, "Do you realize how many people you've inspired?" She rattled off a list, "People are saying, 'If he can do it, I can do it!'" I smiled as I heard that. I can relate to saying that, too. I feel as if I'm now pulling others into my world of joy. Having this power of influence surprised me. It showed me that others had blocks they needed to get over like I did. They saw what I achieved and they were inspired by it. I didn't have anyone to mentor me or guide me; yet I had *become* that person for others.

During training, people came up to me and said they watched me during my workouts and were inspired by what I was doing. They wished they had the motivation themselves to go after their goals, yet didn't think that they could do it. Being around someone who does is infectious! Slowly and surely, people start to believe they can achieve their goals and the inspiration builds until, one day, they commit to action. We should all surround ourselves with people who inspire us to action. People who push us into greatness as they see past our blocks and open us to our life's potential.

Create your schedule, go after your goal, and cross your finish line.

Ignite Action Steps

If you want to complete a triathlon, get a clear picture of two things: Knowing you can do it and the training itself.

1. Set a goal that is exciting enough but not so hard that you will give up.
2. Find a schedule (or make one) that is harder than the distance you plan to do.
3. Fit the schedule into your week. Shift your day around so you will have a block of time to train every day.
4. Work out everyday!

Focus to such a level that even the smallest shred of doubt cannot creep in. You can form this level of focus by completing the fourth step mentioned above. Every day, you're looking at your goal. Every day, your attention is focused on the workout and you feel good just thinking about it. These two things make up the sweet spot of accomplishment. Allow yourself to become obsessed; it is the easiest way to stay on track. Even if triathlons are not your thing, I hope my story inspires you to set a goal and realize that you are holding all the keys to any door you want opened in life.

Brian Schrieber - United States of America
Endurance Athlete, Professional Engineer, Certified Lympologist
@ @energytitan

WARRIOR

DEAN GRAFOS

"The powerful warrior acts from peace, love, and gratitude in the most challenging situations."

My intention is to show those with a deep fire that it can be transmuted and used for transformation and creation; that it's a *choice*. I want to show those of you who are going through extremely tough challenges that there is hope, joy, growth, and creation on the other side.

THEY ARE OUR ANGELS...

I have always been a warrior. My very first memory was me picking up a ruler — at least that's what my Mom said it was — and throwing it at our plumber, breaking his front tooth. I can still remember the anger I felt in that moment, though what led to it and what came after are gone from my memory. Yes, that was the warrior inside me striking out for a reason I can't remember. Moments like that have happened my entire life — a life filled with reactivity, destroyed relationships, personal anger, and deep regret.

I had burned many bridges and regretted it, not able to figure out how to rebuild them. I had so many negative emotions inside of me. Anger, frustration, rage, hatred, disappointment. I felt isolated by it all, and those burning bridges further isolated me. My parents, the quintessential Greek parents whose son could do no wrong, bailed me out from the problems I was creating for myself. My family loved me unconditionally; the only people who did. I felt so alone, not good enough, and that, too, made me angry.

I learned to use my warrior to my advantage. When I wanted to change the energy of a situation to my favor, the warrior instincts were extremely effective. If I felt threatened or in danger, the warrior always turned on and found an exit. When I needed to manipulate any situation, the warrior was overly powerful. But the ultimate price was high — no joy, no confidence, no control. The warrior was allowed to roam my life untethered.

In my early 40s, married with a beautiful daughter, my life looked pretty perfect. From the outside looking in, I had a strong conscious business in a sweet community, a relationship that others looked at with inspiration, and an incredibly loving and joyous family. The list goes on and on, but at that point in my life, the picture I presented was not the truth. The warrior fiercely kept the actual truth inside, cloaked in secret, fearful of ruining the façade. While I was maintaining outward appearances, inside the house the warrior would rage for hours at a time, scaring my beloved wife Lisa and instilling fear in little 3-year-old Vivi. The warrior was only doing what he was trained to do — protecting his image by raging only in secrecy to get all the emotions out.

It was a very stressful time as we were involved in a litigation against us and our business. My inner warrior didn't know how to cope with the stress, fear, and betrayal in any other way. Stressful isn't even strong enough to describe how awful the situation was. It was pure despair and hopelessness, every awful emotion you can think of, and they were fighting with each other to become stronger.

And then, in an instant, my Inner Spirit spoke to me and something inside me changed. I overrode the warrior, listening instead to my soul, not knowing where it would take me. I only knew I was about to embark on a journey with an unknown outcome.

And... it was my choice.

It was an impulsive and unpredictable choice and went against my 43 years of conditioning. At that moment, I must've known I had come to the end of the line. I was failing. The warrior was scared. And I was dying inside and hurting those closest to me. I needed a different path; and when it was presented, something inside me said, "I'm coming."

This was not the first time I made a choice that would alter the course of my life. The other was at the start of my love story. Lisa and I had both attended the same law school, but we never knew each other. It wasn't until after we graduated and took the bar exam that we finally met. I was traveling through

Europe with a few guy friends to wait out that interminable stretch of time between writing the bar and getting my results, and she was doing the same with a few girlfriends. In a budget hotel room in the beautiful city of Santorini, Greece, our eyes met from across the room. I walked over and she handed me a plate of olives and a glass of wine. In that one look, I knew that she was the one.

After spending a heavenly month travelling through Europe with my new love, a crossroad appeared. Her girlfriends had already returned home and the group dynamic had shifted. She shared that she needed to get away from the group and head out on a new adventure. I went with her to the travel agent. She looked at the board and chose the cheapest flight.

Lisa told the travel agent, "One ticket to Leipzig."

Without thinking, I said, "Make it two," throwing down my close-to-maxed-out credit card onto the counter. This wild, out-of-character decision was made from a place of love, lust, joy, fun, and adventure.

We traveled *everywhere*. We flew to Leipzig and rented a Mercedes to drive to the Netherlands. We attended Octoberfest, then went to Amsterdam. Basically we went all over the place, enjoying the adventure and enjoying each other. And everywhere we went, Lisa talked about this book she was reading.

I made fun of it — this book by some guy named Neale Donald Walsch and his *Conversations with God*. But Lisa was so earnest and had such an optimistic and refreshing spiritual essence to her. She had such a fresh outlook. I literally had never met anyone like her before, so positive and thinking so deeply. And the lens with which she saw the world — I had never heard *life* spoken about in that way.

Four years later, she agreed to be my wife and we began building our family. Lisa was so deeply, spiritually connected to the Universe; and I was… not. My fear, worry and dysfunctional coping made me hit rock bottom in my life. Twelve years later, all the stress and worry from the litigation unleashed my warrior within. I was not connected to my spirit and that had me fighting all the time.

Lisa once more turned to the wisdom of Neale Donald Walsch. He was offering a fabulous and free 5-day seminar. My wife, in an act of her own desperation, signed up for the seminar. She was determined to go. She was leaning in to the one thing that brought her hope. I of course knew of her love of Neale from the moment we had met 18 years earlier, and she had made me read his book before we got married (which I naturally read and then quickly ignored), but this time, rather than ridicule it, rather than ignore it, I grasped at a glimmer of possibility.

This time, it was a feeling of hope; a feeling not in the warrior's consciousness. I said, as I had so many years before, "Make it two tickets. I'm coming."

Her eyes lit up and I could tell she was wondering if she heard me correctly. She was shocked, but being the more spiritual one in our relationship, she was hopeful of what might come of this journey. As for me, I felt desperate and more hopeful that this choice would lead me out of hell.

We were signed up and on our way. On a new spiritual path, one that she had traveled alone while waiting patiently for me to join her. This new path was the start of our greatest adventure into the unknown, one that was exciting, new, and *together*. Looking back now, I think of our wedding invitation, which asked, "Are you ready for our next adventure?" At the edge of the pit of despair, I knew I was now more than ready.

On the first day of the seminar, my inner warrior was triggered and emerged in a rage. "You are fucking naive, Neale," I shouted in offense. The warrior was once again in full force, ready to burn the room down.

Of course, this did not go over well with the Neale fanatics in the group, but I just couldn't swallow what I was being told. The five scoundrels who were involved in the lawsuit against us, lying, stealing and plotting ways to take everything I had worked so hard for, attempting to bankrupt my family, costing us 25K a month in legal fees to defend against this fraud… they were acting from LOVE?!

Sitting in that room, I felt even more isolated than before.

At this point in my life, I was completely disconnected from myself, my family, and my business. Our household was filled with screaming and yelling, causing fear that I can still see in my daughter and how it has shaped her confidence and her ability to trust. Every single aspect of my physical and emotional being was suffering. This could not possibly be the result of what Neale calls LOVE!

On day three of the seminar, the scoundrels back home did the unthinkable: they amended the lawsuit to include my wife's loving 75-year-old parents. They knew how close we were and knew this would be devastating to our whole family. I clearly remember the moment. We were having a picnic in the park in between sessions and I said "Honey, we need to leave."

Being more enlightened than me, she stated "I support you, but I'm staying." A complicated rush of feelings rose up in me when I heard her words. In that moment, I had a choice, again a significant one — either run home alone to deal with this new revelation, to fight the enemy threatening my family, or stay, hoping there was some level of peace at the end. She was determined to remain. The warrior in me wanted to stand up and fight.

Underlying that complicated mess of feelings was one that surprised me: I was relieved.

I chose to stay.

The warrior was subdued and I was instead driven by hope. This moment was crucial to my entire life. Not one I could see at the time but looking back... Wow! This was THE moment. Her hope, her light, her certainty that there was another path left an opening for me to follow. One path was going to lead to a life of constant anger, fear, and lonely unhappiness. The other — the enlightened path — would lead to self-reflection, joy, and an unconventional life filled with love, true friendship, inspiration, and limitless possibilities.

On the final day of the seminar, something extraordinary happened.

During the final lecture, it all clicked. Neale was at the front sitting in literally the ugliest chair I had ever seen. I was about half way back, sitting right in the middle of the crowd. By now, people had had tears and breakthroughs and all the things that come up. It had been an extremely emotional week for everyone. For me, it had been frustrating. As people talked about the trauma in their lives, I kept thinking, "Just shut up and deal with your stuff!" I was not the most sympathetic listener. Neale, seeing right through me, had nicknamed me 'angry bearded guy' during the sessions. But in that moment, something happened. An overwhelming sense of gratitude and peace overcame me. It all made sense! I got it! This was *for* me, not against me! The people suing us did that so that I could awaken spiritually. Thank you, thank you, thank you.

I stood up in the middle of the room that I had formerly set on fire with my anger and expressed my gratitude for every moment of the pain and struggle. Neale cried, tears rolling down his smiling cheeks. Everyone was happy for me. People were crying. They were cheering. It was a great moment in my life. I expressed that Neale was right. It was not personal, what the scoundrels back home were doing with this lawsuit. They were doing it out of love — love of money and love of power. And I was the direct recipient of the immense growth unfolding from that very moment. It was transformational.

From that moment on, Lisa and I agreed, "They are our Angels." They were the spark and the catalyst for my ultimate transformation. The situation they created set me forth on my spiritual journey.

Even though my family lost over a million dollars to that lawsuit, what we *received* was invaluable — a whole new life. Their love also gave me a wonderful new tribe of supportive friends. At that seminar, another attendee showed me a video for a group of conscious entrepreneurs at an event called A-fest. We went home and applied, and attended the very next event. Now six years later, that group of amazing souls makes up my closest friends, my innermost circle of love. This was all the result of the choice I made to step into the unknown and stand powerfully in the fire during the most challenging moment of my entire life. Just stepping onto that path has enhanced my friendships, my spirituality, my entire *being*. My outlook on everything is completely different. I see the world — the same world — from an entirely new perspective.

As I am finishing up this chapter, the whole planet is in a deeply challenging crisis. Once again, I am grateful for the training that has prepared me for this. Not financially or systematically prepared, *emotionally* prepared.

I've stood in the face of the crisis and transmuted the fire of the warrior. I'm not denying that the warrior hasn't won a few battles in the past few months. Of course not, that would be amazing, but it's not my reality *yet*. Every day, in every minute, I make my choice. Every day, in every minute, I am grateful to *have* the choice!

My entire company is shut down for an undetermined amount of time, leaving me no income, and I still have business obligations to meet and people relying on me. I have in-laws living with me and we are tasked with keeping them healthy; so yes, I've had some dark days. However, each time I let the fire energy rule, I step back and reflect, learn, and forgive myself. Even when I make the wrong choice, the not-so-spiritual choice, I atone for it in myself, in my apologies, in my forgiveness. Yes forgiveness. I am a spiritual being living a human existence. I am not perfect. But it is always my choice to make, and more and more I choose to keep my power. I choose to stand in the fire with a calm, loving spirit. And in this particular crisis, I am choosing to *create*. Out of a deep sense of gratitude, I am creating; not for money, nor to take advantage of this crisis, but to inject positivity, love, and transformation.

This is the power of transmuting the warrior fire into gratitude, benevolence, joy, and manifestation. In the midst of turmoil, acting from peace, from love, and supporting others during the most challenging times can see you through into the next chapter of your life. You can transmute the fire within you so it becomes a source of honoring your own warrior within.

Ignite Action Steps

I'd like to share a meditation I use to harness the warrior energy for creation. It all starts with the breath. Take at least 10 long, slow, deep breaths in through the nose, filling your entire belly and chest, and releasing the air through the mouth. After you finish your deep breaths, settle into a gentle breath. Make sure to stay present and not let the mind wander. As you are breathing, start by tapping into the energy of gratitude. Think of three things you are grateful for. Then tap into the energy of love. Again, visualize three things that bring you the sense of love. Lastly, tap into the energy of joy. Visualize three things that bring you joy. Now you are in the space of presence necessary for creation. We create from a place of gratitude, love, and joy; not from the fire. Put your focus on the core, for this is where the warrior energy resides. Ask the questions, "What is my passion?" "What lights my soul on fire?" "What wants to come through, activated by the fire of the warrior energy?" Listen for the message. When the message comes through, journal it instantly and immediately take one step forward. This is how you access your Inner Spirit's warrior energy for creation. Do it from your fire, your passion, your soul, after you are in the state of presence.

Dean Grafos – Costa Rica & Netherlands
Co-Creator Core40 San Francisco/Amsterdam,
Co-Creator CycleVIBE, Co-Creator Transformational Fitness
core40.com

Alexia Gillespie

"One small change can create a powerful ripple effect."

In sharing this part of my journey, I hope you will be inspired to make one small change in your life, trusting that it will generate momentum and create a powerful ripple effect. You are not alone. We are enveloped in and guided by a divine love that is far greater than what we see with our eyes. By taking one step at a time, following your joy, and trusting your intuition, you will keep moving forward.

Returning Home to Myself

It was a warm summer day. The long grass was tickling my 4-year-old legs. I was lying beside my dad in the back field of our farm, attentively listening to him do his best to answer my question about how babies were made. The sense of ease and wonder that I felt in that moment was a close companion throughout my early childhood. I knew I was dearly loved, not for anything I did or didn't do, just simply for being me. If only every child grew up with the abundance of love and greatness that I'd had poured into me by the many adults in my life. I grew up with deep roots in a multigenerational faith community and a sisterhood of intelligent, adventurous, and ambitious girlfriends.

As a free-range kid, I developed a love for the outdoors early in life. Climbing trees, building forts, and riding around on my bike were common components of a worthwhile adventure. Summer nights were often spent cocooned in my sleeping bag and nestled among friends as we drifted off to sleep under the vast expanse of a starry sky. Being in nature made me feel alive, and it filled me with awe and a sense of freedom. Nature has always felt like sacred space, the place where my connection to myself, to humanity, and to God is most palpable.

Finishing high school at the age of 17, I confidently left home, excited to go to university and venture out on my own. Things had come easily to me and life was unfolding precisely as planned. My goals were simple and my vision was clear. I wanted to live a life of contribution and have a positive impact on the lives of children. By the time I was 21, I had graduated with a teaching degree in elementary education. I was happily married and my husband and I were part of a vibrant and active community. For two years, we shared a house with four friends. As one moved out, another moved in. It was a hub of activity and connection, and we thrived with shared meals, live music nights, Saturday hikes, and weekend getaways.

Eventually ready for our next adventure, my husband and I decided to move to Prague, the capital of the Czech Republic, to teach for a year. The charm of living in a fairy-tale city and the novelty of living abroad wore off as I slowly settled into the routine of a heavy teaching load. Isolated without a close community and with the added challenge of a significant language barrier, day-to-day life began to feel lonely and monotonous. Weekend adventures and traveling during school breaks were not enough to fuel my soul for another school year and I yearned for home. However, as often happens after university, our community had gradually dispersed, so we decided to relocate to Vancouver, Canada.

Funds were tight and although teaching English to adults wasn't my dream job, it would create some stability while I figured out my next step. Being a leader was part of my identity. Whether it was in the classroom, on a sports team, or among friends, my natural inclination had always been to lead. I was flattered when the director of the school where I was teaching asked if I would consider taking the interim position of Academic Director. I saw this as an opportunity to try something new and move in the direction of leadership. The learning curve was steep, but I was excited by the challenge.

When my boss called me in for an early morning meeting a few months later, I hadn't thought much of it. However, the moment I entered the small conference room, the tight-lipped smiles and lack of warmth I saw triggered panic. Without pretense, they told me I was being 'let go.' The sudden pressure on my chest made it difficult to breathe. The knot in my stomach intensified as I failed to hold back the tears. I felt like a bird frantically trying to escape its cage.

My departure was effective immediately and I was directed to leave the premises without collecting my belongings or speaking to my teaching colleagues. My mind raced: "Who gets fired? Who treats people like this? What had I done wrong? What will people think of me? What will I tell them?" The humiliating walk home that morning, with tears streaming down my face, felt like the longest three blocks of my life.

With no experience to draw on, I didn't know who to call or what to do. The thought of telling anyone what had just unfolded made me want to shrink and disappear. At the age of 23, openness and vulnerability were not in my tool box. Speaking about rejection, personal struggles, or setbacks and how to move through these things hadn't been modeled for me as a child. I lacked the humility to ask for help or allow others to see me floundering. The belief that I was capable of figuring things out on my own hadn't matured to integrate the understanding that interdependence, not to be confused with codependence, would support a much richer life than my fierce independence.

Blame and shame consumed me like a roaring fire and the ashes settled deep within my soul, creating a rich environment for new narratives to grow. I started avoiding friends and connecting less often with family. In moments of stillness, restlessness overwhelmed me. Everything and everyone close to me made me feel trapped and vulnerable. I wanted to escape my shame, the city, my marriage, my family, and my friends. Looking for a socially acceptable way out, I accepted a teaching job in Mexico for six months. I convinced my husband that we needed an adventure, but in all honesty, it was a perfect opportunity to further distance myself.

When we returned home, I found a new teaching position. I stopped taking risks or trying new things, hoping to avoid criticism and failure. My new narratives played on repeat. "I'm not cut out for leadership. My dreams were unattainable and naive and I wasn't capable of making them happen anyway." The stories I was telling myself went unchecked and unchallenged. One brick at a time, I built a wall to protect myself from ever having to experience those feelings of shame again. With each brick, I buried my dreams a little deeper. I guarded my heart and learned to wear the right mask for each occasion. I found a new way to exist and in this way, six years passed.

In the short-term, affirming student evaluations and performance reviews sustained me, but eventually my stagnant existence began to feel mundane. I wrestled with the idea of a career change but I was at a loss as to what direction to go in. I prayed for an epiphany. I wondered if having a child would give me the deeper sense of purpose that I longed for. In floating this idea past my husband, it was clear that the timing didn't feel right for him. I questioned if we would ever feel ready for a child and what our life might look like if we decided not to have children.

When my dad invited me to accompany him on a work trip to Nicaragua, I jumped at the opportunity for yet another adventure. The staff at the hospital where he worked had established a relationship with two grassroots organizations that focused on increasing access to primary health care. We arrived in Managua with two big bags of medical supplies and very little appreciation for how difficult it was for community health-care workers to acquire such basic supplies. Our gracious hosts invited us to accompany them as they went about their day-to-day work. We witnessed children of all ages digging through smoldering garbage at the city dump in hopes of finding something worth salvaging. We accompanied a doctor to a remote village, where he assessed a little boy who had severe burns from falling backwards onto an open cooking fire. His family had no access to local medical care nor basic supplies to treat the burns. I was moved by the compassionate care and education offered by the health-care providers. My epiphany had arrived. Upon returning home, I started taking the prerequisite courses for my journey toward becoming a nurse.

Two years later, I waited alone in my doctor's office watching the second hand on the clock tick, tick, tick. Those few minutes felt like an eternity. As she entered the room, I knew what was coming before her words even landed. "You're pregnant." Our eyes locked as she watched me take in the news. "What?! How did that happen?" I flashed back to that day in the field at the age of 4. "No, wait, don't answer that. I know how it happened. I just thought we had been careful enough to prevent it." As much as I'd hoped that one day we would feel ready to welcome a child into our lives, my nursing school program was scheduled to start the same week as this baby was due. Taken aback by my doctor's question as to whether or not I wanted to proceed with the pregnancy, I responded with an emphatic, "Yes."

The bus ride home that beautiful spring day is forever imprinted in my memory. I had never imagined raising a child in a one-bedroom apartment in the heart of a big city. What would my husband say? Had we been careless? This certainly wasn't part of my carefully laid out plan and yet there was a deep sense of joy within me. Joy — an old familiar friend I had lost touch with. This baby was in fact my heart's deepest desire coming to life inside of me.

At my 20-week obstetrical ultrasound, we learned that we were having a baby girl. A girl?! I held my breath as the tightness in my chest settled in. I had convinced myself we were having a boy, somehow thinking it would be easier and that I was better suited to parenting a son. Flashbacks of my 14-year-old self overwhelmed me with their vividness. Mean girls. Teenage heartbreak. Fights with my mom. Compromising myself to feel a sense of connection and belonging. All my insecurities. I had thought those insecurities would fade away in adulthood but they lingered, morphing and evolving in complexity.

The little miracle in my belly was like a spark rising from the ashes. Even before she was born, she awakened my soul with a love more potent than anything I had ever experienced. As my body stretched to make room for this new life, I was gently reminded of what it felt like to be strong and adaptable. The power of my body to grow, deliver, and provide for this baby girl filled me with wonder and hope.

Holding her in my arms over the first few days of her life, I was enchanted by her perfectly formed body. I realized that my parents had loved me with this same fierceness that filled me to the brim and that their love had buffered me from so much.

Without a doubt, I knew this baby girl had in fact arrived at the perfect time. She was an unexpected gift and a beautiful interruption, inviting me to embark on the long slow journey of returning home to myself.

As my daughter stepped into toddlerhood, the desire for community began to stir in my soul. It took some time, but we eventually found a small church to attend. Hoping that nobody would talk to me, yet also longing for connection, I would orchestrate the timing of our arrival just as the service was starting. Week after week, as I quietly slipped into my seat and the harmony of instruments and voices washed over me, I would begin to weep. It felt like I was being cracked open and the tears were slowly eroding the wall that I had worked so hard to build. Initially, the source of this outpouring of emotion was a mystery to me, but with the tears came a strange sense of release.

Over time, I learned to surrender to the process. As the tears flowed, my hard edges began to soften. All the hurt and shame that was buried deep in the well of my soul was being released and slowly rising to the surface. Cracks formed in the wall creating space for light and love to move in and do its work. Forgotten dreams began to resurface, catching me by surprise. As I cautiously experimented with taking the masks off and allowing myself to be seen, I started to make new friends.

Just after my daughter turned 6, a friend asked what was next for me. "I think it's time to explore leadership." I responded without a moment's hesitation. As soon as the words escaped my lips, it hit me. When did I stop thinking of myself as a leader? Instantly, the defining moment was crystal clear. Being fired had triggered an innate fear of rejection in me. It was not the magnitude of the event itself that had determined the outcome, but rather the resonance of something deep inside me and how I reacted to those emotions. I had allowed it to define me and alter the course of my life. I also knew in that moment that I was the only person who could navigate my way back to the path that I had veered so far from.

I started an intentional practice of looking for beauty every day. At first, I found it in nature. Then, I learned to see it in others. Eventually, I was able to find it within myself. I began to pay attention to the things that sparked joy in me and stirred my soul, taking one small step at a time toward those things and giving myself permission to follow my curiosity and trust my intuition.

Sitting by the water's edge with my feet in the sand watching my daughter delight in the simple pleasure of an ocean swim, there was a stillness in my soul. Over time, it had replaced the persistent restlessness that had resided there for so long. With bright eyes, arms stretched wide, and a big smile on her face, she called out, "Mom, this is where I feel close to God!" "Me too!" I called back as she plunged below the surface again with full awareness that she was enveloped in divine love.

I wish I'd known at 23 that we're always just one decision away from a different life. Our habits and mindset are contagious and we are wired for connection. Being part of a healthy community of people who were consistently learning, growing, leading, and dreaming inspired me to try new things, step out of my comfort zone, and let myself dream again. Through a series of small sustainable changes over time, surrounded and supported by people who love and encourage me, I slowly found my way home, back to my true self, my path, and my purpose. Trusting that my dreams have been given to me for a reason and that I am being supported and guided by a loving God gives me the courage to continue moving forward one step at a time.

Life rarely unfolds as we had planned or imagined. I hadn't chosen to get fired or to become pregnant. In the first, I reacted. In the second, I responded. Staying on our own path and embracing our purpose requires us to respond rather than react, again and again, as the path unfolds. In order to thrive, adaptability and resilience are required.

Throughout your lifetime, invitations to grow will continue to present themselves. It is not the events of life that define you but how you react or respond to them that determines the outcome. You are the co-creator of your life. One small change can create a powerful ripple effect. With each new healthy habit, your identity and way of being evolves, your confidence grows and you generate momentum. A one degree shift sets you on a new course, ultimately leading you home to yourself.

IGNITE ACTION STEPS

Hold the vision — Your dreams and desires have been given to you for a purpose. Allow them to guide you. Imagine them in as much detail as possible. What does it *feel* like when you imagine that they have already happened?

Trust the process — Life is happening for you. When you encounter challenges, ask yourself, "What can I learn from this?" You are not alone. What evidence do you see that you are being supported by something greater than yourself?

Look for beauty — It's all around you. What you focus on, you find. Where do you see beauty, in nature, in others, in yourself?

Cultivate joy — What excites you? What moves you? What inspires you? What sparks joy? Let these things guide you. Intentionally make space for them and follow them with curiosity.

Love the journey — Honor your effort and progress. Celebrate the little wins. What are you grateful for today?

Ignite your life — What five things are most important to you? Are you living in alignment with your values? Does your life reflect your priorities? What is one small step that you can take toward your dreams, trusting that this will generate momentum, stoke the fire, and create a powerful ripple effect in every aspect of your life?

Alexia Gillespie – Canada
Speaker, Educator, Coach
www.stronghealthykids.ca

HINA MAHINDRU

*"It is only in absolute darkness that we become aware
of the power of our own inner light."*

**My intention is for you to awaken to deeper self-awareness, self-acceptance,
and self-love. To see yourself as both the intentional giver and receiver of
that love, and to practice connecting with yourself through play. I hope
you find joy in the many simple 'acts of love' you give yourself each day,
just like you would give to someone else. My most sincere desire is for you
to receive the love that already surrounds you.**

LONGING TO BE LOVED

My husband of almost 15 years moved out the year I turned 40. We had been
living 'separately' under the same roof for eight years by then. I felt nervous,
but there was also a sense of anticipation, like I was beginning my life anew.
Despite the efforts that we were able to make together, we could not reconcile
our differences enough to salvage our marriage. We knew that if we kept waiting to feel the ever-elusive "ready," we would end up just more resentful and
miserable. More importantly, we would leave a skewed, unhealthy impression
of marriage on our only child, our 10-year-old son.

The eight years of 'purgatory' were not all spent in vain, however. While our
views on intimacy and depth of communication continued to remain disjointed,
we were of one mind about cultivating a sustainable harmony between us before
splitting up. My ex-husband and I are good people who were civil with each

other, and functioned well enough for it to be a half-working marriage. We had learned to detach versus argue and fight, to agree to disagree and seek a common ground, or step out of the way when we couldn't walk together. It was a coping mechanism that worked for us, but coping mechanisms work best when they have a time limit. We were as ready as we were going to be, as supportive of each other as possible while living together. We had managed to salvage enough of a respectful friendship to have an amicable separation.

Looking back now, two years later, I can see that it was my Inner Spirit that had been poking and prodding me along, leading me to that place of separation, but I wasn't quite so consciously aware of it just yet.

I had never lived without family. I was raised in a fairly traditional Indian culture, living in my father's home before marriage, and my husband's after. Both my father and my ex-husband are modern men. I was, in all practical senses of the term, a privileged independent Indian woman. However, our culture is in our DNA, and the Indian culture is, at its core, a patriarchal one. I had the tools to be independent, but I didn't have enough real-life experience to stand up on my own. When I started living alone, I began to realize that while my ex-husband wasn't a traditional patriarch in our marriage and family, through my own subliminal conditioning, I had slipped into the role of 'dependent' by default, deferring to him on many matters, because that is what a good, qua-si-traditional Indian wife does. It's what I saw around me, or in the Bollywood movies I had grown up watching!

Living alone for the very first time in my life felt like a mixed bag of curiosity and excitement about all the new possibilities, as well as fear and insecurity of walking down an unpaved path through what felt like hostile wilderness. It was a whole new level of feeling like a grown-up! I felt empowered by my absolute autonomy — no more need to negotiate day-to-day things with anyone else, or to make compromises on how I choose to live my life. But, that was not for long!

I began to realize that I had held a very romanticized idea of a 'lone-wolf' life. I used to be jealous of my friends and peers who had the opportunity in their younger days to live on their own. I was never denied such an opportunity, it just never came to be. Living alone as a consequence of a broken marriage, however, had turned out to be not quite as exciting as I had imagined in my younger days.

I felt insecure and inadequate in my ability to manage my day-to-day life entirely on my own. I was now fully responsible for myself and my son while he was with me. Since he spent equal time between his father's home and mine, there were strings of days when I lived completely alone. It was the hardest during that time! Not having anyone to negotiate and discuss with, to defer to and lean on to make even the simplest choices and decisions felt difficult, risky; a burden too heavy for me to carry alone. I realized I didn't trust myself! I recall the first few weeks feeling tremendous anxiety while buying groceries of all things! I remember standing in the checkout line at the grocery store trying to decide whether to leave the line and get another item. My agitation grew as I struggled to make a decision. I felt the depth of my insecurity and frustration. To decide what *only I* would like to eat — I simply did not know how to think *just for myself*!

The empowerment and excitement that I had initially felt was quickly poisoned with overwhelm and self-doubt, followed by a bout of depression and anxiety. For the first time in my life, I didn't have any default companionship in my home. I had spent 40 years being somebody to someone else around me. My day-to-day exchanges happened simply by another person's default presence. There was always someone to talk to. What I would not give in those days to have the 'privilege' of someone talking back to me, to hear another sound around me and not feel smothered by a dark, dense cloud of silence. I came to feel loneliness on a whole new level!

During the last eight years of my marriage, as my husband and I progressively grew apart, I found myself becoming more socially introverted and reclusive. I was friendly and sociable with people when I had to be, but I increasingly avoided social interactions because they felt fake. Some of my friends and family members knew a little bit about my marriage situation from my personal conversations with them, but it was never acknowledged in a group setting. It felt like a big secret I was carrying all alone, the weight of which got heavier with time and wore me down.

My social introversion led me toward what seemed like a very self-absorbed life, delving into the world of deeper self-inquiry and self-awareness, searching for the real answer to the mystifying question, "Who am I?" As my self-awareness deepened, I began disengaging from inauthentic engagements and interactions for the sake of self-preservation. I was trying my best — and often in vain — to not offend anybody along the way. People pleasing, I was discovering, had been my way of life all along.

By the time I was on my own, my close friendships had morphed to fit my more reserved nature. There were many days in a row when I didn't talk to or meet anyone, and no one called me either. When I was married, silence and solitude were my way to escape the noise and reconnect with myself. I had wished so long for people to leave me alone. Once it had finally happened, I understood the sageness of the warning, "Be careful what you wish for, you may just get it!"

I wondered what would happen if I had a heart attack, for example, and died. No one would know! I imagined being discovered dead in my home days later, after someone eventually missed me. I felt abandoned. I felt disconnected!

A year after the separation, some things were better — my son's adjustment to our new family structure and dynamic, as well as my ex-husband and my communication related to co-parenting. I managed to go through the motions of a 'moved-on' life by numbing the suffocating silence I lived with when on my own. I slept a lot. I coped with my feelings by eating them. When I was awake, I watched a lot of TV and scrolled an endless social media feed, seeing happy people creating happy memories. I didn't remember how it felt to be one of those people.

That year, my son was with his dad in the time between Christmas and New Year's Eve. The three of us had just spent Christmas morning together at my place, and I was feeling proud because I had done well at making it a lot less awkward than the previous year. And then I was alone again.

One night that week, I got off the couch grudgingly because I could no longer ignore nature's call. I had just spent 13 hours in front of the TV binge-watching *The Crown* on Netflix™, smoking pot, and eating easy-to-access food for sustenance — breakfast cereal, salsa and chips, peanut butter from the jar. The only light in the room was from the TV. As I stumbled my way around the coffee table, I caught sight of a big pile of shiny crumpled gold-foiled Ferrero Rocher™ chocolate wrappers. Beside the pile sat the empty 48-pack box my parents had given me for Christmas. I felt completely disgusted, pathetic, and ashamed.

I turned on the light and looked around me. Every surface I could see had evidence of a life being *tolerated*, not lived. I walked around my condo apartment and saw more evidence of the same — dirty dishes overflowing from the sink onto the counter, piles of clothes needing to be folded and put away, a bed unmade for weeks. I was standing in the midst of clutter and an insurmountable mess that was my home, and my life.

I returned to the couch, curled up in the fetal position, and cried. I wailed and sobbed. I hadn't been able to cry like that for years, and my tears weren't stopping. I allowed all of it to move right through me, feeling gutted to the core! I let myself cry out loud, my voice pushing up against the silence that had smothered me for so long. I listened to the sound of myself crying, and cried more at the realization that no one was there to comfort me — no one to sit with me, to hold my hand, to bring me a glass of water or a cup of warm soup to soothe my despair.

And then it dawned on me: *I* was with me. I was my constant companion, and I had been treating myself exactly as one of the many people I had accused of abandoning me. The evidence of my abandonment of my own self was all around me in its stark undeniable messy truth.

Surrendering to the depths of my darkness that night helped awaken my Inner Spirit and reignite its little light. I wiped my tears, turned off the TV, and walked into my kitchen. For the first time that week, I cooked for myself — a simple all-day-breakfast meal of scrambled eggs with sauteed spinach and avocado toast. I made myself a cup of tea and sat at the dining table, *with* myself for the first time. I cried the whole time I ate, my tears adding extra salt to the eggs! But this was a different kind of crying. It had a tenderness to it, a vulnerability of receiving. I felt washed over with warmth. It surprised me how nurtured I felt by a little act of love toward myself — making myself a simple warm meal — with the pure intention of taking loving care of *me!*

I put my dishes in the sink above the pile that was already there. I started emptying and reloading the dishwasher, slowly putting things away where they belonged. Then I decided to go to bed. I went to turn off the light in my living room, but just before switching it off, I paused a moment to look around. I moved my eyes slowly, acknowledging every piece of clutter around me, seeing each item for what it was, separate from the big blob that clutter feels like. *I will take care of you in the morning*, I promised them. I switched off the light, brushed my teeth, and got into bed. It had been a few days since I had slept in my bed without the blue light and sound coming from the TV in the background. This time, the darkness, stillness, and silence felt good. It felt tender, like coming home.

I cried one more time that night as I fell into slumber. I allowed myself to accept that I needed to ask for help. Somebody who loved me would help me if they saw me right now. In that moment, **I** saw me in all of my truth, the light and the shadow! *I will help me*, I promised again. *I will help my 'Self'!*

In seeing myself in all of my truth, the light, and the shadow, I had to acknowledge my unconscious stigma around seeking help for how deeply depressed I was. I felt shame in admitting not being able to manage it *on my own* — it is the biggest myth about being strong and independent!

The day my son went back to school after the holidays, I dropped him off and drove myself to see my family doctor. I sat there and cried the whole time, coming clean about possibly having depression. I felt lighter. I felt supported. I followed my doctor's guidance regarding therapy and medication, and started taking further responsibility for my health after being diagnosed as prediabetic a couple of months after that appointment. I returned to yoga practice, which for me combines exercise, body work, and prayer. I also introduced intermittent fasting as a lifestyle I could sustain to manage my diet without too much deprivation.

I would love to tell you that my life has turned around 180 degrees and I have mastered self-love in all its magnificent power! But that would be a lie. I still struggle with clutter, but it's getting smaller. I still leave dishes undone in the sink, but they rarely overflow onto the counter now. I do make my bed every day, sometimes even if it is just before getting right back into it for the night. It's true!

I will, however, share with you a poignant lesson I've learned: Self-love is a *practice*, a way of life, like yoga, or any discipline such as intermittent fasting. Self-love — like anything worthwhile — takes work. And work, any work, feels too difficult when dealing with depression. So I too fail a lot, and often. However, with help, I have become an expert 're-starter'! Restarting is part of a practice, isn't it?

For now, I am on the other side of depression. Can I guarantee that I will never be in it again? No, I hover near the edge often enough to not be that arrogant. But, as an *expert re-starter*, I return to my self-love practices, every one of them, with a little less resistance, with quicker recovery, and a whole lot of grace each and every time. I acknowledge my restarts with the proverbial 'pat on the back.' I would encourage someone else who consistently made small yet mighty strides toward their healing, their growth, wouldn't I? So why not myself!

I no longer feel 'abandoned.' Instead, through practicing self-love, I found that I was becoming more present, more receptive to love that was already and always around me. It's evident in my relationships, which are healing beautifully.

You too may look around and sometimes find evidence of being alone or abandoned, but I urge you to open your heart, to see and receive the love that is around you in all its imperfect and beautiful glory. You'll feel it, you have it; you *are* it!

IGNITE ACTION STEPS

Practice becoming *present* with yourself. Self-love is not one thing. It is a culmination of many gifts of presence we can give to ourselves each day — acceptance, appreciation, trust, forgiveness, and grace, to name a few.

Practice noticing what feels like *play*. Ask yourself — *What would I want someone who loved me to do for me, or with me, right now? What would I do for myself right now if I was someone I loved dearly?*

Do your best to fulfill what your answers reveal, what you may be longing to receive — a foot massage, a summer afternoon at the beach with *you*; even a little love note on your bathroom mirror saying "Pssh... I love you!" Just play! Find and give yourself whatever feels essential for your inner light to stay aglow!

Practice a new *practice*. What tiny, new practice can you start today? The first one I did was making my bed daily, even if it was just before getting back into it. It was *that* small! When I failed, I restarted. Practicing restarting has made me an *expert 're-starter'*.

So practice that — restarting. You fall down, it's okay. Rest if you need to. Whenever you're ready, get up again. If you need help, ask for it — perhaps someone to carry you, to give you a hand and pull you up, or just to be a strong arm for you to hold onto as you pull your own self up. I realized that people actually *want* to help. So practice asking for help too. Practice may not always make perfect, but it slowly and surely makes change, especially healing, permanent.

Hina Mahindru – Canada
Self-love and Relationship Coach
www.hinamahindru.com

DREAMER

GISELLE JENNAWAY

"It's always too soon to panic."

It is my intention for you, galactic soul, to sense that you are so much more than the story you've lived so far... and to be curious to discover what still lies dormant in you.

BUT WAIT, THERE'S MORE...

It was a practice in the early Middle Ages for rival factions to offer a person, often a child, to each other as a pledge of peace — a hostage. That is the meaning of my name, *Giselle*, and that is how I always felt about being here: that it wasn't really my idea and equally there was nothing I could do about it. More than three decades passed before I began to dismantle that cage.

When I was 16, in my final year of high school, my closest girlfriend Alex and I accepted an invitation to escape Sydney for the week and stay in her cousin's bush shack while he was away on his honeymoon. I'd almost survived my 12-year incarceration in the education system but I was nearing burnout. In our minds it would be a study retreat to rejuvenate and finish our essays on Keats' poetry.

The driveway was well over a mile long, a white earth track winding past tall gum trees, ancient boulders, and mossy tree-ferned gullies. In stark contrast to the inner city landscape of our daily lives, we drove deeper and deeper into timeless peace. When the driveway opened to a clearing with a half-finished shack, we were surprised to find we would not be alone. Her cousin Chris, a school teacher, had a habit of taking vulnerable students under his wing. A young man, Pete, wearing green dungarees fastened over one shoulder welcomed our arrival with a smile. In a split second our carefree ease became defensive wariness; yet despite our initial shock and suspicion, the combination worked. Our synergy as friends and housemates was solid by the end of that first day.

Birdsong and the sigh of the wind in the trees were the only sounds out there. It was far enough from roads and far enough from any other habitation that humans were forgotten. This was before the internet, when brick-sized mobile phones were still a rare accessory. We were wonderfully alone. Our own daily rhythm within timelessness became the whole world.

On the fifth day, our peace was penetrated by the sound of a car engine becoming louder and closer, which could only mean one thing. People. Intruders. The seeming roar of the motor gave way to silence once again as the engine was cut, then the sound of doors opening, closing, the muted pad of feet on smooth earth. Alex and I sat, tea in hand, around the kitchen table, all senses alert. My antennae were riveted by I knew not what. Pete craned his head out the door and we saw a smile break over his face. Footsteps louder, greeting voices... I saw a single lock of curly blond hair swing forward before the tall young man it belonged to was revealed in the sliding glass doorway. And something in me already knew this was the boy I'd seen and *noticed* in Pete's photographs. Two young lads with nothing better to do had heard their friend was staying up at Chris' place with two girls... The introductions are a blur in my memory. All I could hear was my own heart beating faster as time itself glitched out and a buzz of warm confusion swept through my body. I guess I managed to smile and say "Hi."

We must have been amusing to watch. The instant our eyes met, for just a fleeting moment, it was all over. I couldn't help but stare at him, and then in the moment when I knew I'd been looking too long and really should look at something, anything else, he'd glance up and catch my eyes sliding away. The air between us felt electric. I had no idea what anyone else was saying.

After a Baileys™ coffee, we decided to all go for a bush walk down to Flat Rock. I needed to put my boots on. He offered to wait while I laced my boots and my disbelieving mind managed to understand he was deliberately lingering to be alone with me. We walked fifty paces behind the others, near enough to feel each other's warmth but not quite touching, talking shyly. Down at Flat Rock, his friend did his best to capture my attention with an admittedly excellent foot massage, but nothing could have unlocked our energy from each other. As those boys drove away, I had a warm cat-that-got-the-cream-like smile on my face. He left grinning happily, holding tight to a slip of paper with my phone number. I would see him again in three days, at his friend's 20th birthday party.

A few days later, our tight trio arrived long enough after dark that the party vibe was already established. The second story flat door opened straight into a dated white kitchen full of relaxed people and Prince singing "Kiss." It didn't take long for us to find each other, and my rising anxiety that our mutual interest was my imagination eased by the expression on his face when he saw me. A huge 'spliff' was passed around and we flirted coyly across the deucey board. "Do you play?" he asked me. "No, teach me?" I replied and proceeded to smash him. Five hours later, driven by the midnight munchies clawing at our insides, we sat cross-legged on Bondi Beach enjoying gourmet falafel rolls together, our knees just touching. We had both overcome a last paroxysm of self-doubt to get to this moment. He had seen me talking with his friend, and thought, "Fuck her, I'll have a good time anyway," and walked away. I had watched him walk away and thought, "Fuck him, I'll have a good time anyway…" I'm not quite sure now how we circled back to each other, but by 3 AM we were alone. The sea breeze was chilly and the skin on my bare arms was standing up in goosebumps. He settled his jacket around my shoulders. Our hands touched, our lips met, and our souls settled into the next chapter of our long story together.

Before we met, I was living well enough. I was friends with my parents, learning, teaching, and had a couple of true friendships. But I remember, in that period of stark contrast, feeling as though I had been twiddling my thumbs for the first 16 years of my life, surviving like a good hostage, but often just going through the motions.

Meeting my beloved felt as though my soul got switched on. A deeper layer of meaning to my existence opened up. I would go so far as to say that I felt there was true meaning for the first time. I felt like I was actually alive, that *this* was why I was here. Tracing our stories together we felt like chess pieces maneuvered by the Universe. My life, as I knew it, was finally beginning. In each other, we had found Home.

For the next 17 years, our home was babies and living as poor university students together. Living in beautiful places but never quite on our own terms, chasing the end of the rainbow but never feeling truly free to just live, to just enjoy the sweetness of our love.

Seventeen seems to be my number. My father is 17 years older than my mother. My mother is 17 years older than my stepfather, my stepfather is 17 years older than me. I met my husband in my 17th year, and we had 17 years together. He always sensed there was much more to him, always knew that someday, he'd really step up into his full potential. He had no idea it would be a virulent cancer that invited him to know himself more fully. He had an aura of premature death around him that those of us closest picked up and processed in our own versions of deepest fears — his mother and I had premonitions, our son had nightmares, and yet my husband truly was a tiger with nine lives. The most vital, unkillable man I have ever known. I always thought if the worst happened, it would be an accident, but illness blindsided us all. His 36th birthday party was also his wake.

Without my buddy to do Earth with, my sense of being an exiled hostage returned in full measure. I felt as though I had been chewed up and spat out. My heart was no longer whole, but pulpy pieces beating reluctantly. My stress levels were so entrenched my digestion had pretty much shut down. Bread tasted like sand in my mouth. The only foods I could get down to keep me fueled were goats' milk and fruit.

I remembered the stories of Aboriginal people, families broken and removed from their country, choosing to roll off the back of wagons and just curling up and dying under a bush. It was incredibly frustrating to the English colonists that these natives, even warriors, would sometimes just lie down and die. As I felt my growing disconnection to my own body, it dawned on me how easy it would be to continue to withdraw my consciousness and just leave.

But single mothers of five children don't do that. My ancestors on my mother's side were pioneers and their words, "It's a mother's first duty to stay alive" echoed in my ears. I loved my children dearly. So I chose to stay. It was still under duress, but this time it was my choice to be here. With both the past and the future too painful to contemplate, I made the present moment my Home.

I stayed. But I removed *all* the rules. We packed up the house. And went camping for two and a half years. I'd recognize his energy signature any-where… my earthly husband became our otherworldly guide, and I cultivated moments of magic. Indeed I demanded them. His totem was the wedge-tailed eagle and I don't quite know how he managed it, but eagles guided our path all the way. I remember one evening, the sun sinking low over the desert, we still hadn't found a place to pull up and make camp. An eagle appeared over the road, flew ahead and to the left. We followed, and where it landed was the perfect place to spend the night under a sky full of stars brighter than most people ever see.

Eight years later, we had traded travel for our own piece of land and I had to learn all over again how to find the freedom within, while staying still. Waking up to the same view every day was like Vipassana, but with *lots* of talking. A long series of coincidences and synchronicities had landed me squarely in the online coaching world, my path colliding directly with soul family who would become my friends and mentors. One such cascade of events led me to Avery Hopkins' two day introduction to Alchemy. Usually a sit-back-and-observe-quietly girl, I abandoned a lifetime's habit and took a front row desk.

For two nine-to-five days, as the Brisbane River behind us wound its way to the sea, my entire being drank in the precise articulation of that which I had been striving to remember my whole life. Without realizing it, I had been homing to Alchemy — *the understanding of how consciousness relates to matter and experience.* The threads of my life were illuminated by what he was teaching us, no longer separate pieces but chaos *magick.*

True understanding is of the heart: grasping a concept intellectually is insufficient, it must be experienced. No mere theory, it had to be lived. And I realized I had been living it. Life had been pointing me toward something. Since that first awakening, when I met my husband, I had sought to pull back the veils separating Truth from seeming, as time after time my being resonated with something and my brain struggled to catch up. Connecting the dots on my unusual experiences, I had been moving ever closer to having the words that described my growing understanding. Yet until this day, precise articulation had eluded me. It was like watching a pixelated image resolve into a crisp picture, and I was excited by the clarity.

As our teacher shared his stories, I became increasingly aware of the quiet vastness of his understanding. There was something intangible in the sum total of him that I recognized in myself. I was so alone on this planet, and even though I had been deeply loved, I had never before met someone who reflected back to me what it felt like to be me. It was pleasantly shocking. I had thought myself misunderstood by others. What was being revealed to me was that I had misunderstood myself.

In class on the second day, we touched on the alchemical meaning of the twelve astrological signs. In an anecdote it came up that Avery was Leo. He described a trait of being Leo that I had never heard before — we foray hard, and then retreat hard to digest the experience. I identified with that So. Deeply. Over lunch, the conversation in the group turned to astrology again. I shared how his description of Leo nailed me. I asked what his Chinese sign was. Turns out we share the Dragon sign as well — we had landed on opposite sides of the planet just days apart.

As I scanned his stories in my mind, I reflected on my own experiences at those exact same ages and times… and drew parallel after parallel. Different events in different places, same theme. My eyes widened and an avalanche of understanding cascaded faster than thought.

It's not often I meet another Leo Dragon. I would be lying if I denied feeling a certain kinship in their energy on those rare, random occasions, no doubt that basic human yearning to feel understood. But my path had only crossed one other Leo Fire Dragon like me, and though she was super cool, she had not mastered herself yet either. Sitting inches from to this master Alchemist, the full impact of the understanding that had been building within me hit and changed my inner landscape forever. It was a quickening. Just quietly I noticed all the molecules in my body were vibrating faster. Not shaking, not trembling, but buzzing in heightened frequency. If you had had a hertz meter on me that afternoon, I would not have been surprised to watch the count climbing.

I told him later, in a quiet moment after class. I said, "When I stand near you, it feels like my whole being is vibrating faster." It wasn't flirting, it was a statement. We shared a moment of eye contact, a smile of understanding, a small nod. Once again my whole being was understanding something huge while my brain scrambled to catch up.

I trace this as my true moment of awakening. Everything I had experienced up until that point was just priming me for this moment. And what this being was reflecting back to me — in his presence, in his relaxed confidence, in his sovereignty, in his unapologetic understanding and voicing of knowledge, in his complete lack of neediness for approval or acceptance — was how much I was still dumbing myself down. My abandonment of the status quo, my adventurousness, and my Truth-speaking notwithstanding, I realized how much I still withheld and how much I still doubted my own knowing. I felt all the places I was *not* sovereign. Without a word being spoken directly, his Presence was an invitation to really step into the fullness of *consciousness-knowing-it-self-through-my-expression*. An invitation to Do Me. I felt more seen than I had ever been. Not by him, but by myself. I had found *home* again, but within, and this time it couldn't be taken away from me.

You know, in many ways, I like the old me — the one in love with her soul mate of many lifetimes playing us-against-the-world, the one before tragedy — better; there is a part of me that sometimes still grieves for her shattered dreams, and yet I would not give up the inner freedom I have won since then, pulling back veil after veil in my quest for sovereignty and true peace. Before this bigger awareness awoke in me, despite the magic I have known, what was possible felt finite. Since I walked away from that collision of souls by the Brisbane River, I sense the infinite — the peace, the power, the possibility… that nothing is without, it is all within… and how deeply I live it is up to me. Where I go, I can guide; and now I have a knife in the table for you to know that how deeply you live is up to you.

Ignite Action Steps

Grab a piece of paper and shift your awareness into being a compassionate and honest observer of yourself.

Write down every place in your life you feel needy, any place that you feel the power to change something in your life lies outside of you, anything you believe is ruined forever because of past events, and all the ways you feel you withhold yourself.

My love, these are all places you are yet to discover aspects of self that are veiled, hidden. This is not a list of your limitations — rather each one of these is an invitation to *remember* yourself. Blessings on your unfolding.

Giselle Jennaway – Australia
B.Nat C. Hyp RTT Starseed Mentor & Catalyst
www.indigoimpulse.com

DONATA S ELBER

"When you're in a shitstorm, remember to turn on your windshield wipers."

Your inner voice is there, you only have to dig deep and discover it. Your happiness comes from within you. You have the power, no one else does. Find the courage to pick yourself up and make the choices that lead to happiness. Climb out of that hole and have your spirit glow as bright as the rising sun.

JUST BREATHE

When I woke up that morning, I had no idea that my life was about to descend into a deeper pit of pain, suffering, and death than I could have ever anticipated. It was a weekend morning, in the middle of December, and we had begun our weekend chores, the regularity providing comfort to me at a time in my life that often felt stressful and disconnected in my marriage. My husband had headed out to one supermarket and I had gone to another.

Two hours later, now home from the store, I received the phone call from a police officer that made me lose my breath. My husband's truck had been spotted parked in a gas station by a worker across the street who had noticed that it had been parked for an unusually long amount of time. The police officer described that my husband was in the driver's seat, in a state of semi-unconsciousness and further explained that an ambulance was on the way. I felt as though I had forgotten how to breathe, and all I could do was panic. As I worked in the nearby hospital, I requested he go there. When he arrived at the emergency department, I was waiting and could see that he looked like he had a stroke. His arm was at an awkward angle and I could see his hand turned inwards toward his body. As a nurse, this sent my mind spinning. He was immediately examined, then the doctors came to discuss their findings with me. They were convinced that he had a stroke, a hemorrhagic stroke, which meant he was bleeding into his brain. That was not all the news they shared. They informed me he was in possession of cocaine; it had been found in his pocket during his emergency exam. In his semi-conscious state he admitted to using it that day and the previous few days before. I was shocked — I had no idea that he had been using cocaine. At that point I needed to quickly sit down. It takes a lot to get me off my feet, but I couldn't stand anymore. I didn't even know if I was still breathing.

For many years, as I helped my patients deliver their babies, I would tell them to breathe deeply and slowly. It calmed them and reduced anxiety, bringing them better focus during the birth. Controlling their breathing allowed the situation to become manageable and enjoyable. As my life has unfolded, this is the one practice I always try to remember. I tell myself to just breathe in and out, knowing that things will come into focus as I calm my emotions. I never knew how important this action would be to me at the most difficult time in my life.

When you receive debilitating news that leaves you hanging on a cliff, what do you do first, second, or at all? Well, you breathe. And I kept breathing until I was able to think, which took a while. The severity of his illness grew every day and the calls I received from his friends and co-workers became overwhelming. My heart dropped as I listened to an intimate message that his girlfriend had left for him, not knowing that I would be the one picking up his messages.

After many days in ICU, I had a clear picture of what the future held for him, and me. He had rapidly declined, his memory was poor, he was paralyzed on one side, and he spoke very little. I felt like I was losing my husband in big and small ways every day. As his capacity continued to diminish, my focus rapidly changed from his recovery to where he would live the remainder of his life. I felt numb as I turned my attention to the details of his care and the emotional turmoil my children were in.

Each of my three kids was suffering. They were 14, 15, and 18, and didn't know what to do. We would hold hands and breathe together as I would quote one of their favorite movies, "The Three Ninjas," giving them something they could relate to. "We are stronger together, like the fibers of a rope, than apart." Looking them in the face and holding back my tears was one of the hardest things I had to do. I wanted to present a future that was still promising without their father. They had so many questions and I did not have many answers. They were very fragile and I felt completely alone. Yet, I had a sense of my own strength and my capability to push through. I didn't want my children to feel alone, and I summed up everything I had to support them. Little did I know that this trauma would be the beginning of multiple events that would change the course of our lives.

Christmas and New Year's were a blur. January came and he was to begin rehabilitation to learn to walk, speak, and feed himself again, but this was too difficult for him. Within one week, he lost his memory and could not remember our names. During that time, the kids learned about his extramarital affairs and drug abuse, which was devastating to them. Maybe it was good he couldn't remember. Maybe this would help me heal and let go of all the pain I was feeling.

February came, and he was to be placed in a brain injury home. We lived about an hour away and could visit as frequently as we liked. But the children did not want to. My mother was also facing a debilitating illness that no one could really diagnose and we helped take care of her. She lived with my sister about one mile away, in New Jersey. It was helpful that she was so close. My children's lives became so complex because of all that they were going through, in addition to schoolwork, friends, and adolescence, but it was all out of my control and I felt as though I couldn't protect them. I was both angry and outraged — feeling overwhelmed and not able to prepare them for all that life was throwing at them.

Only two months after my husband's stroke, while we were adjusting to our different lives without him, our world changed again. My mother lost her fight with her illness and was found dead in her bed one night. My only consolation was that my sister was in the house with her. I couldn't tell you the date because my head could not comprehend the loss. All I could do was breathe and breathe hard. We hadn't begun to heal from our last trauma and now had to go through another blow to the heart. I again had to be strong and show my children that our lives would go on in a forward direction. It was hard to look into their faces and see their pain. I felt so broken.

Within the next month, my oldest daughter left college, my second daughter was bullied and became homeschooled, and my son developed chest pain, which we later learned was anxiety.

The trauma continued. The next year, my middle daughter, who had just graduated high school, lost two friends in a car accident and then two others to suicide. More death and pain — our lives were rapidly changing and becoming even more difficult. I wondered, how deep can I breathe to help my children who are stuck and struggling to survive? What can I do as their mother to help bring their lives into some sort of normalcy? We had been surrounded by death, and our life had become a house of horrors, taunting us with what might happen next. Within a month, our next hurdle would be our family dog. She ate an entire prescription of blood pressure medication and then spent the night at the vet. At 6 AM, we received the call and we were at her side when she died. And we cried again. We were not only crying for her but for all the open wounds we were carrying. Two weeks after that, I answered another 6 AM call telling me that my father had been found dead at his kitchen table. He lived in Texas and we traveled from New Jersey to bury him.

How much more were we expected to endure? How much did we have to lose? I kept asking myself, how can I heal this family so we can start to live the lives we were meant to have? These were the many questions I tried to answer. To this day, I have moments that make me wonder how I got through losing my husband, my mother, my dog, my father, and my daughters' four friends in two years. The strength I had to muster each day got me through my life and fueled me to take care of my children, but it also exhausted me. I just kept breathing. I was so afraid of my children's spirits getting crushed and lost forever. More than anything, I knew I had to be stronger than all of our pain. So I kept breathing deep into myself and digging for the strength I needed to take care of everyone.

The grief that my children felt began to cause more deviations in our lives. My first daughter became suicidal and was placed on medication, my second daughter left college and got lost with no direction, my son graduated high school and went to work — each disconnected from their inner spirit. We each attended family therapy, but it got us nowhere. Fate would not allow us to move forward.

That Christmas, we had made plans to visit my husband at the brain injury hospital. But the very morning we had planned to see him, the phone rang. Once again, it was early in the morning. On the other line was an emergency room doctor. My husband had passed away from a heart attack. We all sat together and cried, not knowing what to do. I was numb, feeling shaky all over, and the despair on the children's faces was breaking my heart. We were shocked by this news and didn't move from in front of the fireplace for hours, trying to stay warm.

For the many months that my husband had been in the brain injury unit, his parents and sister had abandoned us. This added to my pain and feelings of being truly alone. At my husband's funeral, my sister-in-law did not recognize her own niece. My in-laws lack of support for their grandchildren was excruciatingly painful. I was shocked and angry that they didn't reach out to us over the previous two years. They had no idea of the pain their grandchildren were going through, and it felt as if they didn't care. I didn't understand it. The children really began to hate them because they felt abandoned by them.

I didn't know how but I knew I had to go on. Defeat wasn't an option. I took a deep breath and realized, it was truly up to me to mend my family. My love for my kids is so deep within me that I dug to that place, connected with my Inner Spirit, and fought my way up out of the hole of pain, anger, misunderstanding, betrayal, and abandonment that my children and I were mired in. I decided that they needed me and despite the sorrow I was feeling, I found joy in my children and loved being around them. They were the reason that I kept going.

I searched for the things that made us happy in our lives and removed the things that did not. We love sushi, so I put that in our weekly dinner plans. The kids would look forward to sharing that meal. Dinner was the meal where we all came together and talked to each other, sharing our day and bonding. This was important to help us heal, and it felt so good to talk and laugh together. I started speaking up and saying no to them. They saw that their mom was not a pushover and this brought them back to reality. The rules still applied and this made our life feel normal again.

Time began to pass, and we started to move forward with a different perspective on life. I went back to college with my eldest to help her move into the rhythm of life again and get back back on track. We took American History together. Well, she wasn't as excited as I was but she did it. My inner spirit was starting to get stronger — all I needed to do was give it some air and remember to keep breathing. Sharing classes didn't last long, and both daughters left college and went to work. We had been surrounded by death for so long that it felt amazing to finally be surrounded by life. I felt my inner voice grow and become stronger every day. I began to connect with my own power to support, to learn, and to fiercely love in a deeper way than I had known before.

But no matter how hard we all tried, we seemed to be spinning our wheels in life, as if we were stuck and life had no meaning. We needed a new beginning and my sister was kind enough to offer us the chance to move in with her, her husband, and son, but it was in Texas. I considered that it might be a good thing — it was a totally new place, new people, new air to breathe, a complete change of venue. We agreed to give it a try, well, all but one. My son did not want to move and my other sister in New Jersey offered him a place to live. I wanted him with me, but we are our choices and he had to learn that. He could always come home to me.

A part of all our healing was selling the house. We needed to start again, which meant we needed to move past all the pain connected to the house. We could make a new start, begin again where no one knew what we had been through. That felt good. Starting something new is like a breath of fresh air. It comes with a renewed feeling of what can be accomplished. The house sold fast and we were on our way to Texas. It was exciting to start over but sad since I had to say goodbye to my son.

Once we got to Texas, it didn't take the girls much time to move out and be on their own. My sister had been telling me for over two years about a neighbor she had met that she believed was my soul mate. I wanted to hear none of this after all I had been through.

I hadn't been in Texas for an hour before she had him come over to introduce himself. After we met, it took six months of friendship before we started dating. I soon had everything in this relationship that was missing in my marriage and it felt good. He is so wonderful. I soon found myself moving again, first across the street into his home, and then to south Texas for a job. This time the move was for me — a new job, a new start, and my new man came with me. We built a beautiful home and I was breathing again. We have been together 11 years now. I was happy again but through it all, I found myself still digging into my heart knowing I wasn't complete yet. Yes, my family life had come together, but I was looking for that thing, the thing that would fill that spot in my heart. Once again, I had to dig deep into my soul and find out what that was. I enjoyed my work, but I wanted more. My Inner Spirit guided me to go back to school, and after three years of incredibly hard work, I received my Master's degree in Nursing. Now I am a Nurse Practitioner. I am full and breathing freely with a lust for life again.

As I sit here trying to remember some of what happened in my life, my memory strains, but the pain in my heart announces its presence with a sinking feeling again. As a tear rolls down my face, I must remember my pain, struggles, and hard times. But when I do, my strength, my inner spirit will come to life, my power to control my own destiny as well as the pain. I may not ever be able to let the pain go entirely, but I can make my inner spirit stronger than the despair I feel at times.

I found my greatest connection to my Inner Spirit through my love for my children. My love is so deep that it connected me to the deepest part of me where the core of my strength lies. Once I found it, it gave me a base to build from, and it helped me connect with myself and climb out of the hole — and the sunlight was there and everything looked different. I'm happy every day now, I feel so good — happy teaching and reaching out. The bond that my children and I formed through terrible times continues to flourish and make all of us stronger.

We hope in life that everything will go as we imagined, and when it doesn't, usually due to unforeseen circumstances, we complicate our lives by taking on that despair. Life can become easier when we realize that we do not own what others have put on us. Do not pick up that baggage, leave it there at the curb. You can choose not to own anger, despair, pain, and confusion. Let go of it and breathe — begin to feel your life renewed. Make this a ritual. Every day, take the time to stop, breathe, and remind yourself how great you are. I have always told my children two things: *just do it* and *let yourself be great*. Now, I encourage you… get out of your own way… take a deep breath… and let yourself *be* great.

IGNITE ACTION STEPS

Prioritize your needs: Remember you have the capability to say 'no' to the things you don't want. Reorganize and change your life to fit you.

Choose happy: First, stop holding on to the bad. Give yourself permission to honor how you are feeling. Choose to love and take care of yourself by trusting your abilities and capabilities. Strengthen your confidence. This battle is in your mind, and it's under your control, no one else's. Stop for a moment and breathe, slow and deep. Create this ritual and take better care of yourself.

Donata S Elber – United States of America
MSN, APRN, FNP-C
donnaern@yahoo.com

PAUL BENSON

"Are you ready to uncover your Inner Wealth?"

Life is short; how would your life be if you fully trusted yourself, were satisfied with who you are right now, and saw that life is about giving gifts — your gifts? I would like to take you on the adventure of how I learned this.

UNCOVER YOUR INNER WEALTH

What is Inner Wealth?

Growing up surrounded by wealth, but drawn toward being happy and content, I turned away from the path my family was on and started forging my own. This led me to research how people feel in their own skin, a lifelong project that I began when I was 18 years old. I've noticed two camps:

The Security-driven Camp – these people get a job, create a safe life, limit chaos, save for retirement… and then what? Often missing the joy of life and trying new things; failing and not really growing. The outcome is that when they reflect on their life, they have regrets for not taking chances. They followed a traditional path, clearly laid out, without following their heart and soul.

The Freedom Camp – these folks choose adventure over security. They include the artists, entrepreneurs, authors, and spiritual seekers who follow a 'calling,' with often little financial reward. Only a few hit it out of the park to financial abundance. Often, they end up living a rich life but without financial resources.

I lived in the Freedom Camp for many years but more recently, I've come to appreciate creating a life of balance that includes both camps. It is important to have a balance with each of them: we need to embrace our freedoms and passions; but also our responsibilities in managing money and creating a healthy financial future.

I grew up a trust fund kid, surrounded by multimillionaires and a billionaire. My dad was a mega-millionaire who came from money. He grew up in private schools and had an Ivy League education. He enjoyed everything from stock brokering to building houses and land developments with his side passions of art and auto racing. Yes, he was quite an eclectic character! I have many fond memories of being in his pit crew in Monterey at the California Laguna Seca racetrack. One of my favorite memories was the practical use of white duct tape to keep the car body parts together during his race outings. One of his competitors was Paul Newman, the famous actor, but I always admired my dad.

One day, Mr Newman had gone into the porta potty (those portable fiberglass bathrooms), and when Paul was in it, my Dad ran up and shook the walls of the bathroom as if there was an earthquake. The door flung open and out came an angry Paul Newman. "What the hell?!!!" It was pretty funny. They were quite a contrast, my dad, loud and outrageous, and staring at him in disbelief was 'Cool hand Luke,' the polished professional actor.

My dad was like that. Everything was about fun and having a good time. Whether it was auto racing, searching for hot springs along the west coast, or building cool houses. I still remember his infectious laugh and whooping for joy in the morning as he listened to his big band jazz and rock music. There were many traits I loved about my dad, but I also felt very embarrassed by his loudness as a kid. He was like a god to me, fun loving, but a little over the top at times. But still, I loved his playfulness. I remember summertime when he took all of us kids to the beach. We ran around playing on the sand dunes and then all went out to dinner; priceless times together.

I chose not to go into business with my Dad. It wasn't for me. However, I had always loved learning because it meant I didn't have to be in the workplace. I decided to study Psychology at UC Santa Cruz. Postcollege, my dad invited me to join his business, but I had another agenda going on — my search for happiness and spiritual fulfillment.

I started following the path of a spiritual seeker and searching for inner peace. That was a pivotal Ignite moment in my life. I left a life where I felt like I was not enough and I felt miserable. On my new journey, I started finding gratitude and contentment in everyday things, like enjoying the sun shining on my face in an early morning walk.

For the next 17 years I soaked up whatever I could learn with a number of spiritual teachers before finding my own inner fulfillment and happiness path. An important moment happened while with friends in the Saline Valley, California, a natural oasis with palm trees and hot springs next to Death Valley. As if a lightbulb went off in my head — a doorway opened, I had received what I had searched for over the previous 17 years — *how to be happy.*

Was I enlightened? Ha-ha! Nope! I realized something important — I didn't need to fix myself anymore. I felt that happiness was about knowing that I was enough — and I did know that. I understood I was more than enough, I'm plenty! I had learned so much from my spiritual teachers, but now I found the answer in myself. Trusting myself.

Essentially, happiness is an inside job and no teacher can give this to you.

In hindsight, there were times when I felt as if I was the actor Simon Pegg playing the main character Hector in the 2014 film, *Hector's Search for Happiness.* Like Hector, on my search for happiness, I found it was inside me all along. After reaching a state of deep contentment, it became a tenet to live by. This is why I've included it in my lifelong *inner* business path.

After my 41st year on the planet, I decided to create my own million-dollar company. Investing in my corporate growth, I hired some business coaches and an interim CFO to teach me how to read spreadsheets. There were no spreadsheets provided on my spiritual path!

Soon enough, I learned how to run a large construction company, and after establishing myself with a strong foundation, I later started a second company that was also profitable. Right before the 2008 economic meltdown, the businesses were grossing about three million dollars a year. I employed 35 awesome people in the first of its kind 'green-certified' roofing company. I felt f ***ing awesome!

Hanging by a thread, both businesses crashed in 2010. It was a painful time and like many other Americans, I lost everything, including our home, and I was in over my head with a million dollars in debt. Bankruptcy inevitable, I couldn't hold on to my staff and had to lay off all 35 of them in one fell swoop.

This was a painful time of loss and despair. Imagine being a sensitive introvert, and everyone is pissed off and angry with you. I felt like the walls were caving in on me, but then I realized how the Universe was teaching me *mastery.* When the creditors were calling me for money, I realized I just needed to keep the business moving forward. I offered a payment plan instead of ducking their calls all together. I started thinking about it as a game and it felt more playful.

It became clear to me that I couldn't do business just to make money. I needed to be passionate and more connected to my purpose. My financial losses in the companies and the gains from my spiritual journey reminded me I needed to spend time in both the Security *and* the Freedom camps. Now, I was convinced that to be truly happy I needed to embrace both. I needed to honor my desire for freedom, while living consciously *and* making money.

Once I realized this, I ran my business differently. It stopped being about growing profits — making the next million, and instead, became more about my feelings and enjoying the journey. Each client was a beautiful gift. I was no longer trying to get out of the business. I changed my relationship with the business and fell in love with the process.

I took a page from the Freedom Camp playbook and committed to some quality time. I now have a regular Sabbath, each Wednesday, where I take off and head into the beautiful California Redwoods for four to ten hours, no phone, just walking and enjoying nature. Man, is it ever amazing!

Why did I start this practice?

Sixteen years ago, one of my employees was murdered as I was just heading out of town to go on a 10-day personal Vision quest with about six other individuals. The trauma of losing this person in an act of random violence really shocked my spirit. It made me question the meaning of life and had me contemplating my own mortality. It influenced my quest to the Sequoia National Forest as I started off in a deep, dark mood of inner contemplation.

We spent 10 days in the lush, virgin green great outdoors, at the base of the Sierra mountains. Part of my time was with the group and I spent three days solo, fasting on only water. It was a beautiful magical experience. We shared our nightly dreams with the group, hung out in the cold streams, saw a herd of native bears, and all of us bonded in our collective journeys. In the middle of my three-day vision quest, I felt a change. Up to that point I was searching for enlightenment, realizing it was a waste of time. I quickly felt the need to just live life!

A lot happened on that trip, and I gained the inner wisdom I was searching for. I also recognized from that event the need to do weekly vision quests to keep honoring my intrinsic connection with 'lover' nature. From then on, I have started each day with meditation and a physical workout. I later turned an empty guest room into my 'forest cave.' We painted it avocado green to resemble the beautiful outdoors. This is how I start each work day, and I am proud to say, I have kept this practice going for over 16 years.

I encourage you to uncover your 'Inner Why,' dear reader! This will help you to reveal your true, purposeful calling. Taking this approach has been a game-changer for me to uncover my *inner wealth*. It's helped me to rise up from the ashes of loss, like a phoenix, into a more meaningful and wealthy life. That includes serving others to expand their learning and build their own wealth.

Uncovering my own "North Star," I discovered one of my core themes is adventure. Once recognizing the importance of how adventure motivates and inspires me, I added it to my daily life. It can be as simple as driving to a store, meeting with people, and navigating challenging clients in my businesses. I think I got this love of 'life as an adventure' from my dad.

In making my multimillions and then failing at many other business ventures, I grew emotionally. I learned that when I focused on making money in my business practices, I wasn't as successful. Now, I know that wealth is about connections. Being rich is about the experiences we create. I love the multimillion facets of enjoying life and not having the feelings of being stuck in the Security Camp.

A few years ago I heard a talk by Sri Kumar Rao, a Columbia Business School professor, teaching the course, *Creativity and Personal Mastery*. He urged students to look at business not as a way to just make money but as a way to grow yourself.

In my contracting business, even when I was making almost three million dollars annually, I was still chasing the next million, always raising monetary goals to feel successful. Ultimately, this wasn't satisfactory. Once I realized that I needed to shift how I viewed goals to include my most rewarding values, my businesses changed. The way I do business is based on my purpose and values. Money is secondary, but closely measured. This realization opened up a new avenue of livelihood which is aligned with my inner mission to kindly serve others.

Sadly, many people in their 40s and 50s have overlooked setting up their financial future, so I grew one of my businesses, a personal leadership company, to include offering financial services to small business owners and contractors. As a contractor myself, I know what it's like to have a lot of money flow through your business but not keep much of it.

The wake-up call for me was when we got a large 1.4-million dollar job that we did over two years. On this one job, I netted 750K in profit, but all this money went into the overhead of my businesses. Wow, this was a shock to me, but it also taught me skills that I didn't learn from the resident family millionaires and billionaires in my family. You need to know how to manage your money!

After four decades spent on enjoying adventure, and what many would consider successfully making money, I am most committed to being a constant learner. I keep learning and growing as much as I can. What's really beautiful is I'm now showing others how to build wealth in ways no one bothered to teach me. This work is so fulfilling to me. I support people finding a balance, but also include showing them how to save money and design personal pension funds.

I also work with people who are not so familiar with the American financial system. We have companies we work with that help others set up policies, estate planning, tax filing, and most importantly team building, goal-setting, and long term strategic optimization. To me this is so satisfying because I see how hard people work to support their entire families and in turn create greater, generation wealth. My team is multilingual so we can teach virtually anyone how to manage their money.

True inner wealth is actually listening to both camps of thought. Bringing your passion and purpose into what you do and also managing money flow to pay yourself first. So I challenge you to really think, are you on track to have the best life for yourself? Do you have enough money so when you don't want to work you can be supported? And if something were to physically happen to you, would you thrive?

Ask yourself right now... Are you living a life, where you are giving your gifts to others, and is your life full of rich experiences? Listen for the answers... even go on your own vision quest if you have to. But, make sure you follow your inner desires and honor your 'self-wealth.'

We all need to live in both camps, security and freedom. I encourage you to design a great financial future, but also listen deep to your soul, and craft a life of meaning.

Ignite Action Steps

Sit Down with a Financial Planner:

Either ask me to sit down with you or pick someone you know, and look at your finances. Are you living within your means, or spending too much? Do you have a life insurance policy that also includes living benefits? It is a free-rider that acts like Critical Care but you don't pay any extra for it. If you don't know what that means… It means you need to ask.

Do you have a Trust so if something happened to you, your heirs wouldn't get stuck in probate? If you don't, it is time to do that.

Take 10 percent of your earnings and put in a savings account. If you are in your 50s, it should be 20 percent. Yes that means you!

All these things are great to review so you can make some better financial decisions, versus putting them on autopilot. It can be very confrontative to look at these things but it will create more peace for you. There is so much support out there, go find what will work for you.

Paul Benson – United States of America
Transformational Life Agent & Wealth Coach
www.ItDoesntFeelLikeWork.com

Clint Carleton

"We are the dreamer, and we are the dream."

My intention is to Inspire you to awaken to your true authentic self and to live life fully. Life is filled with infinite possibilities. What has happened in your life is just simply what happened. I hope that you discover an eternal, unlimited version of yourself. It is waiting for you.

And the House Was Empty

When I was a young man, I was deeply concerned with how I was perceived by my family and friends. I wanted to make sure I was at the top of the game of success, and would stop at nothing to continue to propel myself into higher states of wealth in the pursuit of material gain. I drove my bright shiny blue sports car at very excessive speeds, blasting my stereo to make sure everyone noticed how amazingly cool I was.

It was a time in my life when I thought I had it all. The trophy wife, the mansion on the hill, the boat, the sports car, and a thriving business. I had made it, and all at the very young age of 25. I was the most accomplished out of all my high school buddies. Look at me now, Dad. Are you proud of me now? Look at me now, Miss McClure, grade 10 English teacher who told me I would never amount to anything in my life if I couldn't sharpen my pencil — I am a success!

But, it was a reality that could not have been further from the truth. My business had had a serious setback, and now the money had almost completely stopped flowing in. I was carrying a huge amount of stress and worry as I tried to keep us away from the brink of bankruptcy.

I had always been an avid skier and often took to the hills to feel more alive; to feel the intoxication of flying down the slopes, totally in control. On a particular cold and snowy December day, my wife and I returned home from an exhilarating deep powder ski day at Big White Ski Resort. We had just entered the house when the phone rang. My wife ran to answer the call. I put my gear down in the storage room, and as I turned toward her, I could see the expression on her face quickly drop and the color of her skin instantly change. Her legs weakened and began to come out from under her. It was all I could do to rush over and catch her before she crashed to the floor.

My mother-in-law had died in a horrific house fire. The months that followed were some of the most emotionally turbulent times in my life. My wife had been estranged from her mother and grieved deeply, caught up in tremendous guilt. How could anything have ever prepared me to support someone dealing with such loss and regret? And far from family, without the external support we both needed in that time, the pain we both experienced was nightmarish. Devastating. Unendurable. It was then that I realized what it means to have community, and we had none. Not only did we not know how to ask for help, we didn't even know that it was possible to ask for it.

We weren't the only ones who were devastated by the loss. My wife had two younger brothers who needed us, so we stepped up. We adopted them. It was a time of incredible overwhelm for me. Now I was dealing not only with all of the pressures of my own life, I was trying to support and manage the life of two young men and my partner. In dealing with her activated childhood trauma and grieving strongly, my wife fell into a deep depression. Within the first month the fighting between the siblings was almost a daily occurrence, and I would often get pulled into the fray as they would hurl sharp and hurtful words at one another. I was taking care of three wounded children, and I was still just a child myself. I had never experienced such extreme emotions before, and I had no preparation for caring or supporting such deep emotional wounds and grief-stricken hearts. It was too much for me or anyone to handle alone.

The pain and stress took a massive toll on our relationship. A sharp stabbing pain grew each day in my stomach, which felt like I was being gutted with a dagger. The anxiety I felt began to keep me up at night. Then the fighting between my partner and I started. The emotional grief she was experiencing was now projected at me. Over the next couple months, it escalated into bursts of rage that were at times accompanied by flying objects. With the incredible overwhelm, I was feeling helpless. I felt I had nowhere to go for help. My heart was breaking and I didnt know what to do. After having my car repossessed and the bank notifying us that we had either to sell the home or forfeit the title, my wife decided she and her two brothers would move out and get their own place. They left a week later.

It had been months since that life-changing moment when the phone rang. For the first time, I would be returning home to enjoy space all to myself — a moment of peace in the storm that had been my life. It was a bright sunny and cold winter day. As I unlocked the front door and stepped inside, I noticed right away something was wrong. Something was *terribly* wrong. The house was freezing cold, almost like there was a wind coming through the windows. I took a few steps further inside and saw nothing but walls. It took me a few moments to comprehend what I was seeing. Everything in my home was gone. The furniture. The rugs. The Jet Ski™ coffee table. My pinball machine. The TV. I had been robbed, and the thieves had taken everything. A few scattered papers and knicknacks lined the living room floor. I twisted around in disbelief at the empty space before me.

I ran through the house only to find that every room was the same. The backdoor hung open, a trail leading through three feet of snow from the porch. It was obvious where they had parked a truck and gone back and forth many times while loading everything in. I felt utterly violated. My entire Being went numb. I could hardly feel my legs as I sank to the icy floor. I collapsed face down, my cheek pressed against the hard concrete that should have been warm and welcoming. As I lay there, near lifeless, I heard my own heartbeat racing at breakneck speed in my chest. With each breath, I felt like giving up.

I sank deeper into the dark abyss I was free falling toward. It was as if I was tumbling from the tower of lies I had built up around me. Everything was gone. My home, my wife… all that I had acquired as proof I was not a failure. Gone. I had my castle that my ego built itself upon. And now I lay at the lowest of lows, empty, with nothing left.

My mind swirled with each new thought until I was just a hollow shell. A failure. The cold of the floor seeped into me, through my clothing, through my skin, through my bones, and into my soul. It was the coldest I had ever felt. How could this have happened to me. Why? Vast emptiness pervaded my being as I descended down a dark tunnel until I hit the bottom, where a stillness and silence came over me.

As I witnessed the swirling chaos of thoughts flying through my mind, one after the other, I could see that I was not in control of my thinking. I realized something very profound. I realized that I was *not* my thoughts, I was *witnessing* my thoughts. *"How could I be my thoughts?"* I must be something else. *"I must be more than my thoughts."* *"Who was it that was witnessing these thoughts?"* What about this cold loneliness that I was feeling? *"Who was feeling those feelings?"*

Something stirred in me. I quickly became aware that I was not the near lifeless body that was laying there cold on the floor of my house. I was the *awareness* of this body and the feelings of cold that were being experienced. And... if I was not my thoughts and I was not my emotions, then I must not be the material things that I owned, and for sure I was not an accumulation of accomplishments, success, and failures. *I am something that is witness to all of that.* I am something so much bigger than all of that. Something not attached to any of those things. And it was at that moment that something happened within me. I released control. I began to free fall within my own Being — a sensation of expansion and release. I could feel myself tapping into a world of infinite possibilities. Tears began to flow like a gentle mountain stream. All struggle was futile. I surrendered at the deepest level. At that moment, for the first time in my life, I asked myself, "Who am I?"

The answer that came to me was beyond anything I had ever contemplated in my mind before. I realized that there was a space of infinite possibility that was opening up for me. I am not only a participant in this ride called life; I was the co-author. I was emerging from a spiritual cocoon as the co-creator of my own reality. My life began to flash in front of me. I saw a person who was created by the societal norms and the ancestral programming that I was perpetuating. I had built up my life as a way to create safety and protection from being vulnerable in my pain and visible to the lies I was telling myself — the lie I was living. That life was meant to be filled with hard work, struggle, and effort. I had been just living as a program up until that point.

The energy that this charade required had been taking its toll on me, my reptilian survival brain was working overtime, which kept me from witnessing my true inner spirit and inner knowing. To a very large degree, I was rebelling most of my life against a society that felt to me as if it was trying to box me into a very limited perspective of life and my part in it. It gave me a few boxes within which I was meant to find my place. And over time, as responsibilities and personal debt piled on and the survival mechanism within my being took the helm, I began to align to this lie, seeking tirelessly, and I found a place within it. I embraced the hypocrisy and participated in a lower, denser, and dishonest version of myself. This cold floor was my awakening, breaking me free from the shackles that had dragged me into a dark cave. I was free at last. I could feel the gentle breeze of grace begin to fill my reality. I was witnessing my true '*I am*' presence.

I was finally awaking to my most authentic self and the Universe reacted immediately. It was as if a messenger from God himself rang me the next morning. It was Ollie, a longtime friend, who was going to move to the Cayman Islands in the Carribean and wondered if I wanted to join him. Three months later, after selling my home and receiving enough money to pay off overdue bills and finish the bankruptcy documents, I booked my flight.

Ollie and I left on a beautiful spring day, driving toward our new life, taking the road over the mountain to make our way to the Vancouver International Airport. Sitting in Ollie's rusty, beat up Mazda™ pickup truck, I noticed a tape sitting inside the tape deck. Curious, I leaned across the seat and pushed it in. It was the Mystic and spiritual teacher Stuart Wilde. Wilde was a taoist and metaphysician, a spiritual misfit who had written 27 books in understanding the nonmaterial planes of reality. He shared his insights and teachings on dimensions that existed beyond the third density and taught exercises on how to reach those states of being. He spoke about Grace and how to align to grace in your life. I was so excited about what I was hearing that I made Ollie pull the car over! It was like an unquenched thirst I had carried most of my life was finally being sated. I was hearing what I could only describe as truth.

Later that evening, we stepped out of the plane and into the heat and constant humidity of the Cayman Islands. I remember how it blasted through my being. I felt freedom as I had never felt before. Within a few days, I was offered a position managing a small water sports company. My job consisted of renting jet skis, kayaks, and snorkel gear to the wealthy elite at a prestigious waterfront hotel. It didn't pay very much but I was totally in flow. Home rentals in Grand Cayman were astronomical, so I rented a tiny attic. It was in that attic that I pinned a map of the world on the ceiling and, over the next year, with a laser pointer in hand, I planned out my hero's journey — a great awakening journey around the planet. I started a journaling discipline, every day writing down the thoughts that were swirling in my mind. I wrote them as I witnessed them in my early morning meditation practice. I began to shine light on the infinite awareness that is the witness behind the mind. The true 'I am' presence. The 'I am' that I *am*. In the back of my journal, I wrote a bucket list of all of the adventures I wanted to go on, all of the places I passionately wanted to visit.

Over the following three years, I traveled to 38 countries, lived with monks in a Tibetan monastery, spent two weeks meditating in a cave in Thailand, sailed the Carribean Sea, climbed some of the highest mountains in the world, boated down the MeKong river, studied with healers and medicine people in the Amazon, and learned from esoteric teachers many ancient teachings on how to unlock the unknown potential that lies dormant within my Being. I learned to use trance states and deep meditation practices to enter into other inner dimensions. But what I learned and practiced above all else was that through being grounded and present in each moment, I was truly able to manifest my own reality easily, and without effort.

Guided by my Inner Spirit, I continued to let go of old mental programs that were holding me back and awakened to the inner guidance that was always there, behind the scenes guiding me back to my highest joy and the fulfillment of my life's purpose. My journey uncovered many truths for me. I went from living a lie to living my own true soul's destiny. I had been following the stories and dreams of other people and now I had finally started living my own story — the true story of my life, my own life script!

I was smack in the middle of a rite of passage that was telling me to put away one book and pick up a new one. It was an upgrade in my inner operating software. I never had elders to show me how to write my own script, or how to make that story a reality, and so instead of making my own dreams come true, I had spent my life trapped in someone else's dream. What an amazing opportunity lay before me! What do I want to create in this world? How could I best be of service? I knew that I wanted to create things in the world that were life-affirming and life-supporting. My Inner Spirit was no longer willing to participate in anything that was less than this.

I know now there was no other way forward than to take full responsibility for what happens in my world. The part in me that was seeking to build up a false reality around me to prove something to the world now became my ally — the one that brings truth into the world!

When we see our part in the magic of life, we begin to support all life. We serve the highest good of all. The concept of effortless action is one that radically transformed my life. But when we first look at the possibility of life being infinite, it can be scary and you may find it challenging to let go of the struggle; to let yourself sink into the trust that is required to live a life of graceful flow. We must let go of the river bank and let ourselves be in the flow of the infinite without trying to control the outcome. From this place of Flow, what comes into clear view is the true vision and purpose for our lives. We are the dreamer, and we are the dream. We are at the helm, gently dreaming our world into being with effortless ease.

Ignite Action Steps

Ignite Your Dream: Write a bucket list. Make a dream board. Create "Your Hero's Journey" — a script for *YOUR* life. Don't wait for everything to come crashing down. Go out and do it.

First Be, Then Do! Take a moment now to slow down and to relax. To breathe deeply and surrender into this eternal moment. To rest into this moment, finding that comfort and ease, just to let go and naturally be. Our fast-paced world and filled inboxes can have us on overdrive. The mind is like a cup of muddy water, if we don't stir it, the turbulence will slowly settle, and the confusion will purify. What's left is the pure light of truth.

So let's just slow down for a moment now. Take three long, slow, and gentle breaths. In through the nose and out through the mouth. A slight sigh of relief as we let the exhale fall without effort. Just letting it go. Feel your body de-armor and relax into present moment awareness. Be here now.

Start every day with Gratitude: Grace can descend upon us at any moment. We pave the way for grace to be our guide, by first looking into those things in our life that we are deeply grateful for. Take a few minutes when you wake every morning, before your coffee, before you get out of bed, to think of at least three things that you are grateful for. It may be your friends, your family, or your passions. Begin each day with Grace!

You are the dream, and you are the dreamer. Sit in silence every day. Pay attention to your thoughts. Notice, what are the thoughts that I am witnessing? You are not your thoughts. You are an eternal, immortal, universal, and infinite point of awareness. In the infinite ocean of life! Awaken!!

Clint Carleton – Canada
Healer, Spiritual Guide
www.theskymethod.com

LYDIA KNORR

*"In gratitude there exists a knowingness that peace
can be found, even amid the chaos."*

**In sharing my story of finding gratitude in the face of pain, I hope you
will be inspired to reflect upon your own life experiences and uncover the
golden gems awaiting you. By sharing our stories, we have the opportunity
to transform lives and even if that life is only our own, we have the seeds
of an idea worth sowing.**

DISCOVERING Y.O.U. (YOUR OWN UNIQUENESS)

Everybody has a story. I have my story and you have yours, and each story
is unique because it belongs to you and you alone. It's about your life, your
experiences, the lessons you have garnered from those experiences, the wisdom
you have gained, the growth you have enjoyed. And whether those stories are
filled with hope, despair, victories, losses, darkness, or light, they make up
your life's journey, one which is simply about becoming more of who you are.
Your life story creates your authenticity — that which makes *you* uniquely *you*.

This is my story.

As a young girl, I adored everything about music. I loved listening, dancing,
and especially singing along to powerful female vocals. I would spend hours
in my parents' basement full-out performing for no one's ears but my own,
imagining myself as the artist I was listening to, be it Cher, Olivia Newton-John,
or my absolute favorite, Barbara Streisand. I knew I had a desire to be on stage

and loved any small opportunity to be in the spotlight, but sadly I lacked the confidence to stand on my own and openly share my passion, therefore keeping my inner performer to myself.

My parents encouraged a formal education that would lead to a solid career, which led me into the field of nutrition. As a Registered Dietitian I enjoyed many diverse experiences including work in the prison system, the corporate foodservice sector, in academia teaching at a post-secondary level, and my favorite experience of all, a Media Dietitian working in TV, print, and radio. It was in this role that I got to use my voice and my personality to deliver messaging around food and health. Having a platform to engage with people and share an important message completely resonated with me. I felt energized and gratified when connecting with my audience.

I met my husband Mike in my first year of university and we married the year following graduation. He studied aerospace engineering but like me, had a hidden desire, and after working for a few years in the aviation industry, he decided to pursue his true passion for business. He embarked on an entre-preneurial endeavor in the telecom industry and capped it off with an MBA. Mike was always looking for ways to further a business model through the use of technology. He was a big picture thinker who was not afraid to roll up his sleeves and dig in at the ground level to execute his vision. His work ethic awarded him many successes throughout his career but they also came with a cost. Mike's work life involved long days and a lot of business travel. But to everyone who knew him, Mike's first love was myself and our three daughters. Being a family man was by far his greatest joy.

To say we were blessed is an understatement. We really had it all and we treasured that. How could I be anything but grateful? Yet I felt that something was still missing. It was not in my home life or in my career, it was something inside of me. I felt that I was meant to be doing more with my life. It created a restlessness and discontent within me and I feared that unless I figured it out, it might negatively impact those blessings.

Mike would say, "Just do what makes you happy," or "Stop worrying about it and just enjoy the moment." Being happy and being present came so easily to him. I envied that.

Two decades into our marriage, things began to shift for Mike as he assumed the role of President of his company. The demands of the position meant longer workdays, even more travel, and less sleep. The toll it was taking on him was evident. My daughters and I could see how tired he was and noted an unchar-acteristic quietness coming over him. One Saturday, our family had a rare opportunity with no extracurricular activities on the calendar and decided to visit one of our favorite areas of the city. We had lunch, shopped for clothing (which was one of Mike's favorite activities with his girls), and topped it off with coffee and cake in a European cafe. Later that evening, Mike was reflecting on the day and could not stop talking about how special it had been. I agreed that it was a rare thing to have that much leisure time together, but to him, it was so much more than that. There was an obvious shift in his energy. He was very melancholy and it was concerning me.

The next day I dropped him off at the airport for a five-day whirlwind trip to China and as I watched him walk away in my rearview mirror, my heart was so heavy thinking "There he goes on another trip he just doesn't have the energy for."

Three days later, my phone rang at three o'clock in the morning. I saw the name of Mike's boss on the caller ID and immediately knew something terrible must have happened. My pulse raced as thoughts of a heart attack or a car accident entered my mind — NEVER did I expect to hear those words as I picked up the phone. In a broken voice, he said "Lydia, we don't know what happened, but Mike is dead." My husband and best friend of 25 years… was gone. He was 49 years old.

My world was changed forever in that instant.

I suddenly became very aware that I would no longer get to witness Mike's happiness or be on the receiving end of his quirky antics. No longer would I get to hear the excited squeals of our daughters when he came through the door after work while patiently waiting my turn to greet him. No longer would I get to bend his ear for his endless wisdom or sit together over a glass of wine and make plans for our future. No longer would I be Mike's wife.

As I hang up the receiver, it hits me that I am now a widow and a sole parent. I sit quietly in the darkness with my new reality.

My thoughts go to Mike as I imagine his transition, wondering if he is scared, did he know what was about to happen, did he feel vulnerable? Knowing him, I can sense his angst and how he must have fought till the end. I slide over to his side of the bed and wrap myself under the covers, feeling such a strong connection to him. And then a quiet sense of calm and overarching gratitude envelopes me. I feel grateful for the relationship we shared, for the family we created, for our decision to teach our girls to ski and the many family vacations we enjoyed, for our countless poignant conversations, and most especially, for all that we were to one another. I was so blessed to be his wife.

And from somewhere within, I trust I am going to be okay.

The days ahead will definitely be easier with all of the love and support that will surround me and I am also well aware that in the months to follow, there will be some truly difficult times. Yet still, somehow, I know that everything will be alright.

I know this because at this moment, I am not alone. I feel something much bigger at work in my life and I believe it is the Universe in all of its splendor, opening up its doors to me.

Mike's passing became my spiritual awakening.

The validation arrived that first night as I was awoken from my sleep by a white light coming toward me and retreating again, coming toward me and retreating again. I knew without a doubt this white light was Mike's energy. It made me both happy and sad but more than anything, it made me aware that I was dialed into Spirit.

I wanted to maintain this connection so deeply.

Several months had passed when I had a dream that was so profound, it delivered me a firsthand experience of what the afterlife looks like. In this dream, I was at my childhood home when Mike rang the doorbell and entered the hallway. He scooped me up in his arms, spinning me around two or three times before setting me back down on the ground. His eyes were intense and they told me everything he wanted me to know. When I looked into them, I saw and felt a love *so* pure, *so* full of joy, and *so* beautiful. Mike *showed* me what life was like where he now existed. He wanted me to understand the beauty and magnitude of the love there so that I could know that he, too, was okay. I awoke from that dream feeling immense gratitude. Gratitude for my connection to Spirit. Gratitude for being 'gifted' the experience of an immeasurable love.

The months following Mike's death were the greatest period of growth and self-discovery I have ever known, and it was through this that I found the seeds of an idea worth sowing.

Being dialed into Spirit led me to search for a deeper and more continuous connection. I prayed, I meditated, I read story after story on people's experiences with their departed, finding parallels with my own. I journaled about all of the things I was thankful for and made notes of my favorite memories. Mostly though I spent a lot of time in nature, just being quiet and receiving what came to me in the form of thoughts, feelings, and silent conversations. I knew this was me connecting to the part of myself where there exists a *knowingness...* an awareness that can't be found anywhere else — my Inner Spirit.

In getting quiet and connecting with that part of me, I was reminded of Mike's advice to "just enjoy the moment." When I was fully present, I was neither sad about a past that was over nor was I anxious about a future that was yet to unfold. Being in the moment, I felt completely at peace and in finding that, I found my true inner happiness. All of that time I felt restless and discontent, but I had the answers all along. I just had to look inward to find them.

That is what Mike had been trying to get me to understand. Damn, he was wise!

Through this experience, I came to the realization that I was meant to use what I had discovered to inspire others, because like me, I knew there were countless people in this world looking to connect with their truest selves and live a purpose-filled life in peace, balance, and alignment.

Your inner voice, Soul, higher self, whatever you want to call it, is your greatest guide and when it nudges you into action, you owe it to yourself to honor that.

One of the greatest nudges I received came just days after Mike died. There were many 'middle of the nights' when I sat alone, thinking of all of the things I would say to someone about him if they were there with me at that moment. I wanted people to remember his quirky sense of humor, how he had a nickname for everyone he ever met, his 'all for one and one for all' attitude, his open-door policy, his cherished memories and stories of his childhood, and his absolute adoration and love for his girls. I wanted to share all of it and realized I had an opportunity to do just that at his funeral. I could not think of a better way to honor him than by using my voice. To this day it is the most important stage I have ever stood on and the most meaningful speech I have ever delivered. I was so grateful to be able to capture Mike's essence for everyone there that day and knew I could do it unwaveringly because I felt his presence right alongside me — so much, in fact, that as I got up to speak, I remember hearing him wise-crack, saying, "Well would you look at her in her absolute element right now!"

Using my voice became a significant part of my healing. Speaking from a stage with the intent to deliver nuggets of inspiration to my audience was my Soul's calling. I spent the next year working on my messaging, my business plan, my website, and my signature program to find peace, balance, and alignment at every junction in life. It felt amazing! My energy and my inspiration had returned and I felt like my old self again.

Then I got cancer.

I had two surgeries in the space of nine months to remove my thyroid and 30 lymph nodes along one side of my neck. During my recovery, while waiting to find out if my voice would be okay, I had the opportunity to reflect. I knew there had to be a reason this happened so soon after losing my husband.

The answer was obvious.

The fact that the cancer was centered around my throat was a clear sign from the Universe to stop overthinking my 'plan' and just get out there and SPEAK! And that is exactly what I have done and continue to do. Paid, unpaid, on a stage, on a page, it doesn't matter. My mission is to engage and inspire others to live life as the truest version of themselves with a sense of purpose, peace, balance, and alignment.

Finding gratitude in the face of pain connected me to my Soul and helped me make sense of my past, make peace with my present, and create a vision for my future. I have learned that true inner happiness comes from discovering peace in the present moment. My hope is that you will take the wisdom, growth, learning, and awareness you've discovered from your own life's stories because as I said in the beginning and will say it again...

Everybody has a story. I have my story and you have yours and each story is unique because it belongs to you and you alone. It's about your life, your experiences, the lessons you have garnered from those experiences, the wisdom you have gained, the growth you have enjoyed. And whether those stories are filled with hope, despair, victories, losses, darkness or light, they make up your life's journey, one which is simply about becoming more of who you are. Your life story creates your authenticity — that which makes *you* uniquely *you*.

Treasure your stories and use them as a gift to yourself and the ultimate guide for discovering Y.O.U. — Your Own Uniqueness.

Ignite Action Steps

Express gratitude (often).

Being grateful puts you in a state of abundance. It instills the belief that you're thankful for what you have right now, in this very moment, rather than worrying about what you don't have or won't have at some future point in time. Simple acknowledgements like sunny blue skies, the smell of morning coffee, spending time in nature, or watching children at play are just a few examples of how you can acknowledge and express gratitude for what you are experiencing in the here and now.

Your quality of life from your mental, physical, emotional, and spiritual well-being can all be heightened from the simple act of gratitude. You are the sum of your parts and gratitude can benefit each of those individual parts.

Gratitude can also put what you value into perspective when things don't go your way. You can use the power of gratitude to release some of the negative emotions you may be feeling due to a failure or setback by remembering that with every difficulty, an outcome of equal or greater benefit exists. When faced with adversity, ask yourself the following questions:

What can I learn from this? How can I benefit from this? Is there something about this situation that I can be grateful for?

What are *your* silver linings?

For me, finding gratitude in the face of pain connected me to my Soul, and when I stepped into life with Mike's perspective of 'Do what makes you happy' and 'Just enjoy the moment,' I stepped into the truest version of myself.

Lydia Knorr – Canada
Health & Wellness Coach, Speaker, Author
lydiaknorr.com

CHARLENE RAY

*"Listen deeply to the whisperings of your soul; trust and
follow — your inner spirit knows the way."*

**It is my wish that through reading this story you feel supported in allowing
your intuitive gifts to be seen and honored. You are needed in this world.
It is important that you step into your authentic life. Listen. Trust and
believe in your inner wisdom. It is time for you to connect with your wisest
self and allow your gifts to shine.**

RUFFLING FEATHERS

When I was a child I spent countless hours alone in blanket forts. I loved the
one I built on the back porch with a view of the yard, and the one with the fluffy
pillows and blankets in my bedroom. In my childhood Chicago home, during
all seasons, I spent most days inside these cozy caves with my best friends: my
books, my diary, my dog, and my wild imagination. Even in our little city lot,
I would lay a blanket down on the grassy lawn and let the canopy of the old
maple tree be my roof as I lost myself in stories and dreams with my faithful
companions. These stories of my childhood became seeds of inspiration for a
lifetime of work and play in the imaginal realms.

Perhaps this sounds like a familiar story. I wonder if you also believed that
the places you journeyed to, while inside your blanket forts, were real. I knew
that these far-off worlds were as real as the world I saw when I opened my
eyes. Just as I knew that fairies were real and fireflies were evidence of their
nightly adventures in the summertime.

Everyone told me I had a great imagination, but even at a young age, it was clear to me that these were not the made-up fantasies the adults around me thought they were; this was really a capacity to connect with other worlds, *real* worlds.

When I first heard the distant, mystical 'voices' in my head, it was as if they were speaking at triple speed, tumbling over each other in their rush to get out. The sounds were fast and seemed like they were at a different frequency. It was as if the radio was tuned to a station and I could hear mostly static and couldn't really discern the voices. Every so often I would catch a word, but it wasn't until much later in life that I started hearing them clearly. My lack of ability to understand them left me frustrated, curious, and wondering who or what was trying to communicate with me.

One day, I asked my grandmother about the sounds. The color left her face and her eyes opened wide. She stepped back and looked at me, seeming both horrified and alarmed. I was certainly surprised by her reaction. I thought that something must be wrong with me for her to have such a strong reaction. I stood there, lower lip trembling, holding back tears as I awaited her response.

It seemed like a long time but I am sure it was only seconds before she said something. Her voice was quiet but firm, "Don't ever speak of that again. It is your imagination; you will grow out of it." I remember feeling disappointed. I thought it was something good and special but her reaction made it clear that it was something to be afraid of rather than something to celebrate.

My grandmother watched me for a few minutes before she added, "It's really nothing. Ignore it and it will go away." And she was right about that. Dismissing the sounds *did* make them fade away. After that interaction with my grandmother, I also carried the fear that I was mentally unwell.

Other things did not go away. The energy around people and in nature appeared to me in colors and shapes. The trees and the wind delivered messages and wisdom. The fairies danced around my blanket forts and twinkled with the stars.

Once I realized that others did not experience the world this way, these friends, too, left me and went into hiding. My friends did not speak of such things and when I did, they looked at me funny. This fed my apprehension that something was wrong with me. As fear entered my world, I began to fall into a sleep-like trance.

I was drawn to the Lutheran church down the road from where I lived. It was an inviting building, a low and sprawling red brick structure that drew my curiosity. I was only 6, but I took myself in, walking the two blocks to the church in a pretty dress that I imagined was my Sunday best. I asked to meet the Pastor and start Sunday school. He looked at me askance but settled me into a pew right up-front, promising to call my mother after the service. My attendance at church became a regular thing, and I often wandered in on days other than Sundays as well, helping out with various tasks in the church's library. In this way, surrounded by books and the comfort of the building's four walls, I built myself a new fort. In the library, I discovered a book that spoke about speaking in tongues, and this fascinated me. I briefly remembered the sounds in my head and wondered. I explored books about miracles and mysticism before I even understood what those words really meant. I also overheard conversations about pagans and Wiccans talking to trees and worshiping nature, and learned that it was called *devil's work*. Needless to say, I was confused!

I abandoned my own thoughts and decided to follow the Christian religion. I followed what people told me about what a good girl should believe and how I should act. In middle school, I developed a curiosity about the ouija board, connecting with the dead, and creating spells and potions. If the bullying I endured for being a fat girl wasn't enough, I also heard the Catholic girls refer to me as a witch or a devil worshipper, reinforcing my feeling of not fitting in.

Hearing the chants of "Ding dong the witch needs to be dead! Which old witch? The wicked witch" hurt my heart. The girls stole my books, planted cigarettes in my desk at school so I would be punished, and threw food at me. In spite of this abuse, I tried to fully engage with adolescent life: doing well in school, finding a boyfriend, and engaging in volunteer work and church life. My ability to communicate with the unseen world and my intuitive wisdom went into an even deeper sleep.

Every once in a while, a book about clairaudience, psychic abilities, nature, or intuition crossed my path and sparked an interest. Every time I would read one, I would find myself back into the other world that I knew was real, longing for it, to be connected with it, and to have it be a bigger part of my life. It wasn't until over a decade later after I left the church and graduated college that I discovered a book that fell off the shelf. I was sitting in my favorite bookstore in Chicago when the book literally pushed itself out of its place and landed on my lap. Surprised, I looked at the book, *Peace Is Every Step* by Thich Nhat Hanh. I had no idea who this was at the time but I bought the book and added it to my pile for my upcoming trip to the Boundary Waters in Minnesota's wild and beautiful lake country.

In a cabin on Clearwater Lake, I read that book from cover to cover in one day. And so began my journey with Thich Nhat Hanh as one of my teachers, and my exploration of mindfulness and Buddhism. I quickly internalized the soft-spoken and kind voice of this wise Vietnamese monk. I read his words, *"Listen, listen. This wonderful sound brings me back to my true self."* I paused then, struck silent. I ran my fingertips over the impression of ink on the page in front of me.

"Listen." The words resonated through me, a vibration of knowing deep in my heart. They made me want to change my life. They made me want to wake up!

It wasn't long before my husband at the time and I left the bustling city of Chicago in search of nature and a quieter rural life. We found ourselves on Whidbey Island in the Salish Sea near Seattle, Washington. The move quickly opened up my long latent abilities to connect with trees and other "more than human" beings. In the first weeks in our lakeside rental, I met a white Pekin duck who was apparently abandoned to live out his days at Honeymoon Lake. I promptly named him Salvador Ducky — after Salvador Dali — and he became a dear companion during my transition to life in a new place far away from my family and friends. Sal and I developed a close bond that started with morning coffee and duck food and ended with an evening story time and a bed of hay.

When the lake froze over that winter, Sal moved into the garage, complete with an indoor swimming pool and a lovely hay and newspaper bed. He was my companion. With Sal, I felt like those parts of me that had been asleep were waking up. Here was a being that I could be totally myself with. When I talked to him, he would dance around in a circle and flap his wings, sharing his joy in our connection. He was not only a duck, he was a teacher — a spirit guide who had shown up to bring me back to who I am.

He kept me company for over a year, until one day he didn't show up as I pulled my car up after work. I grieved the loss and buried Sal in the spot where we took our morning coffee. I have a lot of gratitude to that sweet duck for helping me reawaken my joy for nature and reinitiate listening to wisdom in whatever form it takes.

Around the same time that I was having adventures with Sal, I visited Port Townsend, a quaint Victorian town just a ferry ride away. I was in the bookstore, of course, when another book seemed to leap from the shelf and land on the floor at my feet. I now knew this was a way that Spirit gets my attention, so I quickly scooped up the book to receive the message. It was *The Artist's Way* by Julia Cameron. I thought it looked interesting and I knew that I was meant to buy it without even knowing what it was about at the moment.

I returned home that day to find an ad in the local newspaper looking for participants to start an Artist's Way group. I picked up the phone and signed up. We met weekly throughout the 8-week process and it was life-changing. I witnessed my own creativity and excitement for expressing myself through writing and collage reemerge. The group met weekly for three years after that initial series of meetings. One of the women in the group was involved in shamanism and introduced me to a journey group where they met to travel to other worlds for guidance supported by the beat of the drum. I remember the first day I laid down on my blanket and closed my eyes and listened to the constant, steady beat thrumming through me. Colors flashed behind my closed eyes and I heard sounds that seemed vaguely familiar. An animal companion, the Puma, joined me on my journeys and I felt like I had come home.

I found another teacher to work with who introduced me to the Foundation for Shamanic Studies and their workshops and training. My Puma began to help me slow down the sounds in my head and turn the knob on my inner radio to a frequency where I could discern the voices of my inner guides. One of them was, of course, my inner zen teacher Thich Nhat Hanh, but I was also able to see that there were teachers and guides of other cultures and even my own ancestors, including my grandmother. And Sal. They helped me remember what I already knew, that this was available to me through my own inner wisdom. I felt as if these were the guides who had been waiting since childhood to communicate with me and support me in my doing my life's work.

As soon as I trusted my own inner guidance, my authentic work and my authentic voice began to emerge. I connected with past lives in hypnotherapy and guided imagery and began to understand my grandmother's fear, which arose because of the long lineage of healers and witches who were persecuted for their intuitive and healing gifts. I am sure she channeled her own abilities into massage and cooking — both beautiful and acceptable ways of healing — because she was afraid of her own power. I still recall a day when I was a small child in the middle of a big Midwest thunderstorm and lightning struck the air conditioner outside my grandmother's window sending a streak of lightning across the carpeted floor ending at my grandmother's feet. As I watched it burn a line in the carpet, I noticed that her eyes were closed. In the moment, I felt like she was in a trance and she knew that the lightning was coming. She had been struck by lightning earlier in her life and as I looked up at her, I thought, wow, even lightning respects my grandmother!

I now understand this sacred power in a new way through the practices that were opening up my own powerful feminine path for me. I now know that I too, am an intuitive, healer, witch, and a mystic. Seeing these words here on the page, living and breathing their power, startles me even now. I hesitate to use the words because of the way they were viewed negatively in my past, yet I know they are true. I wonder why I am afraid of reclaiming this title and the power behind it, and yet I know I must. I am a healer and at the core of my gifts is a deep connection to nature and to my inner guidance. I am a witch and a mystic. And, I allow my inner wisdom to shine forth in everything I do.

My great capacity for my work comes from my willingness to step out of my own way and allow the work to flow through me. When Spirit and my inner guides lead the way, the work has a magic and a capacity to heal that is beyond what my human mind and body could create.

I am no longer a pleaser and a good girl. I refuse to continue to deny my authentic powerful self. I am out of hiding. If I ruffle feathers, then I give gratitude to Sal the duck for teaching me that it is the only way to be. I am no longer hiding in my blanket forts; I am stepping into my gifts more fully. I am inspired as I walk the spiral of wonder, moving ever closer to my authentic path as a mystic.

Always attuned to my wild and creative imagination, I had a dream where I was learning from an eccentric, colorfully dressed, free-spirited teacher named Roxie. She reminds me to be who I am. She has inspired me to pull all the green witchcraft, magic, and nature books off the bookshelves and bring them into my witchy blanket fort. Yes, I still make forts, strong and inviting and full of magic!

Together with my other guides, I am tuning in to my body and soul as I move through my day. I am learning to say no to what no longer resonates with me. I am trusting my capacity to manifest in a new way. I am saying yes to the writer, the creative, the healer, the mystic, and all the magically powerful parts of me.

How about you? Do you have an inner Roxie or other inner wisdom teacher who calls you to live your most authentic life? Can you trust in your wild and powerful expression of yourself and embrace your magic? Is it time to open your heart and your mind to yourself, say 'yes' to your gifts and let them shine? I believe it is. You are needed in this world. I hope you will join me on the journey. Trust and follow — your inner spirit knows the way.

IGNITE ACTION STEPS

It is my wish that you feel ready to truly listen to the wisdom of your inner spirit and bring your gifts into the world. The world needs your inner spirit to shine!

- Reflect on your childhood. Were you ever told that what you believed, saw, or heard was just your imagination? Did you ever hear that you were too much or too sensitive? How did that feel? How do you feel about it now? Write about this in your journal or share your answers with a trusted friend.

- Grab your journal, some colorful pens, and make a list of all the things you long to do, all the things you dream of doing, and all the ways you want to reveal your true magical self to the world. What step can you take right now toward making some of these dreams happen?

- Use your wild imagination to tell the story of your life with abundant embellishment. Create new plot twists and delicious adventures. Then ask yourself which parts of this story you want to make a reality. Allow yourself to dream and have fun with this one!

Always remember to listen deeply to the whisperings of your soul. Trust in magic in whatever forms it takes, be it a white duck or mystical dream figure. Follow where it takes you and let your Inner Spirit show the way.

Charlene Ray – United States of America
Grief Guide, Interfaith Minister, Heart-Centered Counselor,
Spiritual Teacher
www.charleneray.com

SAMUEL FISHMAN

*"Find yourself and savor it; your self-knowledge will
only deepen and enrich your life experience."*

**I encourage you to connect to the Source so that you hear It loud and
clear. This, along with bringing in more color, awe, wonder, and fulfillment through developing your sixth sense (your intuition) will help you
find the adventure of your life. Then you can get on board and begin to
be transformed in such a way as to discover and live your life purpose.**

FINDING CONNECTION — FINDING THE ADVENTURE

Seeking the answers to whether there was God or whether parallel uni-
verses existed was stuff that came out in conversations with my friends during
my adolescent years. I grew up very curious, but I also questioned my value
because not enough people seemed to notice me and recognize who I was. It
was hard for me to see that I was a meaningful part of the world. Because of
this, I didn't really know where my place was on this planet, and I felt I was
in my own sphere separated from almost everyone else.

I remember feeling shut out of the life I wanted — having friends who
could recognize who I was beneath the surface, friends that truly supported
who I was. I couldn't feel joy anymore. I was too timid to express myself. I
wasn't living in my power. I recall this one experience in high school when I
really wanted to talk to my favorite teacher after school, but because there were
other students also casually talking with her, my social anxiety kicked in and

I backed out day after day after day, every time reconsidering and every time stepping short of my ideal. Most of the fun in my life came from playing video games. I played for hours during weekdays and all throughout my weekends, prioritizing that over social relationships. I didn't take the time to develop my love for other people or for life. I was mean and cruel to those I cared about because my life was stuck in being the best video game player and just getting by in all the other areas of my life. I didn't think life had meaning; I thought it was just there and I was experiencing it. Because I was just experiencing it, I had no awareness of my intuition, the beauty of the world around me, or a sense that my life could be an adventure. But, that was about to change.

When I entered college, I began getting out a lot more, mostly because the new environment invited me to explore it. That exploration suddenly replaced my video-gaming life, and that was a *game changer*. One day, I left my dorm room and walked out toward the looped road next to my building. As I was getting close to the road, intuitive information began filling my mind. As a car passed by, the color of the car *meant* something. I *knew* it was a message being delivered for me specifically to pick up on. The same was true for the next and the third car that came down the road. The fact that there were three cars was significant, like the universe was organized by some intelligence through these comparisons and groupings, and not just coming together due to the laws of physics. That experience fundamentally changed my perspective on reality and what life is. It brought me from a lack of awareness of the universe that I was living in to feeling intertwined with a universe that is intelligently designed and can send me clues and messages. I was full of wonder and felt like I had been brought to a whole new level of existence.

Around the same time, I was learning to make important changes in my life. I realized that I felt most connected with other people when we were in a more authentic space in one-on-one situations. This new understanding led me to leave the friend group that I had been a part of, because there were less opportunities to really connect with any of them. I had started to see myself as having value and not just as a third wheel. I began showing up when I was with other people, so I could finally see who I really was. This new style of socializing allowed me to step into my power and changed my life.

The new relationship that I had with the world paved the way for me to become aware of and to live in this personal power. There I began to stand up for myself and others, in my authenticity, and slowly began to live my truth. A crucial early step in this transformation was becoming connected to my intuition. This was like a breath of fresh air where I became more intellectually and philosophically curious about what was in the world and how I could interact with it. I practiced being still and receptive, and began to get images in my head that were powerful and made me curious as to what they meant. Some were clues to my romantic life down the road and the sort of people I would be connecting with, and others were more about myself and potential paths I could take to fulfill my life mission. I began getting this 'guidance' more and more often, and it simply delighted me, filling me with warmth and showing me more cryptic images, such as far-off worlds where there were floating cube islands in the middle of nowhere, or more earthly ones such as seeing a lake with a potential future partner of mine sitting in a canoe. After practicing receiving information, I learned that I could be further receptive by holding space for more information to come through, and that I would receive an intuitive answer to the image's meaning. I felt this was helping me evolve.

Having enough stillness was crucial to being able to receive guidance. Going outside on adventures, exploring nature, and taking walks around my college campus slowed me down enough internally so that I could be calm and connected to receive guidance when I tried to tune in to it. In this way, I built up my connection to Life and to my intuition. Most of my adolescence, I had been online playing video games, and since I was constantly doing that, the stillness and space were resources that I just didn't have.

As I awakened to my intuition, I soon began to realize by instinct that sometimes I was working with my intuition and sometimes I was receiving guidance from the Source. I began to *recognize* this presence giving me information and it gave off a specific signature which I memorized and looked out for because I knew it was the Source. I *knew* that the Source was love, and that it was supporting me fiercely. It was supportive and kind, and grew with me over the years to become hilarious, playful, and witty. It began to make my life extraordinary.

There were many days when I struggled to contact the Creator. The contact was on and off, and sometimes not being able to connect when I wanted to was frustrating. But, one day, as I was leaving my college dorm, I could feel the trees outside resonating with this frequency of ecstasy. I suddenly felt a fantastic energy emanating from inside me, heightening my emotional state and bringing me into intense bliss. This lasted while I was near the trees but faded as I walked further away. I thought this would only be an experience I had once, but it occurred many times over the following two weeks. I soon found myself looking forward to this experience and being captivated by it.

I was mystified and surprised to have such strong spiritual and emotional *experiences* repeatedly when I had never *experienced* anything like this in my life. I made it a mission to keep getting out into nature, even after that particular experience ended. I would walk around the forest behind my school and practice over and over again, trying to let my intuition lead me in one direction or another. I mentally held space in front of myself, giving my intuition the opportunity to say something. I was always looking for a sign, such as some subtle change in the air in front of me or even hearing from a voice to go to the left or right that would point me in the direction I thought I was meant to go.

Soon after this I became depressed. I had had moving experiences, showing me that the world was intelligent and could interact with me, bringing me to new heights of emotion. Even so, I had become unbalanced, taking the spiritual too seriously and getting sucked into self-centeredness where I thought my world trumped the world of others. I became disconnected and lost my way, acting out instead of honoring the gift of playing in the self-discovery that accompanies self-acceptance. At that time I had lost the importance of the meaning of my life, because I thought the point was brazen freedom. I would soon discover something deeper on a trip to Antigua with my family one winter break before my senior year of college.

In Antigua, I was surrounded by the beauty of the teal-colored ocean, the tall swaying coconut trees, and the warmth of the people who greeted us at our fancy hotel. I was happy when I first arrived there, though it was still like I was missing something crucial to my fulfillment. Over the course of the week-long trip, I opened up more to my family and started talking to them about personal issues and emotional topics than I hadn't talked about in the years leading up to Antigua. Then, during one dinner, we all sat down to eat together and I felt this connective energy coming from my core. It hit me then: where there was a void before, this seed of connection provided meaning. What was taught to me through that moment was that connection provides meaning to life and what is truly valuable in the world is always tied back to connection. This truth would guide me in the years ahead.

I went back to college for my final semester and I finally began to grow out of being too timid to stand up for myself. I began transforming into the person I was brought into the world to be, embracing my social influencing power to the fullest. By the time I was leaving college, I had made substantial progress in finding my voice and in expressing myself sincerely.

I had begun to consider my life as an adventure. I felt a gentle encouragement to play and have fun, to seek new knowledge, to see the beauty hidden all around me. Play isn't just for the young, it's for all people regardless of age, and it helps us to be ourselves, to enjoy our experiences more, to be avid adventurers, and to uplift other people. I looked up one day at the subway stop on my corner and saw a design that had always been there but had somehow eluded me, and this filled me with delight. Most of my life I had avoided small details, which is why this experience was meaningful to me. I was walking through the park, and my gaze drifted off a little into the distance, and I realized there was a beautiful blue bird sitting on a branch. Another day, I returned to the park to discover another blue bird sitting on another branch proving to me that all things are connected and part of the adventure.

By learning how to be on the adventure of my life, my days were getting more and more fun. Furthermore, they brought me back to the joy that was ever so present in my childhood.

Then, again, I got lost on my life adventure; I got so depressed about what I would do in life, and scared that I wouldn't find something for me, that at one point I even gave up on having a good future. I jumped from considering being a spiritual counselor to full-time writer to something in HR, to social worker, to nutritionist. Giving up was the least helpful thing I could have done but I did at several points.

I was missing in my evaluation, in giving up, my connection to knowing that I could make my way through tough challenges. To move forward, I had to learn that a better life is always possible as long as I remain open to there being a way forward. Thinking this way was also the only way to prevent myself from continuing to give up. I saw that what is essential to living a better life is getting into my personal rhythm: the way of being that is a reflection of who I really am and practicing flowing from one experience to another in ways that are connected and are important to me. I started comparing things that stood out to me earlier in the day to things that happened to me later to see the flow from the first thing to the next. I saw similarities, developed clearer thinking, and found direction in how to connect with other beings: people, animals, and even plants; to talk to them on the soul level and to find out who those beings truly are. I found connections everywhere. I then became brave enough, through hosting a podcast, to share these experiences with others, and to reveal what life could be like when we all allow ourselves to explore our outer and inner worlds, thus transforming to the point that we're embodying our expression in more creative ways, leading us to feel expansive and free.

I saw that while trying to connect to others I was having trouble staying confident and being my best myself. Eventually I discovered 'flow state': effortlessly writing, speaking, or doing other activities in a state of being that's right for that individual, that fits them perfectly and helps them express themselves. This helped me to connect with others, but it took me what I could only describe as training to consistently enter states of flow. I was the leader of a group of Libertarians called YAL, or Young Americans for Liberty, at my college. Even though I wasn't a Libertarian, I grew passionate about their ideas to value the individual and what benefits them. In that environment, I learned to organize my thoughts and I received a lot of feedback as to which parts of my thinking were solid and which parts were flawed and making it harder to connect. I also learned to respect and open myself up and hold space for other people's thoughts and opinions.

YAL was an adventure in itself, and the way it transformed my thinking opened up my world to going on adventures in general. My adventures kept me interested and engaged with life and educated me about the crucial stuff I was most missing if I wanted to be in and with my essence. I missed seeing value in myself and in other people, and without seeing the value in something, you can't connect to it. Not being able to really see and connect to myself or other people shut me down for many years. I think people not truly valuing or seeing each other is an epidemic. When you begin to really see others, you begin to also see life come alive before your eyes. Things that are personally meaningful start to pop up everywhere for you, even in seemingly ordinary things. It took me three years of striving for my best self every day before I really began to see myself as an essential part of the world, to see others in the same way, and to learn what connection really means to me.

I want you to see how strong you really are through connecting to yourself. I want you to come alive in your life and to be inspired by people and by the world around you. I want you to stand up for who you really are. This all begins to come together when you connect to your life, the world, the Source, and to those around you, and by doing so, your possibilities will be greater than you can possibly even think of.

Strengthen your Source Connection, your connection to Life. The stronger your Source Connection, the better your quality of life, the kinder and more authentic you are, and the more love you'll have in your life. Strengthen it through discovering more of who you really are, through learning to accept other people as they really are, through overcoming life adversity, through engaging with healthy hobbies. A word of caution: you can lose your Source Connection; it's a love relationship with Life itself which is sacred and needs to be supported with strength and connection.

IGNITE ACTION STEPS

At least once a week take a walk and observe the small details of things around you, from the name of a store in your vicinity that you hadn't noticed, to a piece of street art in your neighborhood, to the finer details of nature, such as the leaves on trees and the bugs and birds around you if you live near a park or have a backyard.

Start a practice of asking questions to the Source, Life, God, the Universe, a Higher Power, however you best understand it, if you don't already do this. Develop your curiosity further; practice asking creative questions and holding space to receive answers. This will strengthen your Source Connection and improve your standard of living. Ask questions to solve problems; you might ask how you can resolve a conflict in a relationship. Ask what your Mission is in this life, how you can contribute to the lives of your loved ones and even make a bigger impact on humanity to leave behind a stronger, more compassionate world (yes, you can have a strong influence in this).

Moreso, ask questions to learn more about how the world works. Be bold; ask why the universe was created. Almost nothing is off-limits (just what you can't think of or receive communications from your intuition or the Source about).

Keep in mind it may at first take a few days or longer to receive answers, but with practice and time the information can come to you instantaneously.

Give yourself a personally significant amount of time for stillness. I found that when I took some nights off from watching TV and replaced it with searching my apartment for things that I haven't paid attention to in years, my whole life began to pulsate with more energy and life.

All of these things will keep you in a flow and will guide you toward your highest purpose.

Samuel Fishman – United States of America
Philosopher of Life
https://fishlabs.myfreesites.net/about

TAMMY MCCANN

"Miracles appear when we invite them; make space and allow them to land."

My intention for you as you read this story is to assure you that if you ever felt different, that you didn't belong, or that you are not accepted as you are, it's because you are being prepared for the unique impact you will make in the world. Be open to listening to your Inner Spirit and have the courage to take action and follow it when you hear its message. When you *trust* in following your Inner Spirit, it will gently guide you to make the best choices — for you and for those whose lives you are here to enrich.

TAKING THE QUANTUM PATHWAY

I was racing against time, always behind schedule and constantly playing catch up, but I would discover that this day would teach me something immensely important. I was a mature student in the final year of a Conversion degree in Psychology having quit my corporate job in London a few years earlier. The assignments were coming in thick and fast and I hated that I was struggling to get them done on time. After a half day of lectures and a seminar, I was rushing to my children's daycare, mentally planning my research project for my end-of-year dissertation. As my train came to a screeching halt, I sprinted up the steep hill to the nursery conveniently located 10 minutes en route to my home. Oh boy, another late pickup and £10 added to my bill, but I was overcome with love as I kissed the cherubic faces of my one-year-old twin girls. They were full of laughter and squeals, so happy to see me after another half day at the nursery.

It was an exerting workout forcing their double pushchair up the rest of the steep hill, but I refocused on planning the rest of the day. I calculated that I had just over a couple of hours to myself once I put my twins down for their afternoon nap and before I had to go and pick up their older sister from school. As usual, I was determined to dedicate this time to my studies, but once I reached home and put my twins to sleep, the brain fog crept in. The denseness of fatigue pushed down on my shoulders, making every step toward my office feel heavy, but I kept enduring, knowing all the work that was in front of me. My head was propelling me in the direction of my schoolwork, but my body was resisting. I collapsed into my chair, unaware that my whole life was about to change.

My life has always felt unconventional, unusual even. I was born in a hospital in Seoul, South Korea, a full three months premature and according to doctors, lucky to have survived. My mother had been engaged to a Mexican helicopter pilot but after she accidentally fell pregnant, he felt fatherhood was too much of a responsibility and left her before I was born. When I was two, my mother fell head-over-heels in love with a British soldier positioned in Seoul for six months, and after a whirlwind romance they got married back in England while I stayed with family in Seoul. A few months later, I joined them. My relationship with my new dad was, for many years, a turbulent one. But as a young adult I began to feel and appreciate the gift of resilience I had consequently built up.

When I was five years old, my dad transferred to the United Nations and was posted in Nicosia, Cyprus, where I have many fond memories of camping in the cool Troodos mountains on the weekends. Two years later, we lived in Jerusalem, near the old city, another amazing place, a melting pot of significant religious history — Islam, Judaism, and Christianity. I understood, even as a child, that I was fortunate to have experienced such a rich blend of spiritual beliefs.

After the nomadic earlier years, I moved back to England at the age of nine, to a small town in northern England where my family was one of only two foreign and mixed race families. I started to feel 'different' from everyone else. My mum, a Buddhist, had often felt the presence of Spirit, and happily shared her stories about her encounters. As a teenager, I was embarrassed by this, especially when she felt it was her duty to teach me to set prayer intentions, light candles, to give thanks, and speak to our ancestors and spirit guides. I shunned it for fear of being rejected by my small pool of friends. However, like my mum, I did have intuitive nudges, and a strong sense of what would be; the clairsentient gift runs in her family bloodline. Ultimately, my teenage self-consciousness and desire to fit in made me reject this metaphysical aspect of our heritage, and instead, I turned to evidence-based thinking. Eventually, I would pour my energy into learning about the sciences.

I loved school, got good grades, strived to be the best, and developed high standards. It formed my identity away from home. I was competitive and consistently pushed myself to be an overachiever. Even while pursuing my goals, I was aware of the gentle nudges my intuition kept giving me and it was my inner spirit that guided me to continue on the winning path.

I graduated with a Biochemistry degree with honors, wanting to focus on Health and Well-being. Following my intuitive nudges, some chance discussions with my course tutor led to me being offered sponsorship for a Master of Science program. Consequently, I landed my first graduate position in a prestigious pharmaceutical consultancy, running market research projects with international leading-edge companies. Life was exhilarating, fast-paced, and I was energized to the fullest.

I moved to London in 2000 (with my partner, who later became my husband) and shifted from pharma-based programs to the forefront of technological advancement of the broadband industry. Although it was an exciting time, several years on, it dawned on me it was not what I really wanted to do.

I felt guided to do something more impactful, to help people directly, and decided to become a Clinical Psychologist. On my thirtieth birthday, I handed in my notice and sent the electronic application to London Metropolitan University for a Conversion Degree in Psychology. Synchronistically, the following day the Dean of the Psychology department called me to offer me a place. A new path was forged.

I was happy to embark on the next era of my life: to start a family and study part-time while continuing to work in my old consultancy. I thought I could simply do it all. My friends envied my seemingly 'perfect' life. My then husband found his niche with overseas clients, allowing us the luxuries of what many would deem an idyllic lifestyle: a big beautiful house, wonderful holidays, a nanny to help me with my three toddlers, allowing me precious time to pursue shifting my career to clinical psychology. This is what I thought I wanted my life to look like. But it was a partially distorted view because despite all of this, I wasn't happy or satisfied.

Five years later, the cracks of trying to do it all surfaced. I was struggling. Until then, I thought my resilience would keep me upright, and I accepted that I was going to have to do this mostly on my own. My family and friends were not aware of the growing tensions in my marriage, the arguments and many tears due to my husband's absence, the emotional pressures, and the constant grind that had become my life. I sensed I was physically and emotionally exhausted, and felt a deep unhappiness which several years earlier would have been so alien to the vibrant, life-loving, high-energy me. Somehow, I managed to keep my disposition artificially positive so I didn't have to face the alternative, admitting that I wasn't being my genuine self. Somewhere along the line, I stopped listening to my nudges and I became an overachiever at leading a double life.

What I hadn't realized until too late was that bit by bit I was crumbling and eroding away inside. Despite having provisionally been accepted into a Doctorate program in Counseling Psychology, I was unsure of whether I was on the right path, whether I was doing the right thing. But not only that, whether I was in the right relationship, if I even wanted this life. I felt so torn, guilty in the knowing that most people can only aspire to have what I had. But I felt trapped and was slowly suffocating. This wasn't me.

That fateful afternoon, with the twins sleeping in the adjacent room, I slumped in my office chair and knew something wasn't right. The swooshing pressure of blood behind my ears pounded against my ear drums. I was barely able to move. Reaching out, I clung to the edge of my desk, desperately struggling to take in air from my sharp, shallow breaths. I slowly buckled to my knees, my heart pounding fast against my rib cage, my lips tingling with the lack of oxygen. In my mind I was screaming, "What is happening to me?"

Seconds stretched into several fear-drenching minutes and eventually I screamed in my head, "THIS IS NOT ME, THIS IS NOT MY LIFE… I CHOOSE TO BE ME… I OWN MY LIFE AND WHAT I'M HERE FOR… SHOW ME WHAT I'M NOT YET SEEING!!"

In that flash of a moment, a tsunami surge of energy cascaded through me from the base of my spine up through my body, rising and bursting open into my heart area. I felt exposed yet expanded with the immense high frequency power surge radiating from my chest. It rose further, sticking in my throat, until a cry released through my lungs… I barely noticed the denseness of my body like lead sinking into the carpet.

The flood of cosmic-like power continued to rise into my head and exploded into a vibrant display of color behind my eyes. I was catapulted into a fast-moving tunnel that expelled me into a vastness of what seemed like outer space, with the bright stars not above, but instead around me. I was seeing the solar system, the galaxies, the fullness of the Universe.

What happened next was as if a dark filtered lens had been taken off my internal vision. I started to sense more lightness yet fullness with a visceral wisdom. Without warning, I saw a space in time before and around my birth followed by my childhood events. There was simply a knowing that everything happened for a reason. Every aspect of my colorful life fitted a tapestry of bright 3D visuals of my past, a great holographic masterpiece of images that included all the different experiences of my life and of others' that had crossed mine. Time now stood still. With each vision I was able to comprehend with crystal clarity the reason for each occurrence, how everything was playing out to perfection, for me to witness right now. My abandonment from my biological father and how my life events fitted in place thereafter. *Everything had happened FOR me.*

Then, in a flash the brilliant energy surge traveled through the top of my head and a celestial bright white, yet warm light surrounded me. I felt beauty, peace, bliss, and such brilliant pure love…. everything was just *love*, I *was* this love. Never had I felt such an ecstatic feeling of love and simply *being*. It felt so familiar as if I had been basking in this state of blissful love for eons. I knew this was a divine moment… it was *oneness*.

After that event, I realized it was no longer about trying to fit myself in the current version of my life; it was about totally recreating my life to match the true me, from my core being. I knew I needed to create a different picture; form a brand new puzzle that I fitted into and became an integral part of.

I was not religious, but I held onto the 'knowing' of true life, love, compassion, forgiveness, gratitude, and appreciation. I could see the 'alternative' Eastern philosophy teachings of my Buddhist mum were indeed a precious way of being. The strange nudges I felt, the intuitions which I recognized in my mum, funny feelings, the downloaded 'knowings' and dreams, I could now sense was the call of my own connection with something much greater than myself. My feelings of separation gave way to accept that we are all inherently connected. More and more realizations were uncovered as if I was racing through a manual, speed-reading and absorbing all the wisdoms of the Universe woven into each page.

The implications of letting go of my old life and relationship were painful; to many family and friends it seemed downright foolish, inconsiderate, and illogical. I had to release those friends who didn't understand the real me, who in themselves were looking at my outside world and were still aspiring to have the same. I was ready to give up the trappings of the materialistic world and follow my heart, even if it meant letting go of my luxurious life, having to co-parent my children and start all over again.

During my divorce and transition, I let go of the Counseling Psychology doctorate offer and devoted my time to learning even more about the esoteric field. I studied spirituality, consciousness, and the science of quantum physics. I focused on how to marry these concepts, what I wanted to do, what it would mean for others, but more importantly how it related to my purpose in this life.

I trained in many different modalities, including clinical hypnotherapy, coaching, Neuro-linguistic Programming (NLP), theta healing, and reiki energy healing. I went on to set up a Quantum Transformation coaching business and began to attract clients who understood my message and what they would learn and receive from my interventions, training, and coaching. I started to get into *flow*, and as I began to help others focus on turning their struggles and worries into life transformations, I realized that this work was exactly what I was meant to do.

Allowing myself to be guided by my Inner Spirit and its constant whispers has meant that ten years on, I am now married to my soul mate, business partner, and fellow coach. Owning the real me has led to an 'east meets west' philosophy to our programs. We teach synchronicities and miracles and help clients to see them, believe them, and know that they happen. We have trained hundreds of clients through our Quantum programs for business, relationships, wealth and health transformations, but above all else, *self-transformation* which creates a quantum shift in alignment with purpose.

When we dovetail quantum physics with consciousness and energy vibration work, miracles happen, and this changes lives. Our ego, programmed from childhood, and our intuition will always exist together. It is our responsibility to follow our intuition even when, or especially when our ego doesn't want us to.

But here's what I know to be true: Always trust in your intuition. It may seem counterintuitive to what your logical or conscious mind will tell you, but it will guide you to align to your purpose. Following my intuition has enabled me to have an impact that ripples out into the world. Trust your inner voice and watch your own ripple impact the world also.

IGNITE ACTION STEPS

You are so powerful that you have the ability to change the world. Ask yourself, who would you choose to become, what would you love to experience, what would your life look like if you could live your life by design? Here are some steps that may help you to create quantum shifts in your life:

1. Notice your situation. Ask yourself how happy you are with your life right now. What you are experiencing will give you clues as to whether you are in alignment with purpose.

2. What changes do you intuitively know you need in your life but are reluctant to make or even consider? Write everything down and keep writing until you are finished. Simply hear your whispers, daydream, and envisage a new you; a new purpose in life; a new calling; a new pathway.

3. Notice what your ego (your inner child) is fearing — Listen to the objections, fears and doubts, write these down too. Send yourself love and let your ego know you are safe. Keep doing this until you no longer feel resistance.

4. Explore the new vision, be playful with it — Enjoy it in your mind's eye… give yourself space to dream and feel the new reality.

5. Have courage to take steps forward, one step at a time and notice what happens — things slot into place very quickly when you allow new experiences to FLOW.

Allow these steps to encourage you to follow your TRUE path to discovering your TRUE self and align to your TRUE purpose.

Tammy McCann – England
Quantum Transformation Coach
tammy-mccann.com

PAULA LAWRENCE

"If I can do it, you can do it!"

My wish for you from reading my story is to gain an understanding of the consciousness of the innate guidance system within you to follow, to surrender, and to trust. At those times when you feel lost, afraid, angry, or emotionally frozen, there are specific people who magically appear to educate you along the way into knowing you are not alone. Whatever situation you are in, listen to your heart, trust, and keep going.

MY DANCE WITH THE DIVINE

If asked what is the story in my heart, this is what I would share. My thoughts take me to what I am experiencing now in my life. I feel tremendous relief that my experiences have brought me to being surrounded by people who I resonate with. I appreciate people who demonstrate in their lives the realization of the current magnitude, importance, and urgency of changing the energy on Mother Earth. These people know the inner work of staying on course. Knowing the importance of meditating everyday, being vigilant of owning one's own crap, resolving it, and learning from it. And within their hearts is the intention to serve *from* the heart while being in a state of gratitude to receive this from others. These are the steps in my passionate dance where I am being and living responsibly in this way.

I know at this juncture of my life, I have clarity to take action toward focusing upon a new process to add to my inner work by being a light for others. I am learning to be generous in sharing my life experiences. I am awakening into an expression of this through being a leader, communicator, and teacher. I am stepping into a verbal platform, into the spotlight, by encouraging people to trust their own process, to keep going no matter what, learning to open their hearts to feel the essence of love which unfolds and grows continuously, in what I call Dancing With The Divine. Although the clarity to take action is a strong feeling I have, it is the process that is my challenge to overcome. I am unsteady as I am reaching for the words that have meaning and expressing the voice that I want others to hear, bringing an atmosphere of creative charge and igniting their own divine dance.

This way of feeling started when I was 4 years old. I ran away from home. My grandmother was visiting and my mother had left the house on an errand, and 4-year-old me had the most distinct thought: *I can run away because Grandma can't catch up to me.* Just that quick, I was out the door. I went around the corner and continued down past several houses.

From the doorway, Grandma called, "Paula, Paula, come back! I have a lollipop!" but I ignored her. I just wanted to keep going.

A few houses down from mine, I came out of our quiet neighborhood and into a busier area. The roads turned from one lane to two lanes; cars whizzed by rapidly. The sidewalk ended there on the edge of downtown and I didn't feel safe crossing the street.

I thought to myself, "Okay, *now* what do I do?"

My desire to run away came about during a frightful incident that I overheard while I was upstairs playing.

"You're hurting me, you're hurting me!" screamed my mother to my father between the loud argumentative words they both yelled. I was frozen in fear, not knowing what to do as I had never experienced that before. But, somehow I knew I had to save my mother. That one thought was the strongest thing in my mind as I slowly went down the flight of wooden stairs. Walking cautiously toward them, I could see my father's tight grip around my mother's arms.

"You let mommy go!", I shrieked at him as I tilted my head way back to look up at his six foot tall presence, causing him to drop his grip.

My father released his painful grip on my mother's arm. Watching him, anger flooded in me. I was filled with rage. It was then that I became aware of the dialogue that was stirring in my mind. I began to hear more than others, being tuned into an alternate frequency. I felt a connection with the Universe, and stated to myself and the other presence I felt was with me, "This is a mistake. I don't belong on this planet. You need to take me back."

But the Universe told me no! It told me that I needed to stay where I was. I remember thinking and feeling abandoned and left behind. I knew it was not only my parents that were different; I was different too. I also felt that many people on the planet were not going to relate to me and it was going to be a challenge to blend in. I knew it would take a long time to feel at home and that I belonged. I acquiesced that I was going to be stuck in this situation for my entire life, and it left me feeling empty.

I wanted to leave behind the very disappointing and restrictive situation I found myself in with my parents and get out into the world, whatever that meant to a little person of 4 with one foot in this world and the other foot definitely in another. Having the knowing of how to connect my physical being with my spiritual being brought forth the vibration of love, and became the recipe for connecting me with the interstellar communities. I knew this unique link would be the golden thread of Divine awareness to carry me through my life.

That singular moment, being emotionally upset by my parents' actions, pushed me to make a clear decision. That moment would go on to define my journey through this world. It became clearly evident of all that was *not me* and what *was* me — that sense that I was somehow different from these people who were my parents, and how restrictive it was to be in this house with them and then endure a lifelong bumpy ride. I was desperate for understanding, for a kindred spirit who would share my sense of how the world was meant to be, of how our spirits are meant to live out this divine connection between souls.

That was the first step of my dance and it would be my innate drive that would carry me throughout my life toward clarity.

I began being guided telepathically at a young age, and it continues even now. I could say my life has been a journey of experiential learning while being guided from another dimension. This was a confusing, scary way to my daily life as no one I knew had any conversations remotely close to what I was hearing and experiencing. Not at home, not with friends, not in school. I did gain extreme comfort being in the woods, in water, and around animals, especially horses because I could feel their nurturing energies. Ahhhhhh, breathing in the exquisite musky smells of the woods, hearing the wind orchestrating a chorus with the trees, or swimming in the ocean feeling the deliciousness of it against my body! I could feel the divine connection of life when I was in nature. Being with others sharing these exhilarating moments in time gave me a sense of pleasure and direction for my life. This comfort was a place of peace, harmony, and magic for my growth, and most importantly the understanding of my connection with all.

Although I was extremely young when I became aware of my gift, my mission was clear. I was to be a steward of our planet and an ambassador between us and the many interstellar beings. Throughout my life my heartfelt connections, my golden thread of awareness, has been brought to my consciousness by the people whose lives have crossed with mine. The trust I felt in this conviction inspired me to keep going.

As I reflect upon my struggles as a child into adulthood, I kept following my path when even fleeting thoughts of, "Why do I want to continue?" crossed my mind. This is when extraordinary teachers would show up in my life out of nowhere.

The first was in my 30s. To my delight I received an invitation from a dear friend to join her and her mother for a celebration at an ashram in upstate New York. I always loved sharing adventures with my artsy friend who would inspire me with her creativity, and I didn't want to miss the chance to spend time with the added pleasure of her witty mother. I did not have prior understanding of what I would be experiencing and was excited at the thought of being immersed in a sacred space which would also include receiving shaktipat, the energy of spiritual awakening by an enlightened being.

There I was, sitting upon a round pillow in a large room filled with the beautiful sound of everyone chanting as row by row we approached the spiritual teacher, Baba. I was very excited to be in a position that would allow me to make direct eye contact, or so I thought. As I knelt down in childlike excitement to look up at him, I was gently touched by his peacock feather wand on my eyes and on the top of my head. I had a knowing of the importance of that ceremony but sadly I didn't experience the freeing of kundalini energy within my body that I was supposed to have and was possible after this initiation. It wasn't until years later in life that I realized the importance of that moment. I had no idea that my energy was lying dormant within me until another teacher came into my life.

It was many years later, in my 60s, that this teacher arrived. On the beautiful shores of Garda Lake, Italy, I had the opportunity to attend a 5-day meditation workshop which would be monitored by a team of scientists. I would learn about quantum physics, how to be in a sustained meditative state while being euphorically elated with live music created by an award-winning composer.

My intention for this workshop was to serve, trust the process, and help create a ripple effect of elevated frequencies for the highest good to the best of my ability. While attending the workshop, an exhilarating energy awoke as I was in the precise setting for my intention to surrender to the unknown and receive it. And so it came, starting ever so slowly and increasing with a strong steady tremendous force.

It was like a whirling dervish spinning through my surrendered body. My entire being was rocking so hard, my chair traveled across the floor. My limbs flew about and my head bobbed back and forth so fast my hair tie flew through the air! I was hot and sweaty and it felt really good. I felt like my energetic body was being realigned. I suppose I would have to say by experiencing this, everything in my life took on a further direction of awareness, harmony, and creativity. My understanding of the meaning of love was like a fire that grew brighter, encouraging my spiritual journey and the manifestation of the passions of my heart.

Several other teachers graced my life and their guidance brought me an understanding and further trusting of my telepathic awareness and the power in the energies of song, dance, and drumming, along with understanding of the presence of other beings who are part of our interstellar community.

I was fortunate to gain great learning during an Indian summer in Vermont when I spent time caretaking a spiritual elder (though unbeknownst to me, she was guiding me in my spiritual walk). We developed a loving bond, so much so I didn't want to leave her when the time came as I knew I would not see her ever again. She was like an oasis, quenching my thirst for more. She was a person in my life that I could relate to and that in turn could relate to me. I loved her sense of humor, despite her failing health, and her sweet words of reassurance that I needed to continue my journey out west to learn and then return to teach what I had discovered. At the time I didn't know what she meant, but I later understood the importance of trusting direction without knowing the entire picture. She assured me that everything would be okay because she would be working with me from the other side. "What other side?" I asked her, not knowing it was another dimension she would be communicating with me from.

And so, west I went to the majestic mountains of Colorado. Unfortunately within two weeks I suffered a ski injury which only allowed me to carefully hobble around until my surgery date. (I also had a knowing that there is no such thing as accidents, that this was really a strategically designed inter-vention directed by the Divine, another step in my dance.) The wonderful part of my day was taken up by reading and during one of those trips to my favorite bookshop, I gimped in and stood in front of shelves of books enticing me to pick one out. I silently asked, "Which book do I need to read for my highest good?"

Well I can only say, chuckling, that the book I was to read appeared, and there I embarked on a journey of awareness in the power of ceremonial sound, dance, and the importance these vibrations are to the earth and beyond.

I was thrilled to find out the author and teacher of that book lived two hours from me in Bernalillo, New Mexico. I could experience his teachings at an event there. I wanted to participate so badly, but my knee was swollen. There was no way I could experience the commitment to participate in the many hours of singing, dancing, being in the sweat lodge, and being in a peace chamber. I had surgery scheduled for my knee. To my disappointment, the Universe was making it clear that this was a definite no-go.

I was confused. If I was to learn and couldn't have this experience, what was the point of the book that picked me? Hmmmm! I let it go, however I did wait for a response to my question and eventually it came to me in the mail. It was a brochure introducing me to a visionary, a professional singer and her husband who were associated with the teacher of sound frequencies. They had recently moved to Vallecito Lake, a beautiful place nestled by mountains and pine forests within 15 minutes of my home! It was a wonderful thing. I now had two new teachers to teach me more steps in my dance.

Through them, over a 22-year span of time, I experienced all of what I thought I had missed out on learning by not being able to go to Bernalillo. I had gained the 'presence' of these dear friends in my life. Our friendship evolved throughout the years and has been sprinkled with gatherings and sacred ceremonies, all divinely planned and orchestrated.

I have been so blessed to be a part of this growing community of loving individuals, dedicated and focused upon raising awareness that coincided with my knowing and awareness that ignited at the age of 4. They have helped me see all of us are here, in this time, joining together with all those living in other worlds and dimensions. And that we are harmoniously working together to create places of education to gather together, to nurture, to learn, and to flourish by promoting a home of success for the future and life of harmony for all on Earth and beyond.

I wish for this deep interconnectedness for all human beings and that we each trust in the flow of one's own dance to find one's purpose. I encourage you to surrender to that flow and never give up. Keep going. Be vigilant. The trust of your heart is the choreographer of the dance. Surround yourself with people you resonate with. Seek out and embrace individuals who know their importance just as strongly as you know yours. Those who do the inner work and the outer work of changing the planet's energies will help nurture the harmony in all of us for the better.

No matter what situation you're in, you have the resources to enrich your life and live your dreams. Find your dance, trust the choreographer, let the music of life resonate through you.

Ignite Action Steps

Surround yourself with people who inspire you.

Meditate every day, no matter what. It promotes an atmosphere of clarity, calm, direction, and possibilities. When we meditate, we change the chemistry of the brain and our old patterns.

Use the emotional freedom technique of tapping to move blocked energy and negative emotions every day.

Paula Lawrence – United States of America
Visionary
HarmoniousPaula@gmail.com

JOANNE P. IMAI

"Live life… on Purpose."

My hope is that your soul is *Ignited* into realizing that you are an incredible human being on an amazing adventure. May the words from my story give you the courage to live your life as your true nature intended you to be — walk out of the confusion and into the clarity of who you truly are. In doing so, let life be good to you.

THE AUTHENTICITY OF SELF

The back door to the hobby room was open and a bright ray of morning sunlight streamed through. My mother was working at her sewing machine and I was kneeling near the door on the rough carpeted floor. On the ground next to me, my five pet parakeets fluttered about their wire cage, chirping excitedly as we all enjoyed the warmth of the sun and the scent of fresh air.

"They're telling me that they want to go outside," I naively told my mother in Japanese.

Through the whir of the sewing machine's motor, I heard her respond in kind, "No. Don't let them out, they won't come back."

I squirmed. "They're promising that they will," I insisted.

"No," she responded, while not missing a stitch. My mother was focused on her work. She was listening but not paying attention.

My little brows furrowed as I pushed my face closer to the cage. Like a laser beam, I focused my full attention on my clever friends and I listened to their collective pleas and promises. "We'll come back," they chattered wildly. "We promise."

With full trust in my heart, the door to their freedom was opened.

The shadows moved in clockwise formation as morning turned into afternoon and afternoon turned into night. With hopeful eyes searching the skies, I waited patiently at the back door for hours. But my birds never returned. I was the vision of a crystal vase falling onto a concrete surface — my 3-year-old heart shattering into a million pieces. This was my first introduction to having my trust broken and witnessing abandonment.

A few months later, my grandmother came and lived with us for a year. It was a period of great joy and laughter for me. Time flew by like an untethered kite blowing in the wind and the year came to a quick end. Under the streaming tears of my protest, and without a solid explanation, my precious grandmother left. I was crushed and left unresolved; my heart shattered once more. It was an erosion to my spirit, a sacrifice to my innocent soul.

Like an observant cat living among a pack of dogs, I felt like a misfit that didn't belong on this planet. It wasn't because I was Japanese within a predominantly Caucasian America, but that the lens through which I saw the world was different from the people around me. I understood the language of animals. I knew when people would die. I even saw things that went bump in the night. One Christmas when I was 8 years old, my father commented on an absent holiday card from a family friend who had moved out of state. I matter-of-factly stated, "It's because he died." My parents scolded me for saying such a thing, and my brother ridiculed me. A few days later, news arrived of our family friend's passing. Not a word was said, and I was never vindicated.

I perceived life differently and for that, I was laughed at and got in trouble. To feel safe and limit the damage to the true nature of my spirit or, in more common words, my authentic self, I learned to quell my voice and walk within the straight and narrow lines of convention. I became self-conscious, insecure, and afraid. In effect, by shutting down, my gifts became my tools of self-destruction.

I was a misfit and quite alone, but during moments of stillness, my gaze would turn upward to the night sky. I would transfix upon the moon, stars, and planets as they sparkled like gems and jewels on a surface of velvet black. My heartbeat quickening inside my chest, my breath would slow to the calming scents of the night air. In these mesmerizing moments, I thought, "Maybe, just maybe my real people, family, and home exist somewhere out *there*, in the infinite darkness of space."

The innocent actions of a 3-year-old releasing her pet parakeets followed so closely by my grandmother's departure had culminated into trust and abandonment issues. Going forward in life, searching for connection and acceptance, I found myself in a series of bad relationships. This led to a domino effect of wild bouts of depression, self-image and confidence issues, and even bad hair.

Though smart and gifted in the creative and esoteric arts, I became a shy and unassuming individual as I retreated within a protective shell. I was insecure, often despondent, and somewhat of a nerd. I was the epitome of a self-imposed, unremarkable self-image; my true Being was buried deeply under the rubble of conflicting thoughts and emotions.

More times than not, in the solace of my bedroom, streams of tears would run down my cheeks. Sobs that eventually reduced to an overwhelming sadness; a lamenting grief that would literally make my heart ache. My authentic self required severe damage control in order to escape my prison of the status quo.

Years later, on a warm sunny day in late spring, I was 20 years old and leaving Monterey, a quaint ocean side town about 250 miles north of Los Angeles, California. I was heading back to my tiny guest house in LA. As a poor college student, my only affordable means of transportation was the Greyhound bus.

My seat was firm and the ride was bumpy. The cabin smelled of diesel fuel and that strange odor unique to public bathrooms. I found that sleeping on the long bus ride was a challenge. My best outcome was an induced state of relaxed consciousness as I listened to the mechanical purr of the bus's engine.

Four hours into the southbound trip, I heard the sound of crushed gravel as the bus rolled into a parking lot and came to an idled stop. Over the loud-speaker, I heard the driver announce a 15-minute rest stop in Santa Barbara. Hunkered in my scratchy seat with my head tilted down, I was in a state of suspended animation; staring blankly at the slightly worn fabric of the seat in front of me. "Rustle, rumble, murmur," is what I heard as the passengers walked past me in single file toward the exit. At some point, the exodus ceased and stillness fell over the bus. A thought occurred to me, "Maybe I should go to the bathroom."

With hands planted firmly on the arm rests, I leaned forward to launch myself out of the seat. I succeeded. But what I felt and what I saw were two completely different things. I was sitting upright in my seat, but my senses indicated that my physical body was reclined behind me. I was a transparent

Being released from it's physical body. I was pure awareness and consciousness, the alpha and the omega.

I moved my hands up and down on the arm rests. I felt the motion, but my flesh-colored hands remained motionless. I spun my transparent body around — my physical self was still resting against the seat. I looked across the aisle and saw a gray-haired woman knitting quietly. I was stunned. I was stupefied. I may have even stopped breathing. "Bang!" A flashing memory shot through my brain; a psychology lecture on 'Out-of-body Experiences.' Instantly, shock turned into, "Oh wow! This is so cool!"

I was ready to stand up and float around, transport, or do whatever an out-of-body *experiencer* could do. But as sudden as the feeling of excitement and exhilaration came over me, the feeling of fear overpowered me. I panicked. "What if I couldn't get back into my body?"

The desire to lead an in-body existence was more important to me. Turning myself around, I leaned back into my body but couldn't align my consciousness to my physical form. Fear peeked from the recessed corners of my Being. I felt like I was in a coma. I was inside myself but somehow still not aligned. The only thing I could think of was to try coughing, and so I did. Cough… cough... Deep breath… With a sudden snap, I was back together.

Up to the moment of my out-of-body experience, there existed a small belief that the sensory impressions I received were possibly the results of an overactive imagination. But what I had experienced on the bus that day was not a fantasy, nor a hallucination. I had absolutely crossed the veil into another dimension. Armed with that knowledge, I knew without a shadow of doubt that I existed not as a *body*, but as an *energy form*. A consciousness. A spirit that uses the body as a vehicle while experiencing life on Earth. I had always wondered if the soul was real and if, upon death, there was something that came after, or if we were just gone. Every cell of my body filled with euphoric joy at witnessing my own soul's existence and any fear of death was erased from my Being.

The last few hours of the bus ride were a blur of motion, colors, and thoughts. In a state of bliss, I arrived in Los Angeles. Despite walking the seedy downtown streets, what caught my attention was that everything was saturated in a shower of golden light, magical and breathtakingly beautiful. The world was enveloped in harmony and serenity — the quintessential breath of God.

One would imagine that by experiencing such an extraordinary epiphany, I had unearthed the urns of the Dead Sea Scrolls and discovered the profound meaning to life. Had I? The answer was a resounding, "NO!"

I had developed a faulty belief system through the years and my authentic self and a life of happiness and success were kept at arm's length. Unwelcomed viruses and faulty software had been programmed into the pristine computer that was me. I was living in the network and pathways to a perpetual dead end. "Behave. Follow the rules. Don't make waves." The pressure of society, peers, authority, and years of conditioning from outside factors had done their damage on me. I was afraid to speak. Afraid to express myself. I was more afraid of the people around me than the things that went bump in the night.

All that being said, my out-of-body experience opened my eyes to the mysteries of life like the parting of the Red Sea. The doorway to a plethora of conventional and unconventional knowledge was unlocked. Psychics and tarot cards. Metaphysical books and bookstores. Self-reflective work with channelers, healers, yogis, shamans, and therapists. I learned about energy healing, energy psychology, hypnotherapy, neuroplasticity, and so much more!

What a journey! What an education! What a self-indulgent woman! I enjoyed it all. In my journey to self-discovery, I took myself to a new level of who I am. I have become a better person. I have bettered my life. It is said that knowledge is power and for me, it rang true. On the road to rediscovering my true self, I learned to use the gift of my six senses *as tools* to direct me, like the rudder on a boat. No longer were they used for weapons of self-destruction. I translated them into the thoughts and feelings that would best guide me toward opportunities for transformation, expansion, and evolution. By doing this, I found my voice, my gifts, my courage, and my true self.

From my trainings, conversations, and instructions, I learned one consistent fact: to achieve success in our journey, staying true to the nature of your soul is key. Without this authenticity, the pathway to a happy life will be plagued with problems. Why? *Because it is someone else's vision that is being lived.*

The path of life does not go in a straight line. There are divides and obstacles, twists and turns. One particular path may lead to your destination or maybe to a dead end, but there are always multiple paths to choose from and multiple opportunities to be experienced. I learned that *being interested* wasn't enough; I had to *commit* to putting in the effort to look, learn, and grow.

Today, I am far from that shy and unassuming person of yesteryear; a testament to the transformation and evolution of one's life. In rediscovering my authentic self, I stand in the awe and joy of who I really am — I live life not *with* a purpose, but *on* purpose. It's through *my* particular journey that I experience the opportunities to rediscover the things that matter most to me. Through the successes and the mistakes, the confusion and the clarity. Even through pain, with arms outstretched, I welcome the joy of life.

I read a draft of this story to a girlfriend and she said, "Really? Shy and unassuming? Had no voice?" We had a good laugh because I *have* evolved and connected with my authentic self — achieving the confidence and success that I desire. Today, I have a fulfilling career as an artist and also as an intuitive well-being practitioner. I share my life with an amazing life partner — who lets me be *me*. I found my tribe of like-minded people who 'get' and appreciate me — the ones who my eyes and heart searched for so long ago in a galaxy far, far away. By *my* standards, I have attained a life which is rich and rewarding, and my authentic self places no limit to what I can achieve.

May these words provide the insights you are seeking to rediscover and connect with your true Being. Let my story inspire your authentic self. Trust that this world is here for you to experience all that it has to offer. Create your personal journey and the life *you* want to live. If you get stuck, you are not alone. Ask for help, whether it be from the divine or from the resources of this earthly plane. As you discover who you are, your fears will melt away and you will see for yourself that there is no limit to what you can achieve.

IGNITE ACTION STEPS

- Live life by the golden rule — "*Primum no nocere.*" Do no harm. Treat people the way you would want to be treated — with respect, kindness, and love. Being authentic doesn't come at the cost or destruction of people and the environment.

- View thoughts and feelings as creative tools that will help direct you. Distinguish between meaningful versus meaningless thoughts and feelings in order to enhance your life.

- Ask for support, not a rescue. To be rescued is to remain in the consciousness of a victim. To have support is to experience the mire of the challenge and come through it as a victor.

- If you fall back, give yourself permission to say, "It's okay." It provides the opportunity to reflect, evaluate, and clarify in order to successfully move forward.

- Take a deep breath — and from a place of gratitude, let hope fill you. Have the courage to face the uncertainty of life with love, compassion, and understanding so that you can evolve into the true nature of who you are.

Joanne P. Imai – United States of America
Certified Clinical Hypnotherapist, Intuitive Well-Being Practitioner
www.HalcyonEvolution.com

MELIKE SULE HUSSEIN

"Each challenge can be an opportunity for growth, for discovering our uniqueness and innate perfection, if we have the right tools empowering us."

My desire is to inspire you to free yourself from self-imposed limitations. You matter because of your uniqueness as an individual, not because of so-called success. You are complete when you nourish your health, well-being, and performance together as one. Know that you deserve to live a happy and fulfilling life, and it is in your power to create one through self-awareness and empowered actions.

FINDING THE FREEDOM TO BE ME

I am sitting around a large mahogany table with the representatives of the world's leading financial investors. It is a beautiful sunny day but even the bright light flooding in through the large windows can't change the serious mood in the room. They are our shareholders, and in that meeting, I am representing the company. I am a Senior Manager in finance and have been leading a project on their behalf for many months. Wearing my best power suit, I feel exhilarated, confident, and proud to be in their trust. I can answer any question they may ask as no one has a better command of the detailed analysis or holistic view of the sprawling company than me. My work is mentally stimulating and I am in my element. It's just another day in the office.

I have always been attracted to challenging roles that help stretch my analytical skills. Perhaps this is why I excelled at academia and then in finance as my profession. In my nearly 15 years in the corporate world, in every role I either developed a new product, designed operational improvements, or discovered new ways to increase revenue or reduce cost. I had a special knack for developing imaginative solutions delivering value. But it was not all plain sailing. While my achievements at work became my identity, the question in the back of my mind was, "Who was I without my success?"

As I climbed the ladders in corporate life, I found myself with bigger and more critical responsibilities. I was unable to say 'no' to new work, and I ended up taking on more than one could possibly manage. To keep up with the pace, I gave up the things that sustained me without a second thought. I stopped seeing my friends, gave up hobbies that I loved, and even started to sleep less. During the day, I skipped meals and did not take breaks — all to squeeze more work into a day. Before long, all I had in my life was work. And, I wondered how I got here.

In the society that I grew up in, the measure of success was having a respectable and lucrative job. It was the key consideration in determining one's academic choices and profession. Artistic or athletic abilities and personal preferences did not matter. I was molded in the same way, and I have always felt that my value as an individual was defined by success. Early seeds were sown in primary school. Being a lively child, I was more interested in play-time than classes. Inevitably, I was one of the late bloomers learning to read and write and then was cast aside by my teacher as one of the 'not so bright children' for the rest of the primary school.

Luckily my trajectory in life was changed by my geography teacher in secondary school. One day, sitting in our boxy classroom with 60 other kids, I corrected something she said. She looked at me through her massive tortoise shell glasses and praised me for it, exclaiming what a clever point I had made. I was in shock! No one had ever praised me before! I remember the whole class looking at me because none of my classmates had ever noticed me before. In that singular moment, I tasted success and the difference it made. I finally felt that I mattered. I was hooked. But the question that would bug me all my life emerged in that moment — who was I without success? Before that sudden acknowledgment, I had been invisible to the world and I was painfully aware of that.

My hard work and determination paid off. But with success came intense anxiety and fear. I felt that I was being judged and valued based on my job titles, the companies I worked for, how much I earned, and what I owned. Suddenly I became the collection of these titles. I was so proud of my achievements because I made them happen through my own merit, but they also felt hollow and transient. Constantly I asked myself who was I without these titles that seem to define me? The question was always there.

Both at work and in my personal life, I was under enormous stress and had no real tools to alleviate it. I was time-poor and needed fast-acting, practical tools that I could use anywhere and anytime, discreetly, in seconds — to calm my nerves before a meeting or during a presentation. After all, anxiety does not care where you are or what you are doing. But I had no tools to manage my emotions or the stress I experienced proactively. My health suffered as a result but I kept it private. From the outside, no one could have guessed it. When I was in work mode, I was ready to go, but I had no time or energy for doing anything for myself. Over the years, I lived with a variety of physically and mentally draining symptoms, including insomnia, dizzy spells, and severe headaches and chest pain. I experienced panic attacks and generally felt restless. Through it all, I felt guilt, shame, and frankly considered my health problems weaknesses. How could someone as intelligent and accomplished as me be so unwell? I felt it was my duty to put on a brave face, buckle up, and soldier on. So, I did.

One morning, everything came crashing down. I woke up to find my entire body shaking like a leaf caught in a severe storm. It was painful to breathe, as if my chest was tightly bound by a thousand belts. I could see and feel what was happening to my body, but my mind had no control over it. I was puzzled and scared. When I saw my doctor later that day, he signed me off from work due to stress. I was burnt-out! I knew I was stressed, but a burnout? I was blindsided. It forced me to face reality. I needed to reprioritize my life and take care of my body and mind first. Work had to wait!

Initially trained as a nurse and with medical practice in A&E (accident and emergency), all before my career in finance, I knew that I had to manage my health and make sustainable long-term changes. I explored holistic approaches, trying as many as I possibly could to see if anything clicked. One day, I was recommended to try Transformational Breath®, a specialized form of breathing practice. The idea of breathing as a way of therapy sounded silly, even to someone with a medical background like me, because we only thought of breath as a mechanical function, nothing more. But I was desperate.

My first breathing session was a revelation and it changed the course of my life. My biggest aha was the realization that I was barely breathing. My breath was very fast and shallow. My chest and shoulders were so tight that the air had nowhere to go. When I got my blood oxygen level measured, it was very low – below 90 percent. I wondered how I managed to work so hard over the years with the whisper of breath I had. All my life I had focused on control, on the inhalation. I realized I had never fully exhaled. My body was starving for oxygen. I noticed that many of the symptoms I felt were the direct result of how I breathed. I had no idea that something that was so simple and that I took for granted could be *so powerful*. I knew that I was onto something special, so immediately I shifted all my attention to my breathing sessions.

The first time I managed to take a naturally deep and relaxed breath was the happiest and most enlightening moment of my life. I felt a massive release in my body, as if years of stress and tension lifted with a jolt of energy. My chest and shoulders felt light and ache free — something I had not experienced in well over a decade. My mind was buzzing with energy, yet it was crystal clear with no distractions of swirling thoughts. For the first time, my body and mind felt deeply connected as one. Astounded by what I experienced, I started to self-practice conscious breathing daily. In a short period of time, my insomnia completely disappeared and my panic attacks stopped. I was walking taller, smiling more, and just a happier person. My colleagues and the people around me noticed too. They commented that I was friendlier, much more patient, kinder, and even a joy to work with and be around. My breathing practice was not only changing the way I felt *within,* but how I interacted with the world. *I was awestruck.*

I wanted to understand how and why conscious breathing was so powerful. I became an avid student of science and research in this field. I learned that *our breath, both autonomic and intentional, is the bridge between our mind and body*. How we breathe not only reflects our state of being, but also has the power to *change* it[1]. Simply by changing the way we breathe, we can influence and control our thoughts, emotions, and actions[2]. It is the most naturally powerful self-management tool that we have.

Breathing consciously literally awakened all my senses and helped me connect to myself in a completely different way. Without even trying, I discovered the answer to the question that had been bugging me all these years. I noticed the person I was at the very core — not the person I thought I was. *I came to understand that I am unique, complete, and perfect just as I am. That was my new definition of success. With the right tools in my possession, I was in*

---

1 Respiratory feedback in the generation of emotion. Pierre Philippot, Gaetane Chapelle, Sylvie Blairy. DOI: 10.1080/02699930143000392.Cognition and Emotion August 01(5):605-627.

2 The healing power of the breath. Richard Brown, MD and Patricia L. Gerberg, MD.

charge of my life. From that moment on, I stopped judging any aspect of my personality as good vs. bad — something that I had done all my life to fit in. For the very first time, I felt happy, truly at peace and content within myself. I started to meditate in a deeply connected way. The key was my newfound ability to anchor myself *into* my breathing.

Astonished by the complete transformation I witnessed in my health and mental well-being, I decided to dedicate myself to study these amazing powerful practices. I wanted to empower others with the right tools so that they can take charge the way I did. I went on to train in Transformational Breath® and become a Certified Facilitator. Then I continued my training with Dan Brule, world-recognized expert, and researchers including brilliant Dr. Richard Brown and Dr. Patricia Gerbarg. I became a Certified Breath Coach and an expert in a wide range of breathing modalities from somatic and restorative to transformational. I also became a Mindfulness Teacher to further deepen my personal practice. It felt as if everything came full circle; I was truly being fulfilled by helping others.

Conscious breathing and meditation changed me and my life — 180 degrees — in two profound ways. Firstly, it helped me to train my attention and sharpen my focus. I was still busy with my work, but my mind was not distracted as before and I could maintain my focus on what I chose, as long as I needed. I was able to complete my work much faster and more effectively than ever before — huge performance boost. I discovered a smarter way to work! Secondly, and most importantly, I was connected to my body so well that I could pick up even the faintest early signs of stress and use these powerful tools that I had to take restorative action. This helped me to be calm regardless of the circumstances. Previously I would reach the boiling point and snap at a colleague for making the smallest mistakes. But now, I was able to view the situation with clarity and respond appropriately rather than be swept up by my emotions.

Of course, sudden events can be overwhelming but even then I had the tools to remain calm, regardless of my circumstances. When I was in a serious car accident two years ago, stuck and partly crushed in the back seat, I simply breathed and meditated while waiting to be rescued from the wreck. When the paramedics arrived, I was calm and focused, and my vital signs were perfect. Puzzled by the stark difference between the crash site and my composure, they asked me how I was doing it. When I explained, at first they looked at me with a skeptical stare but then watched me as I was practicing. One paramedic finally said, *"Carry on whatever you are doing because it is working bloody well!"*

I founded my own company, Breathzone, to help others thrive in the same way I did. As my client work expanded, I noticed that something was still missing in how we were teaching breathing and mindfulness as a way to fix symptoms such as stress, sleeping issues, and lack of focus. But what we feel and experience are interconnected and deeply rooted in our physiological, neurological, and mental state of being. As a coach and teacher, I wanted to change the approach.

I created a new holistic modality and saw amazing results. I called it Transformational Conscious Breathing®. It uniquely combined conscious breathing, practical applications of mindfulness, and my medical background, all embedded in science. My philosophy was very simple: *empowering my clients to take charge and thrive in their well-being, health, and performance for sustainable long-term change.*

It is an absolute joy to see my clients being empowered with the powerful tools I share and transform their own lives. I work with people from all walks of life — from executives, who came to me seeking help with the stress they felt, to students who had intense social and exam anxiety, and busy mothers who nearly forgot what a good night's sleep was like. Not only do my clients learn the tools to manage their experiences, they more importantly discover how to lead well-balanced lives and manage their own powerful mind-body connection.

People ask me why I do what I do. It's because I see myself in each of my clients. I had to learn the hard way but they don't need to! But commitment to one's self-growth is a lifelong journey. Just like my clients, I strive to work and live smart. It is very important for me to walk the walk and talk the talk. I start my day with two of my most cherished tools — conscious breathing and meditation. I make a point of being mindful throughout the day — whether I talk to someone or prepare a meal, I immerse myself in that experience. I take regular breaks and consciously give my mind space to unwind. I make a point of connecting to nature, even if it means lifting my gaze to the sky and letting all my senses be present for a few seconds. I make time for my family, friends, and hobbies. All of these sustain me and honor my commitment to myself.

Today, I feel happy and joyful. I am deeply fulfilled and privileged to work with wonderful individuals and visionary companies with a holistic approach to supporting their employees. Every morning I open my eyes to a new day full of excitement and deep joy, buzzing with energy. I feel more alive than I had ever felt before that fateful morning.

Find the tools that will enable you to connect yourself with your innate spirit. You can free yourself from self-imposed limitations and discover your uniqueness and inner perfection. Remember that a balanced approach to your health, well-being, and performance make you complete, and they all must be nourished together. Empower yourself with the right tools and you will create a happy and fulfilling life — the life you desire and deserve!

IGNITE ACTION STEPS

- Build a personal health and well-being toolbox with a variety of practices that resonate with you. Practice them daily with consistency to form a new habit.

- Discover conscious breathing — try a variety of breathing techniques and see which ones work the best for you. Meditate to go within — connect with yourself at least 20 minutes daily. You can meditate not just on a mat, but also while walking or being in nature. Be mindful — bring presence and awareness to your day, the world, and people around you. Approach each activity as an opportunity to be present.

- Visualize. Engage all your senses and bring the life you want to lead alive. Incorporate this vision into your practices and connect to the feeling as if you are already there.

Melike Sule Hussein – United Kingdom
Certified Breath Coach, Mindfulness Teacher, and
Mindfulness in the Workplace Trainer
Creator of Transformational Conscious Breathing®
www.breathzone.com
 @breathzone
 @breathzonelondon
https://www.linkedin.com/company/breathzone/

BOOKS AND RESOURCES MEANINGFUL TO THE IGNITE INNER SPIRIT AUTHORS

Beejal Coulson
Raise your vibrations with *Love, Peace and Light* theta meditation track created by Beejal Coulson and eM. Download from www.beejalcoulson.com

Chris Plough
Resources for Liberation: I use each of these and have invested in some of them.

Chris' Projects:
- Getting Ploughed - https://gettingploughed.com/
- Project Liberation - https://projectliberation.com/
- My One Last Talk - https://chrisplough.com/onelasttalk

Adventures:
- AdventureX - https://adventurex.com/
- The Adventurists - https://www.theadventurists.com/

Communities:
- Archangel Academy - https://archangelacademy.com/
- Dream Circle - https://dreamcircle.co/
- Mastermind Talks - http://mmt.community/
- Maverick 1000 - https://maverick1000.com/

Exploring Your Mind:
- Ammortal - https://ammortal.com/
- Floatation tanks - https://lovethefloat.com/
- Journal - https://cosmicjournal.com/
- Psychedelic Therapies - https://maps.org/
- Sens.ai - https://sens.ai/
- Unified Mindfulness - https://unifiedmindfulness.com/

Financial Freedom:
- ExU Digital Asset Fund - https://exponential.io/daf
- Peer-to-Peer Lending - https://www.thehaloapp.com/
- Sanity Desk - https://sanitydesk.com/
- Wealth Factory - https://www.youtube.com/channel/

UC0Jj6_GAujF7MPIPB5YcmCg

Understanding Yourself:
- David Neagle - https://successfulmindpodcast.com/
- One Last Talk - https://onelasttalk.com/
- Panache Desai - https://www.panachedesai.com/
- Philip McKernan - https://philipmckernan.com/

Esther López
- *Goal Mapping: How to Turn Your Dreams into Realities* by Brian Mayne
- *Self Mapping: How to Awaken to your True Self* by Brian Mayne and Sangeeta Mayne
- *Life Mapping: How to Become the Best You* by Brian Mayne
- *Sam The Magic Genie* by Brian Mayne
- *Mind Power Into the 21st Century* by John Kehoe
- *Quantum Warrior | The Future of the Mind* by John Kehoe
- *The Biology of Belief* by Bruce H. Lipton Ph.D

Giselle Jennaway
www.kymiaarts.com

Katrina Roads
Radical Remission by Kelly A Turner Ph.D

Melike Sule Hussein
- *The Healing Power of the Breath* by Richard P. Brown, MD and Patricia L. Gerbarg, MD.
- *Just Breathe* by Dan Brule
- *Breathe Deep, Laugh Loudly* by Judith Kravitz

Olivia Ódor
www.quantumlifetechnique.com

Paula Lawrence
- Dr. Joe Dispenza
- Julie Jacky Mindset Coach & EFT Practitioner

Samuel Fishman
www.themiracleschool.net - to learn more about how to live the adventure of your life and come into your own

Santiago Rafael Pascual
- I highly recommended you watch *the Map of the Hero* in my Youtube channel: Santiago Rafael. - https://www.youtube.com/c/SantiagoRafael
- If you need an Akashic Record Consultant to work with you, you can find a list of available consultants on my website www.LAFAM.org

Tammy McCann
A free resource from my website is the following Masterclass: https://tammy-mccann.com/5-secrets-to-6-figures-and-beyond/

Traci Harrell
- *The Seven Laws of Spiritual Success: A Practical Guide to the Fulfillment of Your Dreams* by Deepak Chopra, 1994
- *The Power of Intention, Learning to Create Your World Your Way* by Dr. Wayne W. Dyer, 2005
- *The Path Made Clear: Discovering Your Life's Direction and Purpose* by Oprah Winfrey, 2019
- *Choose Them Wisely – Thoughts Become Things* by Mike Dooley, 2010
- *The Holy Bible (an American Translation), Abbreviation* by William F. Beck, 1976

PHOTO CREDITS

Alexia Gillespie - *Savannah Taylor Photography*
Amy Hackett-Jones - *Luciano Salazar*
Cat Flowers - *Jason Abraham*
Charlene Ray - *Shonda Hilton Photography*
Chris Plough - *Matt Prior*
Esther López - *Tomy Domínguez*
Giselle Jennaway - *Seraphine Emanuel*
Hina Mahindru - *Averill Lehan & Camilla Bignell*
Katrina Roads - *Sonja Wrethman Fine Photography*
Michael Tyler - *Charlyn Arizona Photography*
Olivia Ódor - *George Verdz*
Paula Lawrence - *lillypondphoto.com*
Samuel Fishman - *Baris Selcen*
Susana Sebesteyen - *Lauren McColl Photography*
Traci Harrell - *Bigger Than Me, Media*
Yendre Shen - *Alan Canagasabey*

Thank you

A tremendous thank you goes to all those who are working in the background teaching, editing, supporting, and encouraging the authors. They are some of the most genuine and heart-centered people I know. Their devotion to the vision of IGNITE, along with their integrity and the message they convey is of the highest caliber possible. They each want you to find your IGNITE moment and flourish. They all believe in you and that's what makes them so outstanding. Their dream is for your dreams to come true.

Production Team: Dania Zafar, Peter Giesin, and JB Owen

Editing Team: Alex Blake, Andrea Drajewicz, Nicole Arnold, and Chloe Holewinski

Project Leaders: Yendre Shen and Beejal Coulson

A special thanks and gratitude to the project leaders for their support behind the scenes and for going 'above and beyond' to make this a wonderful experience. Their dedication made sure that everything ran smoothly and with elegance.

A deep appreciation goes to each and every author who made Ignite Your Inner Spirit possible — with all your powerful and inspiring stories embracing this idea of the inner spirit found within each and every one of us.

To all our readers, we thank you for reading and loving the stories; for opening your hearts and minds to the idea of Igniting your own lives. We welcome you to share your story and become a new author in one of our upcoming books. Your message and your Ignite moment may be exactly what someone needs to hear.

Join us on this magical Ignite journey!

Leading the industry in Empowerment Publishing,
IGNITE transforms individuals into
INTERNATIONAL BESTSELLING AUTHORS.

WRITE YOUR STORY IN AN IGNITE BOOK!!

With over 400 amazing individuals to date writing their stories and sharing their Ignite moments, we are positively impacting the planet and raising the vibration of HUMANITY. Our stories inspire and empower others and we want to add your story to one of our upcoming books!

If you have a story of perseverance, determination, growth, awakening and change... and you've felt the power of your Ignite moment, we'd love to hear from you.

Go to our website, click How To Get Started and share a bit of your Ignite transformation.

We are always looking for motivating stories that will make a difference in someone's life. Our fun, enjoyable, four-month writing process is like no other — and the best thing about Ignite is the community of outstanding, like-minded individuals dedicated to helping others.

Our road to sharing your message and becoming a bestselling author begins right here.

YOU CAN IGNITE ANOTHER SO JOIN US TO
IGNITE A BILLION LIVES WITH A BILLION WORDS.

Apply at: www.igniteyou.life
Inquire at: info@igniteyou.life

Find out more at: www.igniteyou.life